DECISIONS AND DILE.........

In the field of mental health law, we entrust decisions with consequences of the utmost gravity—decisions about compulsory medical treatment and the loss of liberty—to doctors and approved social workers. Yet, how do these non-lawyers make decisions where the legitimacy of those decisions derives from law? This book examines the practical, ethical and legal terrain of duo-disciplinary decision-making: given identical cases, what dilemmas do psychiatrists and approved social workers encounter, do they reach the same or similar decisions and, most critically, how are those decisions justified? At a time of ferment in mental health law this book, through its narrative format, aids a better understanding of the dilemmas posed.

By the same author

Tribunals on Trial
Inquiries after Homicide

Decisions and Dilemmas
Working with Mental Health Law

JILL PEAY
London School of Economics

·H A R T·
PUBLISHING
OXFORD – PORTLAND OREGON
2003

Published in North America (US and Canada) by
Hart Publishing
c/o International Specialized Book Services
5804 NE Hassalo Street
Portland, Oregon
97213-3644
USA

Hart Publishing is a specialist legal publisher based in Oxford, England.
To order further copies of this book or to request a list of other
publications please write to:

Hart Publishing, Salter's Boatyard, Folly Bridge,
Abingdon Road, Oxford OX1 4LB
Telephone: +44 (0)1865 245533 or Fax: +44 (0)1865 794882
e-mail: mail@hartpub.co.uk
WEBSITE: http//:www.hartpub.co.uk

British Library Cataloguing in Publication Data
Data Available
ISBN 1–84113–343–4 (paperback)

Typeset by Hope Services (Abingdon) Ltd.
Printed and bound in Great Britain by
Biddles Ltd, *www.biddles.co.uk*

Foreword by
Lady Justice Hale

When asked to write a Foreword to Jill Peay's new book, I was delighted to do so, and not only because of my long-standing academic and practical interest in mental health law (as I write, we are hearing an appeal about the legality of the seclusion policy at Ashworth special hospital which also raises questions about the status of the guidance given in the Mental Health Act Code of Practice). As an admirer of the author's earlier work in this field, I looked forward to a stimulating read and was not disappointed. When mental health law is again in a state of flux, this timely study reminds us of the real practical dilemmas faced by professionals in their everyday practice as well as the difficulties faced by policy-makers in devising laws which will work both in principle and in practice.

The first part of the book vividly describes the findings of an 'in vitro' study of decision-making between pairs of doctors and social workers under the Mental Health Act 1983. The second part is a discussion of how such research in general, and this research in particular, might inform the current debate about a new Mental Health Act. Although the author suggests that the book is not really written for lawyers, there is much food for thought for any lawyer working in the field. I suspect that any comparable study of lawyers' reactions to these same case studies would reveal exactly the same differences of emphasis and opinion as did the care professionals in this study. The lawyers might be clearer about the legal principles involved, but they would still be torn by exactly the same dilemmas about how to fit the perceived needs of the individual case into the prescribed legal framework. Their objectives in each case would probably be very similar to those of the professionals portrayed here. The level of consistency in their decisions might well be no higher. Honesty and objectivity in decision-making are more attainable virtues than consistency.

One difference between lawyers and care professionals is that the multi-option decision-making required in many health and social care settings is always harder and more complex than the either/or decisions required by most litigation: in other words, in litigation we have an elaborate (and very expensive) machinery for making quite simple choices. In health and social care, there are rather more rough and ready ways of making very complex choices.

Those of us who apply the law in our everyday lives, whether as lawyers or non-lawyers, should be in no danger of forgetting that 'application of the law is

fundamentally an interpretative exercise', as the author reminds us at various points. If we want to understand what this means and how it shapes what we do, we could all do worse than read this fascinating book.

Brenda Hale
London
May 2003

Fundamentally, I think the question is what do people want from mental health and psychiatrists? When I worked in a big Victorian asylum it was dead easy, they were either in or they were out. OK it wasn't as graphic as that, but the point is, what do you want, at the moment? I feel that a whole bunch of people who are out there are at risk of killing themselves, of hurting themselves or hurting somebody else; there are loads of them and we walk around every day discussing them at team meetings, thinking what might happen? It's true, isn't it, we do it all the time. On the one hand the legislation says that you may or may not deprive somebody of their liberty on the basis of certain criteria and so on and then, on the other hand, there is why didn't somebody pick this up and do something? I'm sure we should have done something, but we have no power to do anything just because they are miserable and wretched, or they didn't quite fulfil the criteria, whatever your criteria happen to be and we didn't think that this was a massive problem. But it was there and 49 people over the last 3 years in our district out of a population of about 250,000 killed themselves. That is 15 a year or whatever the number is. We are never going to target them, never in a thousand years with any Mental Health Act. And then there is something about the thinking, about what level of tragedy are we prepared to accept and tolerate. What do we want psychiatrists actually to be doing? And we must be clear about the legal framework to enable them to do it, for those they target to be most at risk. If you were to take a very broad approach and say, look in general, just keep them all in, Mr Wright or whatever, just do it to keep them happy; or do you say, there is a very small number of people who you have to put through very strict criteria. If that's the case then the others aren't your responsibility, you can try and work with them but if you can't, it's not your problem.

A psychiatrist from pair 14 discussing whether to discharge in the case of Mr Wright

Preface

Lawyers are fond of asserting that 'no two cases are the same'. Indeed, for some, the *raison d'être* of their work is to establish differences between cases and thereby avoid a particular result through the application of the doctrine of precedent. It is equally commonplace, however, to assert that even experienced lawyers will disagree about the interpretation and rightful outcome of specific cases. Decisions made in the Appeal Courts where the most senior judges consider the same case at the same point in time and yet still cannot agree on the proper outcome are powerful testament to the law's persona as a malleable beast.

If there is not a uniform view amongst lawyers, why should we expect non-lawyers applying the law to be any more consistent? In short, we don't. But in the field of mental health law we do nonetheless entrust decisions with consequences of the utmost gravity to non-lawyers; namely, doctors and social workers. Their decisions to admit a person with mental health problems under compulsion to a psychiatric hospital and to treat him or her thereafter, potentially without that patient's consent, are taken with the authority of the law, but in the absence of lawyers. Yet these decisions can have a profound impact on an individual's life, restricting his or her liberty and, perhaps as importantly, that individual's freedom from intrusive and unsought medical treatment. Equally, decisions not to use compulsion entail their own consequences, potentially detrimental to both the professionals and, critically, the patients.

Treatment under compulsion entails a number of paradoxes; first, that we impose treatment on those who reject it sometimes in priority over those who seek treatment but cannot obtain it; second, that we concern ourselves increasingly with questions of risk and less with issues of health; third, that a long-standing acceptance of professional discretion is being progressively outweighed by demands for accountability and a fear of responsibility, in short, trust is no longer a given; and finally, contrary to what might be expected in an enlightened age, that the gulf between the treatment of those with physical and mental disorder is widening and not narrowing. For, whilst the treatment of those who retain capacity is imbued with concepts of autonomy, even if death is the result, the treatment of those who have mental disorder, regardless of whether they retain capacity, *can* be dominated by a paternalistic imposition of the choices of others. These are dauntingly big issues. Yet this book does not approach them head on, but rather from the side, focussing on how the detail of practitioners' thinking enables them to reach or reconcile decisions where others might see the decision as simply unreachable.

In tacit recognition of the responsibility which accompanies the nature of these decisions and of the vulnerability of individual decision-making, mental health law seeks to ameliorate the impact of individual predilections or prejudices by first, requiring these non-lawyers who are charged with such decision-making to be 'approved' or 'recognised' as having some special training or expertise in mental health law. And second, the law's procedures adopt a belt and braces approach by assuming that two (or three) heads making joint decisions are better than one (lawyer) alone. Indeed, two heads from different disciplines and with different outlooks are assumed to be even better. But, is this true? Moreover, is it even true that a formal training in or understanding of the relevant law will ameliorate the influence of individual factors in these very difficult decisions?

This book concerns these issues. It is based on a study that examined the terrain of duo-disciplinary decision-making by mental health practitioners under the Mental Health Act 1983. The study examined whether, given identical case materials, individual and paired professional decision-makers reached similar decisions about the application or non-application of the law; and, more critically, whatever the nature of the decisions made, how those decisions were justified by the parties making them. Thus, the adage 'no two cases are the same' was reversed as the study sought to examine whether 'any case was the same to any two practitioners'?

The detail of that decision-making study constitutes the empirical heart of this book. The fieldwork element was conducted in 1998–9 with Nigel Eastman, a forensic psychiatrist from St George's Hospital Medical School and the work formed part of the Department of Health's programme of research addressing the operation of the Mental Health Act 1983; it was also funded by them.[1] The research programme was prompted by a desire on the part of the government better to understand the workings of the 1983 Act with a view to informing the early stages of an on-going process of law reform in mental health. Indeed, a number of meetings took place between the various researchers and the relevant parties at the Department to up-date the latter about the progress of the research projects. The final results of this decision-making study were submitted in June 2000, a date that fell before the government finalised its plans for mental health law reform.[2]

Taking part in the original study were psychiatrists approved under section 12(2) of the 1983 Act as having 'special experience in the diagnosis or treatment of mental disorder', approved social workers (ASWs)[3] and a second group of psychiatrists who also held the formal position of second opinion appointed doctor (SOADs).[4] In total, 106 such practitioners participated. Each was

[1] Department of Health 2000.

[2] It notably fell between the publication of a Green Paper (DoH 1999) and a White Paper (DoH/Home Office 2000) which set out the shifting terrain of the government's then intentions in respect of law reform.

[3] To become 'approved' a social worker must undertake approximately 3 months of specialised training in mental health, which includes training in mental health law (CCETSW 1992).

[4] These psychiatrists are appointed by the Mental Health Act Commission. They exercise an independent judgement in respect of some decisions under Part IV of the 1983 Act to administer

required to make decisions alone and as a member of a professional pair, with psychiatrists being paired either with approved social workers or with other psychiatrists, namely, the second opinion appointed doctors. The individual and paired decisions required of them related to three commonplace scenarios. First, the decision to admit a patient to hospital under compulsion; second, the decision to discharge a detained patient from hospital; and finally, the decision to give medical treatment to a patient on a compulsory basis. Three hypothetical but entirely fictitious cases were devised which addressed these scenarios. In making the decisions, both alone and in their professional pairs, practitioners had access to extensive case materials and video evidence; their decisions were also subject to interrogation and deconstruction as part of the research exercise. In studying decision-making in this way, the focus of the research was not so much on establishing *what* decisions the practitioners reached, but on *how* those decisions were reached. Given that there were very divergent outcomes, what were the justifications and reasoning processes adopted? Thus, the book strives to identify the range of strategies employed by real-life practitioners to resolve these three cases, and in so doing explores the ethical, legal and clinical conflicts posed by 'everyday' dilemmas in mental health practice.

This is an odd book. For many, it will fall between two stools, having neither the methodological rigour of a research report nor the analytical rigour of a scholarly legal text. This is intentional, for it has been written with a desire to avoid what are sometimes arid and inaccessible terrains. Mental health law is a sufficiently daunting interdisciplinary topic without making matters worse for those who may come across this publication. Rather, my intention has been to attempt to recapture the sense of anxiety, excitement, curiosity and discovery experienced by those participating in the research. For, whilst trained (to a greater or lesser extent) in the content of the law, the practitioners who took part repeatedly acknowledged that their understanding of the law was less than ideal. In the process of being required to justify their own decision-making, it became evident to the psychiatrists and ASWs that they had rarely engaged with the law's inherent problems or, even more rarely, articulated their own difficulties. Applying the law in practice in these cases required them to do just that; confronting these common dilemmas brought the subject alive for them.

compulsory treatment to patients who may either lack the capacity to consent to treatment or who are refusing it.

[5] Peay (ed) 1996.

[6] Letter 13 June 2001 from Professor John Cox, then President of the RCP to Jacqui Smith MP Minister of State at the Department of Health.

[7] Budd 1999.

[8] DoH/Home Office 2000. [9] Monahan *et al* 1999, 2001.

[10] Høyer *et al* 2002.

[11] DoH 2002.

[12] Alan Milburn, opening the second day of the debate on the Queen's speech, announced that a Bill would be brought forward during the course of the session once the Department had finished considering around 2,000 responses to the Draft Bill; Hansard, 14 November 2002. This statement made curious reading in the light of his assertion earlier that day on BBC Radio 4 when he used the time-honoured phrase that a Bill would only be brought forward 'when time permits'.

Of course, being true to their attempts to grapple with the dilemmas is a messy business and whilst the book has striven to impose some structure on what took place, much of it is itself confusing, as examples are given of how practitioners set about the task required. However, if I am not to place a false gloss on what occurred, this mess is, if not intentional, certainly inevitable. Moreover, in an attempt to replicate for the reader the processes of decision-making and discovery through which the participants went, the materials are presented in the same narrative format (with a synopsis of the video material) as they experienced them. The first three chapters of the book should therefore be treated in this way, as an unfolding of issues and dilemmas.

It also worth stressing that the research, and the process of law reform, was undertaken at a time when the relevant professional groups felt some trepidation about their roles, responsibilities and respective future working lives. For the professionals the climate was dominated by a fear of 'getting it wrong', either clinically, practically or legally. The era of the Inquiry after Homicide still dominated;[5] 12 per cent of Consultant posts in psychiatry in England remained unfilled[6] and ASWs were alive to the possibility that they might lose their independent role under the 1983 Act. Moreover, social workers and nurses were, amongst employees, two of the groups most likely to be subject to attacks or threats of attack by members of the public.[7] Finally, this was an era when risk took precedence over health, most tellingly as revealed in the government's White Paper on mental health law reform;[8] the pressure generated by a policy dominated by the fear of unknowable consequences was almost tangible.

The first three chapters deal in turn with the issues of admission, discharge and compulsory treatment through the cases of Robert Draper, Clive Wright and Hazel Robinson. These chapters have a common format. They start with the narrative of the cases and include a detailed case history. All of the case notes, correspondence and medical reports are reproduced in the same format as was sent to the participants. This documentation includes many of the ambiguities, uncertainties and contradictions common to such written materials, complete with grammatical errors, infelicities and missing data. Then there is a description of the key elements of the patients' current situations as they emerged in the videos seen by the participants; together these two elements comprise the case materials available to the section 12(2) psychiatrists, ASWs and SOADs to resolve the problem of 'what, if anything, should be done next?' Third, there is a brief analysis of some of the problems raised by the each of the cases. Fourth, an analysis of the decisions reached by the participants both individually and in pairs. Fifth, there is an explanation, from these practitioners' perspectives, of the reasons lying behind these (divergent) decisions. And finally, a discussion of the ethical, clinical and legal dilemmas entailed. Thus, the contextual and analytical questions emerge, as they did in the original exercises, from the detail of the cases.

Moving on from the specifics of these chapters, two context-setting chapters, on research and on the law and policy, follow. Had this been a conventional text, these would have preceded the empirical work. However, as has already been intimated, this is an odd book; its format is driven by its experiential ambitions. Thus, chapter four, places this research study into the context of decision-making in mental health law and its research basis. Whilst this review of recent research is primarily UK based, it makes reference to comparable international studies; in particular, the MacArthur studies in the USA on competence, coercion and dangerousness[9] and the Nordic studies on coercion.[10] What main lessons are there for developing an understanding of how practitioners apply law?

Chapter five reviews the developing legal and policy context from 1983. The chapter looks at aspects of the recommendations of the government's expert advisory group, the Richardson Committee and the government's Green and White Papers; both of the latter conflicted with the Richardson approach and, to some extent, with one another. It is important to stress at this point that I was a member of the Richardson Committee and, as such, was fully signed up to its fundamental approach; namely, one which favoured law reform based on principles of non-discrimination and patient autonomy. That the government did not share this view reflects the fundamental dilemmas that have continued to dog the field of mental health law reform. And, despite considerable opposition, in June 2002 the government produced a Draft Mental Health Bill[11] that perpetuated its earlier proposals and built-on other legal provisions developed in the 1990s that emphasised mental health care as a route to, or at least a justification for, public safety. In so doing, the government signalled its intentions to favour an Act which would be even more broadly drawn than the 1983 Act and one that supports an approach directed more at public and patient safety than at patients' rights. However, as I write, the situation is in some turmoil. To considerable surprise, the Draft Bill was dropped from the Queen's speech in November 2002 and, whilst the Secretary of State has proclaimed the government's intentions to bring forward a Bill,[12] its provenance must remain uncertain.

Chapter six concludes this examination of the process of law reform. It pulls together the conflicting themes that have emerged from the empirical study and the analysis of policy development. Whilst the chapter does explore whether the findings of the current study have relevance to other decision-making fora, its focus remains robustly on mental health. Can the gulf between the law's aspirations in this field and its implementation be narrowed? Is the proposed direction of mental health law reform wise? Is it even properly informed by the range of research findings? And, is the next Mental Health Act likely to be any more effective (or less ineffective) than the current one? Or, is the driving force of risk one that cannot be counterbalanced by professional ethics and a growing desire, by professionals and academics alike, to put mental health law on the same footing as medical law? Will mental health care become inappropriately imbued (in form, if not in application) with a criminal justice/risk-infested agenda? Indeed, can the gulf between policy, politics and mental health care practice, where each side pursues an agenda so little informed by the concerns of the other, ever be crossed?

Thus, the book is a smorgasbord. For those who are drawn to the practicalities of mental health law what follows is a combination of story telling, dilemmas and decision outcomes. Whilst objectively there are only three stories, 106 individuals imposed their own interpretation on those stories and 54 professional pairs argued between themselves as to how these stories should be resolved. If the old adage is true, that no two marriages are the same, then the disclosure that the professional pairs were as diverse in their approaches, reasoning and decision-making as any two marriages will do nothing to ruin the book's ending, but rather will alert the reader to the complexity of what is to follow.

There are, however, elements in the book with a more traditional format. The two chapters on decision-making research and then the law follow a more familiar academic pattern and adopt a 'law in context' approach. And, at the end of the book, there is a series of appendices. The first of these reproduces selected sections of the Mental Health Act 1983 and two others detail the methodological niceties. Again this is intentional, since this level of detail would have distracted from the momentum of the core of the book had it been placed any earlier. However, this detail is there to enable those with boundless energy and an inquiring mind of the 'how, exactly?' variety to satisfy their curiosity. In the last appendix, the decision outcomes are presented in tabular form, so that the reader can crosscheck any numbered individual's or professional pair's decision against those singled out in the text. Finally, for those with a historical bent or a reforming zeal, one central question runs through *Decisions and Dilemmas*; namely, are the problems posed by mental health law likely to be more readily resolved in the new legal era?

To end, I must acknowledge the part that Nigel Eastman played in the research. Dr Eastman had a major hand in the preparation of the case-materials, giving them an authenticity that would have been difficult for a non-clinician to replicate. Equally, his role in the fieldwork provided a practical edge that I would have struggled to achieve alone. Whilst acknowledging his influence on the direction of the earlier work, I take responsibility for the analysis and interpretation of the study offered here.

JP December 2002

Contents

Acknowledgements

A number of people have contributed in various ways to this book and I am grateful to them all. First, the 106 people who agreed to take part in the study; nameless to readers and largely to one another, their openness and patience was remarkable. Second, my colleagues at the LSE, and in particular, Caroline Roberts, George Gaskell and Nicholas Allum who all helped with the analysis of the data, and Elizabeth Durant, for the horrible task of fiddling with the text. Third, I would like to acknowledge the funding received from the Department of Health, and, in the early stages of the research, advice from them, the College Research Unit at the Royal College of Psychiatrists and two anonymous referees. Fourth, a number of people have had the text thrust upon them in its developing and developed stages; Andy Ward, Oliver Lewis, Genevra Richardson and Brenda Hale have all been willing victims. Their ideas, encouragement, humour and warmth have sustained the project. And finally, for long-term logistical, technical and much other support, Al.

Abbreviations

A&E	Accident and Emergency
AMHP	Approved Mental Health Practitioner
ASW	Approved Social Worker
BASW	British Association of Social Workers
CCETSW	Central Council for Education and Training in Social Work
CHI	Commission for Health Improvement
CMHT	Community Mental Health Team
CPN	Community Psychiatric Nurse
CPS	Crown Prosecution Service
CTO	Community Treatment Order
DoH	Department of Health
DSPD	Dangerous People with Severe Personality Disorder
ECHR	European Convention on Human Rights
ECtHR	European Court of Human Rights
ECT	electro-convulsive therapy
EEG	electroencephalogram
GP	General Practitioner
LSE	London School of Economics and Political Science
MHA	Mental Health Act 1983
MHAC	Mental Health Act Commission
MHT	Mental Health Tribunal (under Draft Bill)
MHRT	Mental Health Review Tribunal
NICE	National Institute for Clinical Excellence
NSF	National Standards Framework
OT	Occupational Therapy
RCP	Royal College of Psychiatrists
RMO	Responsible Medical Officer
SOAD	Second Opinion Appointed Doctor
s 12(2)	Psychiatrists or General Practitioners approved under s 12(2) of the Mental Health Act 1983 as having 'special experience in the diagnosis or treatment of mental disorder'
WHO	World Health Organization

1

Robert Draper: A Case for Admission?

WOOD PARK HOSPITAL
LONDON N.22

ADMISSION SUMMARY

Name: *Robert Winston Draper*
Date of Birth: *1.4.1971*
Date of Admission: *3.2.1993*
Date of Discharge: *21.3.1993*

HISTORY

History of Presenting Illness

Mr Draper presented with a 6 month history (given mainly by his mother) of increasing suspicion of others, refusing food because he said it was poisoned and the belief that some of his neighbours were interfering with his hi-fi. He said that he was angry with 'particular people', who he would not name, and that 'something would have to be done'. When asked what it was that would have to be done he said 'they will have to be stopped . . . and it's getting worse, and they are checking on me to make sure that I can't get back at them . . . but I will, they are destroying my life.' On further questioning he said that he was sure of what 'they' were doing because he had seen programmes on television which were about him and that 'they were making sure that they were transmitted'. He said that the programmes would also have to be stopped.

On direct questioning he said that he could hear voices of people commenting on his thoughts and that others knew what he was thinking by doing 'particular things' which could connect them with him. He also said that there was a conspiracy to stop him from being able to play music and that he was sure of this because of the way in which a band called 'Steel Life' sometimes sounded on the radio. He said that the radio producers altered how the band sounded when they wanted to warn him of the danger to him and that 'very special ways of playing' would indicate who it was he should protect himself from. He said he was angry with what was being done because he was, himself, a very successful musician who had won 'golden disc' awards and now he could not play properly as a result of things that were being done to his brain. He said that he had been recommended for the award by Diana Princess of Wales.

A history taken from his mother indicated that the changes in her son had occurred gradually but that he had always been a bit suspicious by nature. She said that the death of his father 5 years ago had made him more suspicious of others than usual but that he had not 'lost it' in the way that he has done recently. She described him now as 'depressed' and not eating properly, losing weight and having disturbed sleep. He had also cut himself off from his few friends and had both started to smoke more cannabis and taken to drinking alcohol in the morning 'to calm himself down' (see Drugs and Alcohol History below). Also, his appearance had deteriorated and he was no longer washing as he normally did (when he was usually fastidious). Finally, she had noticed that he would stare at the door of one neighbouring flat when he passed it, where an older white couple with whom she was friendly lived; normally he was very civil to them, although not particularly friendly.

Personal History

Mr Draper was born in Trinidad. There were no known birth problems, although he was born at 38 weeks, by vaginal delivery. His early childhood development was normal and he walked and talked at the right ages. He came with his mother and father to England when he was 4 years of age and has never returned to Trinidad. He went to a local primary school where he was described as 'bright'. However, he did not mix easily with other children and tended to be a bit of a loner. He was referred to a Child Guidance Clinic when he was 9 years of age because he was teased and got into fights more than other boys his age and also seemed unhappy. However, he only went a few times and there are no records available about the assessment or any treatment (his mother says that he did not attend on more than a few occasions). In senior school he made one or two closer friends but these relationships petered out when he left school, which he did at 16 years with a few CSE passes.

He worked initially as a shelf packer for a supermarket but this job only lasted a few months because he resented the exercising of authority over him and he tended to answer back, this particularly being a problem after his father's death. After a period of 12 months unemployed, he then worked as a driver for a small local haulage company and kept this job for a few years (perhaps because he could work better on his own). He drove a small van delivering parcels around North London. He would sometimes call in 'sick' for the odd day or two but was generally reliable. He continued in this employment until five months ago, when he said that he was 'fed up with it' and stopped going into work; he was eventually sacked. His mother said that his employers thought that he was a good worker but that he was 'a bit off-hand with people', and could also be 'over the top' when people criticised him justifiably.

In the last five months he has gone out less and less, and taken to smoking more cannabis and drinking more. He has also become irritable and depressed (see above) and, on one occasion, he uncharacteristically struck his mother in the face when she said that he should 'get his act together'. He has also become much more socially withdrawn and now hardly goes out of the house.

Family History
Mr Draper's father was a car factory worker for most of his life. Mr Draper described him as 'a good man, but sometimes he beat me'. He died 5 years ago. His mother is a Nursing Auxiliary in a district general hospital, where she has now worked for many years. Mr Draper has no siblings (his mother said that she was unable to have children after difficulties surrounding her son's birth).

Social History
Mr Draper mainly enjoys music. He plays drums in a group and is good enough to earn some extra cash through doing occasional gigs. His few 'friends' come from that setting. He also used to like running but he stopped this two or three years ago. He lives at home with his mother, as he has always done.

Previous Medical History
As a small child (1–3 years of age) he had convulsions when he was ill with infections sometimes but he has not suffered from fits since then. He suffered from a head injury in a road traffic accident (when he was working) four years ago when he was knocked out for a few seconds but with no significant pre or post traumatic amnesia. Otherwise, he has had his appendix removed (two years ago) and has suffered from hepatitis on one occasion (details unknown, notes apparently unavailable).

Alcohol and Drugs History
Mr Draper started to smoke cannabis just before he left school. His consumption has been frequent but variable in quantity. He said that it helped to calm him, although sometimes it made him 'a bit paranoid'. He has tried 'speed' on one or two occasions and had also had the occasional 'trip'. He has never taken heroin. He started to drink alcohol when he was 13 years, usually on his own. However, he has never, he said, been 'addicted', although, like his cannabis consumption, 'it can go up and down a bit'. He became angry when asked if he was drinking and smoking more at present than usual.

Previous Psychiatric History
Apart from being seen in a Child Guidance Clinic when he was young (see above) he has never been referred to psychiatric services before. However, his mother went to the GP on two or three occasions in the past 3 years saying that he seemed withdrawn and distant from her, and from others. She also complained that he sometimes developed 'odd ideas' which upset him. The GP reassured her that 'he was just growing up and finding his way'. He has never been on psychotropic medication.

Premorbid Personality

Mr Draper himself said that he was 'a very powerful man' who 'could take care of himself' and he didn't need doctors, or anyone else, to tell him what to do. However, his mother said that he was usually kind to her and his recent assault on her was entirely out of character, although she acknowledged that he had been in trouble at school with and that some people said they found his aloof nature 'threatening'. Otherwise, she said that he had few friends 'outside of his music' and that 'he liked to keep himself to himself'.

Forensic History

Mr Draper was convicted of possession of cannabis at the ages of 17 years and 21 years, receiving only fines. He was convicted of possession of an offensive weapon two years ago when he was picked up by the police and found with a 'Swiss Army knife' on him late one night; he received a six month suspended prison sentence. He also says he was convicted of burglary of a chemist's shop when he was a late adolescent and he then had some form of contact with the Probation Service.

MENTAL STATE EXAMINATION

In **appearance** Mr Draper presented as a somewhat dishevelled young West Indian man with stubble on his face, smelling of sweat; his clothes did not fit him very well and the looseness of his trousers suggested that he may have lost a significant amount of weight. His **behaviour** showed suspiciousness and he also looked at times either depressed or angry; there was no psychomotor retardation, however. His **speech** was lacking in spontaneity and he had to be pressed for answers to questions; there was sometimes the suggestion of a mild degree of loosening of association, although it was difficult to be sure of this; there was no evident 'knight's move' thinking and generally no clear evidence of a disorder of form of thought. His **thoughts** were generally inaccessible to the interviewer but the combination of some history from him plus a good deal more from his mother indicated the presence of persecutory paranoid and grandiose delusions, as well as primary perceptual delusions of reference; there was also evidence of thought broadcast. His **perceptions** included apparent auditory hallucinations in the third person. His **mood** was suspicious, angry and depressed. **Cognitively**, he was oriented in all modalities. As regards **insight**, he had none into the possibility that he might be mentally ill but conceded that he was depressed as a result of the persecution which he was undergoing; the latter meant, he said, that he might come into hospital in order to 'gather his strength'.

PHYSICAL EXAMINATION

There were no physical findings of any note; there were no neurological abnormalities and no evidence of physical effects of drug abuse.

PROGRESS ON THE WARD

Mr Draper agreed, with some persuasion from his mother, to come into an open acute admissions ward of the hospital. His mental state remained much as it had been on admission during a medication free period of two weeks. He co-operated minimally with staff but gradually the symptoms described by his mother became evident also to nursing and medical staff, although he remained very reticent about talking about what was worrying him. Investigations revealed a positive urine screen for cannabis from a sample taken two weeks after admission but not for any other drugs. On one occasion he became very angry with one junior nurse who somewhat forcibly confronted him with the falsehood of his beliefs and he threatened to 'hurt her' and subsequently he appeared always to be suspicious of her, although it never became clear that he had incorporated her into his delusional beliefs.

He was then started on chlorpromazine, 150mg qds and gradually both his beliefs/hallucinations receded and his hostility lessened, although he never became friendly and always remained somewhat suspicious. He accepted the medication only somewhat unwillingly at first, although he appeared ultimately to be consenting and it was not thought that, for this reason or because of any unwillingness to remain in hospital, he needed to be sectioned under the Mental Health Act. He therefore remained an informal patient throughout his stay in hospital. Towards the end of his stay he was switched to a depot preparation because of concern about his long term co-operation with medication, although his mother emphasised her intention to ensure that he took medication.

On discharge back to his mother's flat he was much improved and he agreed to co-operate with community/outpatient follow up from the Consultant and a CPN, Mr Sandle.

DIAGNOSIS

Probable paranoid schizophrenia; not entirely possible to exclude a drug induced schizophreniform psychosis; background personality of a paranoid/schizoid type.

TREATMENT AND FOLLOW UP

Outpatient follow up, initially 4 weekly, with the consultant
Regular weekly CPN follow, with home visits.
Modecate 25mgs three weekly

SAMPLE OUTPATIENT LETTERS TO THE G.P.

20.4.93

Dear Dr Howard
I am pleased to tell you that Mr Draper is still doing well and has settled back into life at home with his mother. He has essentially no symptoms to speak of and is compliant with medication. He is fortunate that his personality is well preserved and there is no evidence of negative symptoms of schizophrenia (indeed, they tend to occur much later in any event). Indeed, he is an articulate young man who has a wry sense of humour. However, he has not been able to return to work and he has now lost his job formally. I am therefore asking Mr Sandle, the CPN (with whom Mr Draper seems to get on reasonably well) to try to arrange some daytime activity for him, perhaps even involving his musical interests. Hopefully he will eventually return to some form of work, even if it is of a sheltered type.
  He remains on Modecate 25mgs three-weekly.
Dr Jones

.
.
.

22.1.94

Dear Dr Howard
Bob remains well and is attending 'Sound Minds', a musical group at the hospital, twice weekly and also goes to a day centre for black patients twice weekly. He is entirely co-operative with his depot, which remains at the dose which it has always been. Unfortunately, although he is so well and presents as kempt and articulate he still has not managed to find paid employment and, as you know, he has rejected sheltered employment.
Yours sincerely
Dr Jones

.
.
.

1.7.95

Dear Dr Howard
Bob came to see me today and was clearly not his usual self. He was suspicious of his neighbours, not eating properly and worried by the radio. He was also angry with me for suggesting that he might not be entirely well and said that perhaps we ought to increase the dose of his depot. He was also very concerned about his mother's health (as you obviously know from your own care of her, her heart condition has deteriorated and she has developed a considerable

degree of heart failure). In spite of all of his worries he was still well dressed and his usual very articulate self. It then transpired that the CPN, Mr Sandle, had made an error in handing over care for his summer holiday and that Bob had not been offered, or received, his depot for 6 weeks. Bob had then become angry and somewhat hostile when an attempt was made to restart the medication.

Fortunately, Bob had come with his mother and, knowing what had happened, she was herself concerned that he must restart the depot (she said to me 'he's a bit like he was in the early stages of his illness last time'). With much persuasion from his mother Bob eventually agreed to restart medication, at the same dose (which I hope will be enough).

I will see him in two weeks' time.

Yours sincerely
Dr Jones

.
.
.

23.8.95

Dear Dr Howard
I am please to say that Bob is showing definite signs of improvement now that he is back on medication. He is much more co-operative and his abnormal thoughts have become much less intrusive and important. I am particularly pleased because he told me that, when he last saw me, he had been thinking about having to do something to stop his elderly neighbours from persecuting him.

I will see him in 4 weeks.

Yours sincerely
Dr Jones

.
.
.

22.9.95

Dear Dr Howard
I am delighted to tell you that Bob is back to his old self and has returned also to his daily programme.

Yours sincerely
Dr Jones

.
.
.

14.6.97

Dear Dr Howard
Bob continues to do extremely well and, given how well he has been for most of the four years since his admission, even the previously favoured diagnosis of

schizophrenia may be in some doubt, particularly when I remind myself that a drug screen which was negative for drugs other than cannabis was not taken until two weeks into the admission. Even his apparent deterioration when he missed medication in July 1995 occurred at a time when he was probably worried about his mother's physical health and it is possible that he was coping with this with the aid of drugs of some sort.

In any event, given his mother's continuing ill health, it would probably not be wise to attempt a diagnostic drug free trial at this point.

Yours sincerely
Dr Jones

.
.
.

1.7.97

Dear Dr Howard
After doing so well for two years and without symptomatology I am a little worried about Bob. As you know, his mother has had a second myocardial infarction and her heart failure is much worse. He is understandably very distressed and has started to blame other people for what is happening to her. I have increased his medication to Modecate 37.5mgs three weekly and have asked Mr Sandle (with whom he has a very good relationship) to engage in some focused counseling which will help Bob to cope with the now much greater uncertainty about his mother's future. I should be grateful to be kept informed about any relevant developments in Mrs Draper's condition.

Yours sincerely
Dr Jones

.
.
.

7.1.98

Dear Dr Howard
After coping so well with his mother's illness and her untimely death at Christmas, Bob told me today that he wants to go back to Trinidad 'to discover his roots'. I am sure this relates to how alone he feels at present and so have asked Mr Sandle to try to increase his input and to find other ways too of increasing the support around Bob, although this will not be easy.

I will keep you informed.

Yours sincerely
Dr Jones

.
.
.

8.3.98

Dear Dr Howard
Bob is still finding life without his mother difficult and I feel there may be a touch of 'arrested grieving', although it is rather early days to conclude this. He seems rather depressed and lethargic, although otherwise he remains well as regards his schizophrenia.

Yours sincerely
Dr. Jones

.
.
.

24.4.98

Dear Dr Howard
In Dr Jones' absence on sabbatical in S. Africa for the coming two months, I saw Bob in outpatients. Unfortunately he started to insist that he no longer wanted to take his medication. He said that he had been upset by his mother's death but that now he was better and, as a consequence, no longer wanted to take medication. I tried to persuade him otherwise but to no avail. He will continue to see the CPN (more frequently) and he has agreed to come to see me again in two weeks' time.

Yours sincerely
Dr Young, SHO to Dr Jones

.
.
.

20.5.98

Dear Dr Howard
Bob has now not come to two appointments with me and is becoming increasingly resistant to seeing the CPN, Mr Sandle. I will send him a further appointment but both the CPN and I are worried about how he is, particularly since he is off medication and I note from previous records that, when he accidentally went without his Modecate for six weeks some years ago, he appeared as though he might be becoming unwell again. On that occasion his mother persuaded him to go back on medication but, of course, she is no longer here to help.

Yours sincerely
Dr Young, SHO to Dr Jones.

FILE NOTE

4.6.98

I received a telephone call from Bob's elderly neighbours today complaining about him and saying how worried they are both for him and for themselves.

They say that his milk has been outside the door untouched for over a week, that he has not come out of his flat in more than 10 days and that he appears suspicious. He has also been shouting and playing music loudly. They feel somewhat intimidated by him.

I think that he needs a medical and social work domiciliary assessment given that he has been off medication for a few weeks and he is showing signs of relapse as he did some years ago when he came off medication for about six weeks. Also his mother's death at Christmas hit him hard and in any event she was his mainstay carer. I am also worried that he might be taking drugs since there was a suspicion of this in the aftermath of his father's death when he was only about 17 years of age.

His consultant is still on sabbatical in South Africa and I shall be on leave for a week from tomorrow. I have therefore telephoned his GP to ask if he could assess Bob at home tomorrow, with the possibility of psychiatric and social work assessment thereafter.

Mr Sandle CPN

FILE NOTE

5.6.98

*Bob's GP Dr Howard telephoned me this afternoon after having seen him at home. Dr Howard is concerned that Bob **may** be relapsing, although he is clearly concerned that any change in Bob might be explicable through drug abuse. It is obviously necessary for there to be assessment by a s.12 approved psychiatrist and an ASW.*

Given the lateness of the hour I don't think this needs to be done tonight, but an assessment over the weekend is required.

Mr Sandle CPN

Current situation—as portrayed by video

Mr Draper lives on a 1960s estate in a second floor apartment. Extensive building work is taking place on the surrounding premises with a prominent skip and scaffolding. Builders are hammering tiles into a half-completed roof. Children play on a central area of grass and amongst parked cars; washing hangs on the flats' balconies.

Mr Draper's elderly white female next-door neighbour is on the telephone expressing concern about Mr Draper's isolation. Her husband is in the background and can be heard saying that Mr Draper 'worried his mother to death and he's trying to do the same to us'. He also complains that Mr Draper is 'making all the noise' and that 'he is a bloody raving lunatic'. The tension between the husband and his wife, as she tries to speak on the phone, is evident. She appears to be towards the end of her tether saying that her own husband has not been 'too well of late' and that 'they can't be doing with all of this'. She concludes 'it's all very frightening'. Meanwhile, her husband, still clutching his toolbox, can be heard saying 'if he tries it on just one more time, I'll swing for the bastard, I swear I will'.

Dr Williams, who is a male duty psychiatrist, and a female ASW—Julie Redmond—arrive at the complex. She tells Dr Williams of Mr Draper's previous informal admission to Wood Park Hospital and of his history of compliance with medication. She explains that Mr Draper had recently asked to come off medication; she confirms that, as far as she is aware, there is no history of violence.

She rings the door-bell but Mr Draper, whom she can see inside through the letter-box, does not answer. She calls to him saying that his GP has asked her to come and, if he does not answer the door, she will simply keep on coming back. Mr Draper says, without opening the door, that he has already told his GP that he is OK. She persists in asking him to open the door; he asks for identification and she shows her ID through the letter-box. He opens the door and spots Dr Williams, asking 'who is he?'. Julie Redmond explains and Dr Williams puts out his hand saying 'hello Bob, how are you?'. Mr Draper declines his hand and responds that he is OK. On asking why they want to come into his flat, Dr Williams explains that the matter is 'confidential'. Mr Draper emerges from the flat, looks along the corridor, says that 'he understands' and motions them inside.

The flat is clean and tidy, a pile of newspapers is neatly arranged on a table, and there is a bottle of whisky on the window-ledge with several empty glasses. Mr Draper looks physically well. His clothes are ironed and well fitting. After a brief mention of the building work, he takes the initiative and says to them 'You think I've got a problem and you can help me with it, but I haven't and you can't. I'm OK'. He then offers them a drink, reaching for the bottle of spirits and pouring himself a drink. They decline, but Dr Williams asks if he normally drinks whisky at this time in the morning; Mr Draper responds with 'No, normally I drink vodka'. Dr Williams explains that Mr Draper's neighbours are very worried about him, to which Mr Draper asks why they, as psychiatrists, don't go and do something about them then? Dr Williams says that he has been heard shouting, to which Mr Draper responds 'They are always snooping around, checking up on me and asking questions'. He suggests that his neighbours probably write it all down in a big book, even when he goes to the toilet, as the walls are as thin as paper. But he also says, not looking at the ASW and psychiatrist, that 'What they don't seem to realise is that I can hear them too, talking about me'. When Dr Williams asks what it is that Bob has heard them say, he stands up and goes over to the pile of newspapers, tidying them again. Dr Williams persists with the neighbours' concerns about him shouting at three and four in the morning and shouting through their letter-box that he would 'do them in'. Mr Draper retorts that Julie Redmond had shouted through his letter-box. He then goes on to say that he will not go back to the hospital and that that is, after all, what they (the professionals) want and why it is they are in his flat. Then he says to the seated pair 'Now I want you to get out of here, both of you, go on, get out' raising his voice as completes his sentence.

DECISIONS AND DILEMMAS

THE MATERIALS PRESENTED above replicate the information available to the professionals taking part in this case study, which concerned the possible compulsory admission of Mr Draper to hospital. Five sections now follow; an analysis of the problems faced by these decision-makers; a synopsis of the decisions they made; an analysis, largely from their perspective, of how those decisions were made; a review of the ethical, legal and clinical issues arising; and finally, a summary of the key findings in this chapter.

Precise details of the methodology adopted for this exercise are set out in Appendix 2, but they are not central to an understanding of what follows. For the professionals who took part in the study, the question posed to them at the end of the exercise, after the video had been shown, was 'what would you do next?' These professionals had first to decide what they individually would have done, and second to agree a joint course of action with their paired colleague, whether that be a section 12(2) psychiatrist or an Approved Social Worker (ASW).

At this point some readers might want to pause to reflect upon their own actions if they had found themselves facing this situation with Mr Draper. For those who just wish to press on . . .

1. The Nature of the Problem and the Options Arising

Having left the apartment several possibilities faced the professionals. These depended on a number of factors, including how urgent they thought it was to take some action. The options ranged from those that were not very intrusive to the most dramatic option (from Mr Draper's perspective) of an emergency compulsory admission to hospital. This latter course would have entailed (in real life) completing the necessary paperwork on the basis of the information already gleaned and possibly, calling an ambulance with police back-up to convey Mr Draper to hospital. The use of such procedures, with all of the drama for relatives, friends and neighbours it entails, is infrequent. However, section 4 of the Mental Health Act 1983, authorises detention for up to 72 hours on the basis of the authority of the ASW and one doctor's opinion. This section of the Act, together with the details of section 2 (a 28 day assessment and treatment provision) and section 3 (a six month treatment provision) are set out in Appendix 1.

At the least intrusive end of the range of possibilities was the option of doing nothing and just walking away from the situation. None of those taking part adopted this course. However, a number would have approached the problem in a relatively non-intrusive way, by either attempting to support Mr Draper in the community or trying to re-engage him in further discussions about restarting his medication or raising the possibility of his being admitted to hospital as a voluntary patient (that is, a patient who consents to go to hospital and who may also choose thereafter to leave hospital).

Lying between these two extremes of a section 4 emergency admission and supporting Mr Draper in the community were the options of admitting him to hospital under compulsion using either section 2 or section 3 of the Act. Both sections require the paperwork to be completed by two doctors and the ASW. However, in this scenario, obtaining a supporting opinion from another doctor, usually the patient's GP, was not perceived as problematic, since it was the GP who had already asked them to assess Mr Draper. The factors relating to the choice between section 2 and section 3 are discussed further below. Suffice it to stress at this stage that the criteria for admission under section 2 are somewhat broader than section 3, but section 2 only lasts for 28 days, rather than the 6 months authorised by section 3.

The questions on which the resolution of these choices will turn include:

—Is Mr Draper likely to comply with treatment in the community (most likely, the resumption of his medication)?
—Is he willing to be admitted to hospital as a voluntary patient?
—Has he the capacity to refuse admission, and if not, can he be admitted as an informal patient (that is, a patient who does not consent but who does not resist admission either)?[1]
—If he is admitted as either a voluntary patient or an informal patient will he accept medication in hospital?
—Is he suffering from a mental disorder 'of a nature or degree which warrants the detention of the patient in a hospital for assessment' (part of the criteria for admission under section 2)?
—Is he suffering from a mental illness 'of a nature or degree which makes it appropriate for him to receive medical treatment in hospital' (part of the criteria under section 3)?
—Ought he to be detained for his health, his safety or for the protection of others (under section 2)?
—Is it necessary for his health, his safety or for the protection of others that he should receive medical treatment in hospital (under section 3)?

All three of the terms concerning the patient's health or safety or the protection of others raise complex questions of risk; namely, clinical risk (will the patient's condition deteriorate or become more resistant to treatment?), the risk of self-neglect and the risk of harm to others (either physical or psychological harm). So, a further question arises:

---

[1] See the judgment of the House of Lords in *R v Bournewood Community Mental Healthcare NHS Trust ex parte L (Secretary of State for Health and Others Intervening)* [1998] where assent was held to be sufficient for informal admission to hospital under s 131 of the 1983 Act.

—Is there evidence in the presenting history to sustain a belief in any of these risks to a degree that would satisfy the terms of the 1983 Act?

However, as the Act fails to specify any particular threshold that has to be satisfied before the presence of a risk meets the notion of 'necessity', the terms remain a matter of individual interpretation. For this reason they are also vulnerable to an understandable tendency for professionals to find them satisfied by meagre evidence in circumstances of uncertainty.

The questions require the ASW and the psychiatrist to address a number of specific issues. Some of these lie most clearly within the domain of the psychiatrist; for example, whether Mr Draper is experiencing a re-occurrence of an established illness (which may favour a decision to detain under section 3) or whether this is some new phenomenon, for example, a grief reaction to the death of his mother combined with some abuse of alcohol or drugs (which may incline the psychiatrist to favour a section 2). More prominent for the ASW are questions concerning the availability of community support and whether Mr Draper's problems are fundamentally more of a social than medical nature (for example, arising out of his deteriorating relationship with his neighbours).

2. Decision Outcomes

There are two striking features of the decisions made. First, there was considerable variability in outcomes both within and between the two professional groups. The same case was perceived in very different ways and seen as requiring very different forms of intervention by different individuals. Secondly, in respect of the difference between individual and joint decisions, the pattern of the latter more clearly reflected the decisions the ASWs would have made individually, than those of the psychiatrists. Thus, the psychiatrists' preference for section 3 admission is not reflected in the joint outcomes, whereas the ASWs' preference for 'other' decisions was clearly mirrored there. A crude summary (a more detailed breakdown appears in Appendix 3) of the 80 decisions made individually by ASWs and psychiatrists shows there were:

40 ASWs	*40 Psychiatrists*
—1 to admit on s 4	1 to admit on s 4
—12 to admit on s 2	12 to admit on s 2
—4 to admit on s 3	17 to admit on s 3
—2 to admit informally	0 to admit informally
—21 other	10 other

For the 40 decisions made jointly by the ASWs and the psychiatrists there were:

—0 to admit on a s 4
—12 to admit on a s 2
—6 to admit on a s 3

—2 to admit informally
—20 other

The category 'other' was made up of 20 pairs all of whom together 'agreed' that it would be necessary to seek further information from, for example, the GP, the neighbours, the CPN, the hospital team or the patient's case file, and/or to revisit or reassess Mr Draper. However, the urgency with which they wished to do this varied greatly. For example, one pair believed that, come what may, Mr Draper needed to be in hospital that night, whilst another were content to leave matters for up to two weeks whilst the ASW attempted to re-engage Mr Draper. What the pairs wanted to achieve through a further visit to Mr Draper also varied; for example, arranging support for him in the community, trying to get him to take medication at home or at another venue if he preferred, persuading him to go to hospital informally, or attempting to gain re-entry to the flat in order to undertake a formal assessment under the 1983 Act (assuming that these pairs considered that the interaction that had just taken place between the ASW, the section 12(2) psychiatrist and Mr Draper did not constitute a formal assessment).

Whilst the joint decisions varied between those wanting to use compulsion, those being prepared to use it should another strategy fail, and those being adamantly opposed to its use altogether, such joint decisions also disguised preference shifts. Generally, as the exercise progressed, the ASWs as a group became less sure about using compulsion, and in particular, less sure about the use of section 3 as opposed to section 2. However, the psychiatrists shifted in the opposite direction, favouring section 3 more as they gained more information. The differential distributions in decision outcomes between ASWs and the psychiatrists after viewing the video of Mr Draper is statistically significant (see Appendix 2). And, whilst there is nothing remarkable in decisions being altered by the addition of the new information (namely, that which could be gleaned from the video rather than from the case notes), divergences in the 'direction of travel' of decisions between individuals or groups is of interest.

Since the joint outcome generally favoured both section 2 over section 3, and the use of other non-compulsory measures, the ASWs appeared as a group to have a greater influence on the outcome. Indeed, a crude analysis of 'who wins?' in the discussion revealed that ASWs prevailed on 22 occasions, psychiatrists on 9 occasions, and for the remaining 9 the decision was evenly balanced. Statistical analysis of these joint outcomes indicates that the tendency of ASWs to prevail over the section 12(2) psychiatrists does not occur by chance (see Appendix 2). This is not surprising, given the ASWs' formal responsibilities in initiating the sectioning process; however, psychiatrists do occasionally prevail. This is a counter-intuitive finding, since it suggests that the psychiatrist has been able to overrule the opinion of the ASW, despite the fact that the process of sectioning a patient under the Act cannot proceed without the ASW taking independent action (and, if they are professionally opposed to this and have not been persuaded by the psychiatrist to change their view, a question remains over the true multidisciplinary nature of the decision to use compulsion).

It is also notable that whilst there were decisions across the spectrum of possible outcomes (that is, to use compulsion and not to use it) confidence levels in all decisions were generally high. Thus, whatever was decided, the decision was conceived as the 'right' choice; indeed, it was often characterised as the only choice. The use of 'terminology of constraint' is common in the decision literature (that is, participants claiming that 'I had no alternative but to. . . .') even though it is evident that others faced with exactly the same information felt equally constrained to do something entirely different. Thus, whatever constraints the professionals perceived, they were largely self-constructed.

It is perhaps less surprising that, as a group, the ASWs generally grew in confidence as the exercise progressed, as they obtained more information and had the benefit of a discussion with their paired psychiatrist. However, the psychiatrists, who started the exercise with higher levels of confidence, seem to have had this eroded by contact with the ASWs. Was this because they didn't 'get their way' as often as they would like (and hence had less confidence in the joint decision) or because the ASWs caused them to think again about the appropriateness of their own medical approach? It is not possible to answer this question definitively, other than to observe that the psychiatrists' individual preference for using compulsion (broadly either section 2 or section 3) was overwhelming (73 per cent) whereas only 40 per cent of the ASWs would have used compulsion in this way. In the event, only 40 per cent of the joint decisions favoured compulsion under section 2 or section 3.

3. Analysis of Decisions

3.1 Joint Decision-making—Are Two Heads Better Than One?

In a perfect world, the decisions made by two people acting jointly should be better than those made by one individual acting alone. The 1983 Act has adopted the adage that 'two heads are better than one' by requiring decisions about the compulsory admission of patients to hospital to be made by an ASW together with one or two doctors. In this perfect world, all parties would bring to the decision their own expertise within their discipline, an adequate understanding and knowledge of the law and an ability to apply that expertise to the particular factual situation posed by the patient. Thus, the psychiatrist should be expert in assessing mental disorder,[2] in understanding the common history and prognosis of such disorders and should possess an ability to assess its presentation in this particular patient. The psychiatrist should also have some

---

[2] This is the term used by the Act, and the one favoured in the Draft Mental Health Bill 2000. However, many jurisdictions prefer the term mental disability, or some other variant.

expertise (as a doctor) in assessing the patient's capacity and the validity of any consent to treatment they might proffer. Ideally, the patient's GP, who would have longitudinal knowledge of the patient, would also be party to the decision as a medical expert. The ASW would bring an expert knowledge of the social factors influencing the presentation of mental disorder and knowledge of the facilities available to support patients in the community, or provide support for them and their immediate network (dependants, pets etc) should the need for admission arise. Ideally, each party would benefit from the expertise of the others, so that any decision reached took account of all of the relevant factors and disregarded any irrelevant factors, and each party's views would have an appropriate impact on the decision so as properly to reflect the range of factors pertinent in that particular case.

This image of a world inhabited by perfect decision-makers seems far from that portrayed by the research. Amongst the 40 joint decisions concerning Mr Draper there was more than one pair who approached this ideal, and particular illustrations of the paired decision-making strategies are given below. However, such good decision-making processes were not the common pattern.[3] Arguably, the research methodology, which required participants to commit themselves privately to an individual view before discussing the case with their expert partner, may have solidified conflict in a way that does not routinely occur in practice.[4] However, it is also arguable that the methodology exposed conflict that would routinely have remained hidden in real-life decision-making. In real life, for one reason or another, parties can become aware of each other's preferences and a joint view emerges without either person having to admit that this is not what they would have done had they acted alone. Of course, it is possible in the research where the parties had come with conflicting views that the discussion preceding the joint decision had been genuinely persuasive, either mutually persuasive or one party persuading the other. But, there were instances where this was clearly not the case. These can be identified where one party had a markedly lower confidence level in the final decision than he or she had had in their individual decision prior to the joint discussion. Thus, the methodology laid bare the sense of unease that one may experience when reluctantly agreeing to a course of action. As we all know, the unease can persist in nagging away long after the decision, with the dissatisfied individual experiencing recurrent thoughts such as 'if only I'd said X or if only I'd thought of Y at the time things might have been different'. The real world is a world of uneasy accommodation.

It is also evident, looking at the individual decisions as progressively more information was presented through the medium of the video, that the outcomes were not dominated by flexibility, compromise or novel thinking. Thus, of the 80 who took part, 50 of the ASWs and psychiatrists had the same individual

---

[3] The relationship between process and outcome is not straightforward; poor procedures can result in fortuitously good outcomes, and vice versa.

[4] See ch 4.

view of the case at the end as at the start. Participants tended to stick with their initial impression, regardless of what that might be (and the original views varied from 'immediate emergency admission' to 'no urgency to do anything other than gather more information'). Equally, in only 8 of the 40 pairs was a decision reached that neither of the parties would have made individually. What appeared to occur was that, in cases of initial disagreement, one party or the other (and in the admission decision the ASW had, as it were, the final word, since they had to initiate the 'pink form' process) obtained an outcome that reflected their view. In short, one head largely dominated.

3.2 *Joint Decision-making Dynamics*

The factors individuals bring with them to a decision-making situation will include not only those relevant ones identified above, namely their discipline expertise and knowledge of the law, but also permutations and variations on these themes. For example, what experience of this type of case has this professional had in the past? Was the outcome experienced as successful or unsuccessful? Individuals will also bring a range of competencies (and sometimes areas of incompetence); and, regardless of the participants' desire to ignore them, innumerable extraneous and irrelevant factors will also feature. Overarching all of these factors will be the professional's fundamental approach to their role. What do they think they should be trying to achieve and how should they set about it?

One of the questions asked of the participants concerned this overarching role definition. Three possibilities were presented; they were termed clinical, legal and ethical styles of decision-making. Although these terms are used here as handy labels, the participants were presented with a lengthy explanation as to what it meant to characterise themselves in this way. For example, a 'clinical' decision-maker was described as someone who was essentially driven by what was in the patient's and/or society's best interests, who looked to the Act only to determine whether there were legal powers that could be invoked in order to pursue these prior best interests. A 'legal' decision-maker was someone who carried around, either literally or metaphorically, an awareness of their legal powers and duties under the Act, together with the framework of safeguards it provides for patients, and allowed predominantly these factors to drive their decision-making. Finally, an 'ethical' decision-maker was one driven by questions of capacity. Was the patient capable of deciding for him/herself? Only if the person lacked capacity would the psychiatrist or ASW look either or both to best interests and/or to the Act. Hence, only incapacity would trigger intervention against the patient's objection. None of these descriptors was meant to be definitive and clearly an argument could be sustained that acting in a patient's best interests constitutes 'ethical' practice. However, none of those taking part showed any great reluctance to adopt one of the three characterisations.

Although the bulk of participants appeared to have little difficulty in deciding 'what they were' ('legalists', 'clinicalists' or 'ethicists'), this was most striking in respect of those who saw themselves unequivocally as driven by best interests within a clinical/social mode. This applied to nearly all the psychiatrists (36 out of 40). The strength with which they adhered to this model varied; however, there were psychiatrists who made it plain that any model that was in competition with the clinical one was subsidiary. By so relegating the relevance of law, these psychiatrists were arguably doing just what others in their profession claimed they should not do; namely 'be an island unto oneself'. A substantial minority of ASWs did not fall into the 'best interests' model (15 out of 40). They presented particular difficulties as regards categorisation. Whilst one or two did adopt a robust stand; hence 'ethics overrides the Act. . . . I don't feel bound by it' or 'I'm not in this business to be legal' making it plain that they adhered to some personal version of a higher authority than law, it often required some close questioning in order to determine exactly how it was that they did perceive their position. In particular, there were participants who claimed to be one thing but, presented with questions that tested their claim, crumbled into another mode, invariably the clinical best interests mode. Hence, a question like 'so, your ethical belief in the primacy of capacity would extend to allowing the capacitous patient to kill themselves, or others?' would most often be met with a shift to a sometimes grudging acceptance that they were *ultimately* a clinicalist who would seek to use the Act because it was available in that situation.[5] Usually, it was possible in this way to tease out what was the bottom-line position for a subject. However, for a few individuals (2 psychiatrists and 6 ASWs) no amount of questioning moved them from a position of asserting that they operated more than one model simultaneously and without ultimate preference.

These numbers are not wholly unpredictable. However, it is perhaps surprising that as many of the ASWs classified themselves in the way they did. Given the nature of the ASW role, the extensive training they receive and the guidance given in the Code of Practice,[6] one might have expected that the ASW role would more often have been perceived by them so as to emphasise their function as a social and legal 'brake' on a doctor's desire to treat. Thus, it might legitimately be expected that ASWs would have been somewhat freer from the clinical model's imperative that treatment *is* in the patient's best interests.

In addition to the part played by their overarching characterisation of their decision-making approach, other factors can influence the joint decision-outcome, for example, the role of personality. Some individuals are naturally more hawkish in their decision-making, others more doveish. Indeed, some are more prepared to tolerate a degree of risk, others are more cautious. Last,

---

[5] Whilst this question appears stark there are, of course, other methods of restraining people who are dangerous to others than to resort to the 1983 Act.
[6] DoH/Welsh Office 1993, 1999.

although this does not exhaust the range of possibilities, there will be interactive effects between these factors. What happens when a hawkish ASW is paired with a highly experienced psychiatrist and presented with a complex medical situation in a context of perceived risk of harm to others?

Thus, it is readily apparent that whilst the facts of Mr Draper's circumstances remain the same, their interpretation will depend very much upon the individuals who are required to assess him. Or, whilst 'no two cases are the same', no single case is likely to look the same to any two individuals.

The range of outcomes reflects these permutations. In contrast to the 'perfect world' approach, there were occasional pairs who did not appear to be up to the job required, with neither party compensating for the other's deficiencies, either in respect of their legal or professional specialist knowledge. More common were the pairs where both parties quickly identified and agreed upon the course of action to be adopted; in these pairs there was little discussion of the factual or ethical difficulties posed. In pairs where there was explicit conflict, the reasoning processes were more exposed. In some the conflict was resolved by resort to one party having the formal power to make or implement the decision. In others the outcome was counter-intuitive, namely, the psychiatrist 'got their way' in the face of a dissenting ASW. This could occur either by the psychiatrist invoking clinical risk, that is drawing on an area of expert medical knowledge that was difficult for the ASW to counter, or by invoking the risk of harm to the patient or others.

Illustrations of each of these themes are discussed by reference to particular paired discussions. A word of caution is, however, timely. The characterisations of the decisions adopted here are not driven by the decision made, but are based on the process by which that outcome is reached. This is because there could be no 'correct' answer to the question as to 'what to do next?'; the analysis accordingly strives to be non-judgemental.

What now follows is a review of five types of paired decision-making.

3.2.1 Consensus Decision-making in an Ideal World

In pair 24 the ASW individually favoured gaining further information over the week-end and returning on Monday for a more formal assessment, possibly accompanied by the police and armed with a warrant which would have had to have been obtained from a magistrate.[7] This would have been necessary if it was thought that Mr Draper would deny the professionals access to his flat on any further assessment visit. The ASW did not think there was any great urgency about the situation and was confident that he had arrived at the right conclusion. The psychiatrist favoured a section 3, although she didn't have any great initial confidence in this option. Indeed, after watching the video she concluded

---

[7] See s 135 of the 1983 Act. This provides for an ASW to obtain a warrant authorising a constable to enter premises if there is reasonable cause to believe that a person suffering from mental disorder is alone there and unable to care for him or herself, in order that they might be taken to a place of safety and assessed with a view to making, for example, a s 2 or s 3 application.

that the situation was not as bad as she had envisaged it on the basis of the clinical notes.

As she put it:

> Before we saw him, I thought we've got a man with a history of schizophrenia who is shouting a lot, playing music and generally making a nuisance of himself and upsetting his neighbours. Then I thought, right this looks like an obvious relapse, we are not going to be able to get in. When we do get in we will find that the flat is a complete and utter mess and that he has been neglecting himself and that everything is going all over the place. In which case we would have to admit him under a s 3. But what we saw belied that. He did let us in, a bit suspicious, but then I don't know how unnatural that is, if two complete strangers come banging on the door saying that they are worried about your health. The flat was alright and there was nothing from what he told us that made you think that there was a deterioration in his mental health. So, what we actually saw probably reduced my fears. **Psychiatrist, pair 24**

After a discussion with the ASW, in which both played an equal part, they made the decision that they would return together on the Monday morning, in order to maintain continuity in Mr Draper's dealings with them, and with his assessment. Meanwhile, they decided to discuss the situation with the female neighbour. They agreed not to 'jump to a warrant straightaway' but on the other hand were alive to the possibility that the history did suggest a deterioration in his mental health and that they wouldn't have any concerns about intervening on the Monday if there was more evidence over the week-end to suggest that action was necessary. However, neither took the view that 'anything dramatic' was going to happen over the week-end. The psychiatrist indicated that 'you can't detain someone just on a hunch' and the ASW offered that 'whilst the Act allows you to detain virtually anybody, in reality you don't. The skill of the assessment is in the way you apply the criteria'. The psychiatrist agreed:

> I suppose it's a reluctance to put people on a s 3, or detain people under the Act, if you think there is any way you can manage them when they are not detained under the Act. I think that there is still a chance that we could manage this man. **Psychiatrist, pair 24**

Interestingly, both parties endorsed the joint plan with a high degree of confidence, with the psychiatrist increasing her level of confidence over that associated with her original plan. Thus, this looked like a genuine meeting of open minds.

3.2.2 Where Risk Trumps

This pair stands in stark contrast to pair 24. Here the ASW initially expressed much the same view as the parties above, namely that more information was required and that the situation did not warrant an admission under the Act. However, the psychiatrist, invoking his medical expertise, started with:

> It is very interesting that I hold a different opinion. I am basing my opinions from what we already know, from what we have read. I think this person has been known to get very ill very soon once he stops medication. He has been ill enough to cause serious

concerns to others in the past. He has a history of violence. At the present time it is very clear that he is hearing voices, he hears his neighbours shout at him in the middle of the night, which clearly can't be true so we can assume that it is the voices that he hears and responds to. I am very concerned . . . the man (neighbour) seems to have got very worked up about what he is doing. It is very likely, I think, that an incident might happen. **Psychiatrist, pair 21**

In response to the ASW asserting that the state of the flat didn't seem too neglected, the psychiatrist continued:

I think that it looked rather too tidy. You see him arranging the papers in order. . . . he has become more obsessive and more rigid about these things. . . . We need to take him in. I think we can think of quite serious concerns about the safety of others, especially the neighbours. He seems to have psychotic symptoms directed towards them. **Psychiatrist, pair 21**

At this point the ASW effectively caved-in and agreed that they would have to apply under section 3 for Mr Draper. Interestingly, whilst the psychiatrist had a very high level of confidence in this decision, the ASW recorded a low level of confidence (35 per cent), indicative of continuing if ineffectual dissent. In further discussion, the psychiatrist rated the nature and degree of the patient's disorder as being amongst the most serious he had encountered and the ASW (whose views were sought second) concurred with this medical view. However, when questioned about this seeming change of mind, the ASW said that she had not been persuaded by the psychiatrist, but rather was very concerned about the neighbours. But she also said, possibly picking up what the psychiatrist had said, 'he is obviously hearing voices'. The ASW was ultimately prepared to endorse all three of the 'health, safety, or protection of others' criteria, whereas the psychiatrist was predominantly concerned about risk to the male neighbour. Indeed, his scenario of what might happen if they did not admit Mr Draper to hospital under compulsion, turned on the neighbour initiating some violence in response to Mr Draper's abuse and then Mr Draper responding. Being younger and stronger, physical harm would ensue. Hence, his view of the risk posed by Mr Draper was based on the presence of intolerant frail neighbours. In another situation, with other neighbours, Mr Draper's condition would not merit compulsory admission. However, the seemingly compliant nature of the ASW did not equip her well to rebut the psychiatrist's analysis.

3.2.3 A Brake on Clinical Fear?

This pair illustrates direct conflict between an ASW opposed to the use of compulsion in Mr Draper's circumstances and a psychiatrist who thought immediate admission was necessary under section 3 in order to medicate him. Thus, their discussion commenced:

I suggest we leave him for a few hours and I will go back and see him on my own to see if he is prepared to sit down with me and talk things through, basically to assess what is bothering him and how we may help to assist him. There are a number of options open to us. We could invite him to out-patients, invite him to see a professional therapist, or we could involve an out-patients team or the home treatment team. **ASW, pair 28**

... the neighbours are complaining, the neighbours feel threatened. Mr Draper has not been complying with his medication, listening to him it is clear that he is quite paranoid, he is suspicious of the neighbours, the way he looked around when we came in. He is abusing alcohol as well, so the concerns are for his health, there are concerns for the safety of the neighbours. I suggest he is admitted to hospital straightaway under s 3 so that medication can be instituted. **Psychiatrist, pair 28**

And their exchanges continued in this fashion with the ASW playing down the case's potentially worrying features, for example, that Mr Draper 'slapped his mother once when she made a critical comment' (the notes record that he 'struck his mother in the face') and describing a Swiss Army Knife as 'an ordinary pocket knife.' In contrast, the psychiatrist played up the worrying features. Thus, he made reference to Mr Draper being convicted of ABH when he was 24 (there is nothing in the documentation to suggest this) and of him 'screaming down the letter-box of the neighbours'. Whilst this professional pair did discuss the possibility of informal admission, the ASW made his views very clear: 'At the end of the day I'm not happy to sign the pink form'. In the light of this there was little the psychiatrist could do other than go along with the ASW's plan to ensure that Mr Draper was visited regularly, if necessary twice a day, to monitor him. However, it was evident from this psychiatrist's confidence levels (which dropped from 100 per cent in his own plan to 60 per cent confidence in the joint plan) that he remained markedly unhappy.

In discussion it emerged that the ASW had a caseload with a large proportion of patients with a forensic history. It was commonplace to him for them to use cannabis and carry knives. In contrast, the psychiatrist said that it was 'unusual' for any of his patients to have convictions. Although his concerns were driven by the possibility of something going wrong—'if something happens, something goes wrong, it's me that gets held responsible and therefore I've got to satisfy myself'—it was also apparent that his threshold of what might go wrong was set very low. In response to being questioned about exactly what it was that he was worried about he mentioned verbal exchanges with the neighbours:

What I am worried about, and I know psychiatry has changed over the years, is a perception of public safety. There is a patient on the street who is causing a lot of problems, who may not be physically aggressive to the neighbours. But that is enough to cause concern in the neighbourhood. One needs to take that into account, because in a way that is protection of the public as well. **Psychiatrist, pair 28**

3.2.4 A Counter-intuitive Outcome—Clinical Risk Trumps

The discussion started with the psychiatrist (who was opting for a section 3 admission) making an authoritative statement about Mr Draper's clinical condition:

> He seems to have a recurrence of his psychosis, he has hallucinations, he's obviously irritable with our visit and if the reports of the neighbours are valid, he has been disruptive and disturbed. We are not just capturing one moment of his behaviour. **Psychiatrist, pair 6**

The ASW, who would have opted for some form of further engagement with Mr Draper in an attempt to get him to accept treatment from the community psychiatric nurse (CPN), tried to counter this by making reference to Mr Draper's insight (ie that he was not that unwell).

> I felt there was some level of insight because he knew why we were there, he knew what we were about . . . he understands that we are trying to get him back into treatment and he has made it quite clear that he doesn't need admission to hospital. **ASW, pair 6**

However, the psychiatrist remained adamant that the discussion that needed to take place was not *whether* Mr Draper was to receive medication, but *where* that was to occur. Making reference to the GP's and the CPN's concern, he continued:

> We are now confirming that he has a recurrence of his psychosis, a paranoid psychosis. We know from the history, which is reliable, that it is a relapse of the symptoms. There may not have been any harm to the neighbours, although they are getting increasingly stressed. What do we gain by waiting for three or four days? **Psychiatrist, pair 6**

Although the ASW continued to argue his case, he was prepared to concede that admission under section 2 for assessment might be an option, since there were a lot of new factors and the admission would be as an acute assessment. Would these new factors be taken into account, he wondered?

However, the psychiatrist would have none of this. He used the ASW's concession to contest his logic; thus:

> On the one hand you are willing to say that if he will take his medication now we can manage him in the community without assessment. On the other hand you are saying he needs assessment because it is a presentation of symptoms he has not had for sometime. I don't understand the logic. **Psychiatrist, pair 6**

And, having stressed again that his current symptoms were a recurrence of an established mental illness, the psychiatrist pushed home his view that the length of detention (ie section 2 or section 3) was not the prime reason for admission; what was required was that treatment be re-established. An application under section 3 was agreed.

3.2.5 Procedural Power Trumps

Here, the psychiatrist's level of confidence dropped from 85 per cent to 5 per cent between his individual decision and the joint decision. The 'joint' decision was to pursue further assessment of Mr Draper in the community. However, whilst this was the outcome the ASW preferred, the psychiatrist had been firmly of the view that a section 2 was appropriate. The flavour of the exchange between the two is captured by the following exchange:

> . . . As I say, he's dangerously delusional, you bear in mind that he's threatened the neighbours . . . Wouldn't you agree that we ought to take him into hospital? It would have to be compulsorily, because he refused . . . **Psychiatrist, pair 9**

> Well, I'm not sure that he indicated that he was refusing—but he didn't co-operate with the interview—there's no question about that, but he wasn't actually canvassed about hospital—I don't think the interview really afforded that opportunity. **ASW**

> But it worries me . . . in his state being out of hospital. **Psychiatrist**

> As I say, I would want more extensive information about what's been happening and I certainly wouldn't be prepared to endorse a section just on the basis of what we know. **ASW, pair 9**

Sometimes, as occurred in pair 9, where the psychiatrist wanted formal admission but the ASW refused, this kind of conflict would be resolved by the psychiatrist signing section 2 papers, and the ASW taking the papers, but not agreeing to implement them forthwith.

Finally, the illustrations above show how the relationship between formal authority under the Act and practical authority, based primarily on 'superior' knowledge of factors crucial to the decision to be made, can pan out. Hence, whilst in the admission decision the ASW enjoys a formal power effectively to veto the use of the 1983 Act[8], the psychiatrist has a powerful influence over the outcome (since they are often possessors of and imbued with the 'best' knowledge about the patient's health and risk).

3.3 *Styles of Decision-making and Conflict Resolution*

Given that so many of the participants described themselves as being 'clinicalists', that is, as being dominated by a desire to achieve 'best interests' outcomes, it was inevitable that many of the pairs would be *ad idem* in respect of what it was they wanted to achieve, even if they disagreed about the best course of action to attain that objective. Conflict was accordingly the exception rather than the rule. However, it is notable that the *ALCESTE* analysis (see Appendix 2) did indicate that there were clear distinctions between the discourses associated with the ASWs and the psychiatrists. Thus, whilst the individuals concerned may not have described themselves in markedly different terms (a surprising finding given their core values training) their professional discourse did display different lexical classes, with psychiatrists raising issues which had more to do with the patient's current condition (which has relevance primarily to *whether* the patient's status should change) and the ASWs being more

---

[8] In the absence of a nearest relative for Mr Draper, only the ASW has the authority to initiate the sectioning process.

concerned with case management (*how* the patient's status should change). Although these differences emerged in the discussions ranging between the pairs, in outcome terms the differences were less marked. Indeed, the discussions show how these traditional roles could be corrupted by the paired decision-making so that, as one psychiatrist explained it, 'you almost wind each other up into using the Act'. The perception of the role of the ASW as 'a brake' on proceedings (or the legal gatekeeper) can thus quickly become eroded by clinical imperatives, whether those imperatives relate to an amorphous risk to others or to the patient's own vulnerability. Finally, whilst core value training and role definition were two aspects of what practitioners brought with them to an assessment, it was also evident that some practitioners approached these tasks with a particular mind set; as one psychiatrist commented, 'even being called to a Mental Health Act assessment biases you towards its use'. Others, notably ASWs on an emergency/out of hours rota, had a more circumspect approach, perhaps prompted by their recognition that difficult cases would often be held over until the out of hours team were on-duty; in this context they assessed one difficult case against an array of other difficult cases, perhaps making them somewhat more judicious in their decision-making.

How the discussion was managed by the pairs is also of note. Some ASWs would commence the discussion with an explicit attempt to draw out the psychiatrist, along the lines of 'what do you think doctor?', or 'there's a dilemma', or the more neutral 'did you pick up on whether he had seen the GP?'. Others started with a summary of their impressions or problems, as in 'I was worried we weren't going to get in at all', or 'hopefully we have left an option to come back . . . I don't think we can walk away and just leave it like that'. Others (mainly the psychiatrists) started with a potted case history based on the notes and the interview and then invited comment from their partner. These relatively neutral opening gambits could lead (although not invariably) to a genuine exchange of views between the parties. In contrast, some participants made it very clear from early in the discussion that they had formed a view that was largely immutable, a sort of 'here I stand' approach.

Avoiding conflict could take at least two forms. First, avoiding conflict between the professionals. And secondly, avoiding confronting the problematic aspects of the case itself. One method of achieving the latter was, in effect, to delay the evil day. So, some pairs argued that they would need more information before they could reach a decision; this would entail a series of further approaches to potential information sources (the neighbours, the CPN, the GP, or even tracking down relatives in the Caribbean). Others argued that the situation was not so urgent as to require immediate action; here, one party or the other would be entrusted with taking further exploratory action.

Another strategy for signalling uncertainty (and accordingly, a preparedness to negotiate rather than impose a view) concerned the quantity and type of information that each party would require before they would be prepared to take any given decision, for example, to section Mr Draper. This issue might be thought of as a 'burden of proof' problem.[9] Thus some, often those with a civil libertarian bent, appeared to require more current data (ie the burden was on the doctor to establish overt symptomatology in Mr Draper) and lack of it was interpreted as a 'not proven' situation where no formal action could be taken. In contrast, a 'medicalist' might reinterpret the current data in terms of past data (within a medical disease model, congruent with the notion of repetition of symptoms based on previous recorded episodes of disease). Those dominated by a social model would look at the current (changed) social situation and use that to overturn the medical presumption of repetition of symptoms ('I want more information before I'll accept that he is ill').

However, where the search for more evidence proved futile, there was a tendency to accept the medical model. In some pairs this could be characterised as a frank 'caving-in' by the ASW; yet others had a more reasoned justification:

> I know you can't wait until people become really ill and become really disruptive . . . [yet] when I sign the papers I throw away people's liberties so I can't just sign the papers so easily . . . I'm not here to challenge the psychiatrist . . . but if somebody who knew him really well said he was relapsing, even if it were just a telephone call, then I would feel happier to sign the papers. **ASW, pair 31**

For her, assessment was a process during which she collected further information and/or got to know the person concerned. In the absence of such information, she felt that she was under pressure to sign the papers and, as she put it, 'I would do it at the expense of Mr Draper'. Alternatively, a fruitless search for more information, for example, returning to the flat on another occasion but not being admitted, could be interpreted as evidence tipping the decision in favour of a section (since his failure to open the door on another occasion could be seen as a deterioration in his circumstances). Logically, of course, it need not signal deterioration, but the passage of time combined with 'something needs to be done' seemed conducive to interpreting such negative information as supporting intervention. Thus, divergent views about what inferences should properly be drawn from the current data, including that which the participants could observe for themselves by seeing Mr Draper reading the case file, led to divergent views about how to handle the issues of illness and risk.

Another variation on this tussle between past information and current data relates to the history of previous practice with the patient. Past use of an informal approach can set the tone for a preference for continuation of a similar approach. Thus, as Mr Draper had been admitted before only as an informal patient some practitioners were keen to pursue this, despite his changed circumstances (namely, the death of his mother, a key figure in gaining his co-operation previously) and his overt refusal to go back to hospital. It might be argued (uncharitably) that this represents political correctness, being readily dropped once there was a failure to obtain further information. The available

---

[9] See also *R (on the application of H) v Mental Health Review Tribunal for North and East London Region* [2001] and the remedial order *SI 2001/3712*.

data was then reinterpreted as being sufficient for detention. Others pursued the informal approach seemingly at all costs and were prepared to admit Mr Draper on what was a covertly coerced basis. This was justified with resort to what might be termed the 'reality coercion' alibi, namely that Mr Draper would know that, as practitioners, they would have the option to admit him formally, so his agreement to come in informally was made knowingly by him in this light. As attractive as this reasoning sounds in respect of managing Mr Draper's admission on a low-key basis, it readily fell apart under questioning once participants who would have pursued this course were challenged about Mr Draper's knowledge of, for example, the safeguards he would be foregoing. Others subsequently made plain their reluctance to go along with this form of reasoning, either because it might place them (as ASW) in a vulnerable position during the process of transporting Mr Draper to hospital or (as psychiatrist) because it would not solve the problem of needing to give him treatment against his will on arrival at hospital. Thus, the course of least resistance, whilst initially attractive, tended ultimately not to be adopted where one of the professionals was alive to the difficulties associated with coerced informal admission. As a strategy it represented a form of short-termism that did not survive robust analysis. In practice, of course, such robust analysis does not routinely take place at the point of deciding whether or not to use compulsion, and many patients are admitted informally and then sectioned once in hospital.[10]

In summary, therefore, although there was a wide range of decision outcomes, overt conflict within the pairs was unusual. Many of the participants were anyway like-minded. In other pairs, there was a pain-free and almost imperceptible resolution, where one party gave way (or was persuaded). In a limited number conflict emerged explicitly. Where this occurred a variety of strategies were employed, some of which were not profession specific. However, it was evident that the psychiatrists' superior (or assumed superior) knowledge about the aetiology and prognosis of mental illness enabled them to draw more heavily on the past data, which could then rebut all but the most robustly reluctant ASWs. Social data was 'softer' and the search for further information about the current situation needed to be weighed against any urgency stressed by the psychiatrist. However, there were ASWs who adopted the approach of 'thus far and no further'. In this context, the impasse could be resolved by the psychiatrist making his or her written recommendation and then leaving it with the ASW. In these situations the responsibility for ensuring that 'things did not go wrong' was being overtly handed to the ASW. This approach was also seen by the psychiatrists as 'covering their back' should anything go wrong whilst the ASW 'dithered'. As one psychiatrist commented, 'at the subsequent inquiry I will be able to show that I made the appropriate recommendation'.[11]

---

[10] See ch 4.

[11] The psychiatrist was making reference to the practice of holding an independent Inquiry should a patient, or former patient, commit homicide; see Peay (ed) 1996.

4. Ethical, Clinical and Legal Issues

4.1 Application and Interpretation of the 1983 Act

Since the majority of discussions did not involve overt conflict, there was little need for the participants to resort to the Act or Code of Practice. Nonetheless, it was surprising just how infrequently the participants made reference to the Act and, in respect of the Code, there was almost never spontaneous reference to it. Very few of the psychiatrists made any reference to specific criteria in the Act as relevant to their decisions; rather they appeared reliant on the ASWs for these, both physically (for the doctors almost never came equipped with any appropriate legal sources) and in respect of the content of legal sources. Whilst ASWs often came appropriately equipped, few spontaneously drew the attention of their partners to this information. It is perhaps therefore not surprising that the discussions about 'law' were often ill-informed or based on an intuitive understanding, which was not necessarily correct.

These often acknowledged areas of vagueness by key practitioners paled by comparison with others who had more peripheral involvement with mental health law. For example, during one discussion when the psychiatrist remarked that he felt he would have difficulties bringing Mr Draper within the criteria for a section 135 warrant (to gain admission to Mr Draper's flat, see above), the ASW responded by saying that, in his experience, he would be able to get a warrant without any difficulty since the Magistrates always asked him what they were supposed to do.

The relationship of these non-legal practitioners to the law was imbued with complex issues of uncertainty. First, although the participants were broadly familiar with the law, they in no sense regarded themselves as 'experts'. The law generally remained alien and, worse, subject to change. And, whilst all the participants would have had some training in the law, their exposure was partial and quickly outdated where pertinent cases arose (of which they were aware they may not have been be aware). Moreover, trying to establish what practitioners understood by the terms central to the use of their powers, underlined the gulf between the meaning lawyers attached to these terms and how practitioners used them. Second, mental health is a medical field imbued with uncertainty. Psychiatry has been recently likened to the dregs of a discipline that has yet to locate its proper scientific roots; only once the aetiology of a disorder has been identified can it be allocated to a recognised medical speciality; until such time it remains in the repository of 'mental health'.[12] Finally, the decision the practitioners had to make required them to consider the consequences of both action and inaction on their part. Weighing known facts is hard enough;

---

[12] Surgeon General 1999:11.

weighing the future is an impossibility. The consequence was that uncertain risk, and its consequences, infected all of their thinking. Thus,

> we are trying to make predictions in situations of uncertainty and in a sense we are bound to err on the side of safety. In some ways it's the only error we are permitted to make because we are expected to protect individuals, and we are expected to protect the public. This is part of our overall responsibility and if the balance is tipping towards increasing concerns, I don't think we can put it aside . . . not to do something and wait to find out, well, we might find out what we don't want to find out **ASW, pair 17**

> In some ways I feel that the law gives you that little bit more support. Say he goes on a s 3, it does tighten everything up. I don't think it's so bad to use the law and I'm not saying I don't think twice about it. There are times when I have put people on a section and I've thought gosh I'm depriving that person of their liberty. It's not something that you can take lightly. I think that I do use best interests all round. I think now, almost all of us are so fearful to let things slip, it's almost like you are saying, it's in the best interests for me as well because if this goes horribly wrong then I cop for it. I am the scapegoat. **ASW, pair 22**

Interacting with one another, these three kinds of uncertainly produced a situation that was potentially full of dread; resort to the law provided a kind of prop. And whilst not fully understood, it was sufficiently familiar to provide some element of comfort. The next sections of this chapter relate to first, the situations in which practitioners can and do avoid the use of compulsion, and second, to the use of compulsion itself.

4.2 Avoiding Compulsion—the Use of Voluntary or Informal Admission

Even though the use of compulsion has been increasing, the vast majority of psychiatric patients are admitted to hospital as voluntary or informal patients.[13] Broadly, voluntary patients are admitted with their consent and informal patients, who do not resist admission, can be admitted on the basis of their passive assent.[14] Treatment thereafter can be given with consent, or, for patients who lack the capacity to consent, on the basis of necessity where that treatment is in the best interests of the patient and consistent with a reasonable body of medical opinion skilled in that particular treatment.[15] Chapter 3 deals with these issues in more detail. Where practitioners do not act under these common law arrangements but rather choose to detain patients and invoke the 1983 Act, the patient's capacity to consent to treatment becomes, for most purposes, an irrelevant factor, since the Act permits treatment to be given without consent (and indeed, against the wishes of a capacitous patient who is refusing treatment). Using the 1983 Act to detain patients, and thereafter to compel treatment brings with it a series of legal safeguards for patients, for example the right

---

[13] DoH/National Statistics 2002.

[14] See *R v Bournewood Community Mental Healthcare NHS Trust ex parte L (Secretary of State for Health and Others Intervening)* [1998].

[15] See *F v West Berkshire Health Authority* [1990] and *Bolam v Friern Hospital Management Committee* [1957].

for the patient to have their case reviewed by a Mental Health Review Tribunal (MHRT) and the need, in certain circumstances, for the patient's doctor (called under the Act a responsible medical officer RMO) to seek a second opinion from another doctor (known as a Second Opinion Appointed Doctor SOAD). These safeguards have consequences for clinicians. This, in turn, provides an arguable incentive not to use the 1983 Act (and instead, admit patients with their consent or informally) unless it is deemed necessary by the clinician to use compulsion. The next part of the chapter unpacks some of the circumstances that make clinicians reject informal admission.

4.2.1 Capacity and Consequences

How did the practitioners deal with Mr Draper's circumstances? First, it was striking that the practitioners approached the assessment as a Mental Health Act assessment, and not as a health assessment.

> I'm usually called by the ASW anyway to go and do a section assessment and that's where this winding-up starts. The implication being that the section is primarily in your mind. **Psychiatrist, pair 22**

Thus, Mr Draper's past history of mental illness (even though he had never previously been subject to compulsion) meant that assessing his capacity and his ability to consent to treatment did not seem pre-eminent. This provides a striking contrast with a health assessment, where, if a patient asserted that they did not want seemingly beneficial treatment, the next question in the minds of practitioners might then be, does this patient have the capacity to make decisions with which I, as a practitioner, would disagree? If they do, then that, legally, is the end of the matter. However, in this mental health context, the approach was different. Mr Draper's right to refuse, and his capacity to do so, did not dominate their thinking. It was not their starting point.

Thus, almost no person spontaneously and explicitly referred to Mr Draper's ability to decide about his own admission to hospital. The Act, of course, does not require the patient's incapacity in order to trigger detention and so there is perhaps nothing remarkable in this finding. However, there was evidence of what amounted to some participants resisting taking the decision to override the patient's refusal of admission because of a wish to leave him 'empowered' for as long as possible. This strategy, which appeared most commonly amongst ASWs, was hardly ever expressed explicitly in terms of allowing a capacitous patient to decide for himself. Indeed, it was sometimes pursued in the context of concern that the patient might *lack* the full ability to decide. On direct questioning such participants would quite often affirm the importance of the specific notion of capacity but, once the imperative to admit had become overwhelming, the presence of *capacity* in the patient was rarely seen as definitive. Indeed, when questioned, participants referred back to the absence of any legal need for incapacity in order to justify detention. Even with those participants who appeared to hold some respect for the ethical role of incapacity, it was almost always the perception of risk to the public (specifically Mr Draper's elderly neighbours) that drove the decision. Thus, it was consequences that determined the decision to disempower the patient and not the capacity of the patient to decide. Similarly, although Mr Draper had no history of self-harm, any serious concern about this possibility tended ultimately to override the objective of empowering him. Indeed, there was evidence throughout the study that some participants were affected by having practised against a background of 40 years' history of mental health legislation based upon paternalism.

Yet, there is support from the earlier national survey of mental health practitioners' legal knowledge and attitudes towards mental health law for the contention that doctors (both psychiatrists and GPs) are not in favour of overriding a capacitous refusal where only the patient's health is at stake.[16] Is there then an important distinction between asking the stark ethical question, where an answer in favour of capacity is probably perceived as almost ethically unavoidable, *and* operating that ethical attitude when thinking about a particular case, where the effect of 'learned cognitive habits' is powerful?[17] This would reflect both the commonly found divergence between what people do and what they say they do, and the seeming irreconcilable results emanating from the earlier national survey and this study, its methodological companion, of decision-making practices. In short, practitioners like to think that they would prefer to operate an Act based on issues of capacity, but in practice seem content to operate, sometimes almost unthinkingly, one based on a more paternalistic approach.

The potential complexity of this dilemma, and the relationship between giving some credence to capacity and the overriding impact of consequences, on whether there is resort to the Act, is illustrated thus:

> . . . my advice and recommendation as the psychiatrist seeing you, assessing you, is that this is the course of action that I would recommend. I think this one is best, that one is not so good and this one I really think would be a disaster. I would hope that the patient would buy into my first or second option rather than the disaster. If they are not prepared to buy into a way of dealing with things that would allow something positive to happen, then I would look in the Act. I would prefer to do that with most patients, but it does depend a lot on the circumstances as to whether the patient has the capacity in the dialogue about the choices . . . **Psychiatrist, pair 6**

At first sight this appears to be a psychiatrist who is engaging with a patient; yet, the engagement in practice extends only so far as the range of options that the doctor considers desirable. It is not actually constrained by whether the doctor thinks the patient has capacity (where he/she would then respect their views even if he/she disagrees with them).

In short, whatever participants may *say* they believe about the importance of capacity in decision-making under the Act, their practice was frequently indicative of a very different learned ethical and legal habit. Where Mr Draper was

---

[16] Roberts *et al* 2002.
[17] See also Kullgren *et al* 1996 discussed in ch 4.

refusing admission participants were frank in their disregard of incapacity as being of any relevance. For them, the House of Lords decision in *Bournewood* was both right and justifying of their attitude and practice.[18] If a patient was not objecting to admission, and was therefore compliant, whether or not they retained capacity was irrelevant. Assent did not require capacity, only consent required it and consent was not necessary. Hence, it was unnecessary for such participants even to consider capacity. Such a position had the added advantage of pragmatism, which included the knowledge that, if the patient *did* renege on his/her agreement later in hospital, then the patient could be held temporarily under section 5(2) or section 5(4) of the Act and then, if necessary, an application made under section 2 or section 3.[19]

4.2.2 Hypothetical Scenarios: the 'Ill-informed' and the 'Deluded' Patient

In addition to the question of whether or not informal admission was appropriate for Mr Draper, two further hypothetical scenarios were put to the participants to explore the boundaries of informal admission. First, how did the practitioners respond when they were faced with an essential misunderstanding between themselves and Mr Draper about the purpose of his admission? The example given was one where Mr Draper said that he was happy to come to hospital 'for a rest' when the practitioners knew that the purpose of admission was treatment. Second, what would their response be if Mr Draper gave a very deluded reason for wanting to come to hospital and take medication; namely, that he believed that it would change the weather? This latter example was intended to explore their understanding of the decision of the House of Lords in *Bournewood*, which upheld the right to admit a patient informally, even if they were incapacitous, provided they did not dissent from admission. By using this example it was possible to explore the contrasts in admission practices between those applied to 'demented little old ladies' and those they might adopt with Mr Draper, a young, black, physically strong man.

The pragmatism of an approach based on assent was, however, rarely couched in overt legal terms with reference to the *Bournewood* judgment. Rather, it was presented as a desire to maintain a therapeutic relationship with the patient. For example, in pair 37 both parties would have taken Mr Draper informally, informally for a rest, informally if very deluded (although not the psychiatrist) and would even have accommodated coerced informal admission, where their ability to take him under section produced his agreement to be admitted informally. Thus,

> if he is willing to hold his hand out and say I'll come in for a rest, then it would achieve most of my objectives, at least in terms of keeping him safe and keeping his neighbours

[18] *R v Bournewood Community Mental Healthcare NHS Trust ex parte L (Secretary of State for Health and Others Intervening)* [1998].

[19] s 5(2) is the doctor's 'holding power' which enables a voluntary or informal patient to be detained for up to 72 hours whilst s 5(4) gives a similar power to nurses to detain for up to six hours.

> safe and I would be prepared to settle for that in the first instance, knowing full well that if he changes his mind, after whatever length of time it takes us to make our assessment, to take a decision about what we want to do in treatment terms. The options are still open to us at that stage to do something . . . **ASW, pair 37**

and putting the delusional reason scenario:

> To be perfectly honest, I don't think it will remotely concern me . . . rights can be bludgeons on people at times . . . I haven't sneaked up and ambushed him . . . if he is willing to go that far with me I want to give him that option now, even if ethically it avoids the question. **ASW, pair 37**

Where the issue turned on Mr Draper agreeing to 'come into hospital for a rest', the participants were asked to think about the patient's understanding that he was being assessed for admission under the Act. Most acknowledged that even the initial assessment in the flat would have set a scene in which Mr Draper would have felt either coerced or the potential for coercion. However, for most participants this bore little on whether they were prepared to accept his hypothesised agreement to admission. When pressed as to whether there was any way of testing whether the patient had truly and autonomously 'changed his mind', or had 'chosen' informal admission rather than accepting the risk of detention, or whether he had been coerced into what would be an ethically invalid decision, few practitioners could suggest ways of dealing with this problem.

It was put to some of them that a litmus test might constitute examining whether a patient, if detained, would apply to be discharged by a MHRT. The proposal was that the patient who would not do so was exhibiting consent and the patient who would do so was not truly consenting. Many saw this as a useful aid. Another way of viewing the patient's apparent consent was to subject it to a test of whether the recent snap-shot of his attitude (apparent consent) was consistent with a cine-film approach. Thus, what did the documentation reveal about his overall attitudes to treatment and/or admission over the last few months? Was there a picture of enduring refusal or was there an identifiable progression of thinking (towards consent) which was linked to factors not evidently coercive in nature? Some participants, perhaps the more ethically inclined, accepted these as possible ways of determining the contribution of coercion to the patient's hypothesised change of heart.

One illustration of such ethical thinking arose in pair 35 where the psychiatrist wanted genuine consent before she would take anybody informally; indeed, even the mention of the 1983 Act would make the situation coercive if consent were forthcoming thereafter.

> I'm sorry I don't think that's valid consent. I mean its coercion at its worst or maybe at its best but it's still not a valid consent to come into hospital. **Psychiatrist, pair 35**

For this psychiatrist, the dilemma was even more complex since she distinguished 'reality coercion' (the fact that a patient who has prior knowledge of the use of coercion, or even knowledge of the Act, may experience coercion) from being explicitly coercive. She elaborated:

> I don't have a standard phrase . . . I mean I tailor it to the patient but I don't use threatening language and I hope my body language isn't threatening and the circumstances aren't threatening and I try to go through it quietly and rationally with them. But I don't have a stock phrase, I'm afraid.

Here was a good illustration of a thoughtful psychiatrist showing awareness of the minefield in which she found herself. Thus,

> I think it's the wrong thing to do to mention the Act . . . I say are you willing to come into hospital? . . . Almost the first thing I say to people after I've sectioned them is do you understand what your rights are, do you understand that you can appeal to a tribunal? ... I will encourage all the patients I detain to go to appeal. **Psychiatrist, pair 35**

Similarly, in pair 26, the psychiatrist would have used compulsion under the Act with Mr Draper even if he said he was prepared to 'come in for a rest' because it was important to make plain to Mr Draper that he was coming in for treatment. Indeed, this psychiatrist continued (in response to an ASW who would have favoured using informal admission and 'best endeavours' to get Mr Draper to take medication):

> I don't think it is satisfactory . . . It is not very fair on the in-patient nursing staff either, because you are really just transferring the responsibility of making the decision to them. **Psychiatrist, pair 26**

He would also have gone on to use the compulsory provisions for admission even if agreement was forthcoming after mentioning the 1983 Act 'otherwise he is not really coming in informally, he is coming in under duress'. However, this same psychiatrist would have been prepared to admit Mr Draper informally if he gave a very deluded reason for coming to hospital and taking medication.

> If I was convinced he would take medication then yes, I actually would . . . I think people often take medication for reasons which are complex and due to partial insight. **Psychiatrist, pair 26**

However, a distinction was drawn between a deluded patient sharing Mr Draper's characteristics (that is, young, black, possible schizophrenia) refusing medication (who would be admitted under section) and a 'demented little old lady' refusing medication (who would not). When challenged to explain the difference the psychiatrist first said 'Something tells me there is a difference but I can't rationalise it'. Then he agreed that it might be because of 'custom and practice' explaining that:

> it's not really a legal argument . . . .the context needs to be borne in mind and the amount of distress that this causes to these patients and their families by them being committed to hospital because of the way that generation of people tend to interpret

those things. It's an argument for avoiding the use of the Act even in the context of incapacity. **Psychiatrist, pair 26**[20]

Thus, for some patients, sectioning was always potentially stigmatising. Yet this belief was held without apparent recognition of the protective civil rights effect of detention under the Act.

Taking the very deluded patient on an informal basis potentially created other kinds of problems:

> I suppose it is more of an ethical problem than a legal problem that he has been hood-winked in a way but on the other hand the practical outcome is the same and hope-fully enables the restoration of good health so I would say my practice has always been to admit people informally if they are prepared to accept treatment, but my reading of the literature is that that is starting to change **Psychiatrist, pair 32**

Another psychiatrist had rationalised the approach adopted in a rather different way:

> I find it very difficult and always have done to know what to do with demented patients, because the difference between what happens in practice and what is written down is so great, that in the end I like to think that common sense rules. I know that is not the idea. Demented patients get admitted to our hospital informally. **Psychiatrist, pair 24**

Others didn't see the issue as a dilemma at all. For example, the ASW in pair 35, who would take practically everybody on an informal basis, observed:

> If you have a view of the mental health services as excellent services then those who can be persuaded will be persuaded and those who can't because they are deluded can come in informally anyway. I'm not certain in what context you'd want to use the Mental Health Act because the safeguards become almost redundant if you have a very positive view of mental health services. **ASW, pair 35**

Pragmatism often seemed to lie at the heart of the approach of many of the participants who did not accept the idea of admitting Mr Draper informally, whether or not he was thought to retain capacity. It was frequently argued that, even if he accepted admission initially, his probable psychotic state determined that any assent, or even consent, would be unstable and subject to the risk of a change of disordered mind at any time. So, even for many participants who believed that he retained his capacity, there was a need, pragmatically, for detention *ab initio*.

By contrast, for others, who were more empowering in their general approach and/or who tried to put into practice the notion that treatment should be given in the least restrictive setting, or those who merely wanted to take the line of least resistance, informal admission was acceptable. This was so whether or not Mr Draper was capacitous, again in the knowledge that

---

[20] Research has shown that black men are significantly more likely to be admitted under compulsion than their white counterparts, Audini and Lelliott 2002.

there was a bail-out option in section 5(2) should the need to use compulsion arise after admission.

Thus, when faced with the scenario where Mr Draper was prepared 'to come in for a rest' his change of heart was seen by most as likely to be a consequence of him apprehending the possibility of detention under the Act. Yet for some this decision was likely to be unstable and, since the reason for admission was primarily the need to re-establish treatment, coming in for a rest was not assent, or consent, to what was actually intended. Other participants were also prag-matists but would have accepted the patient's assent or consent on the grounds that it achieved the first goal of getting him into hospital; the issue of treatment could be dealt with once he was there with the presumption being that the therapeutic alliance could be re-established once there was adequate close con-tact with the patient. Again, section 5(2) lay in the background if such optimism proved unfounded. Finally, some participants were not pragmatists of any sort, at least not initially. For them, they refused to accept 'coming in for a rest' as there was essential incongruity between the perceived bases of patient and clinician. It would therefore be unethical to accept informal admission.

Some of those who would have accepted informal admission 'for a rest' would not however accept the 'deluded reason' scenario for his change of heart. This amounted to an upgrading of the potential for any instability of the patient's decision, since the decision would clearly be emanating from psy-chosis; whereas it was perceived that the idea of 'coming in for a rest' could even amount to evidence of some degree of covert 'insight' on the part of the patient that he *needed* hospital. The deluded reason scenario converted most pragma-tists who had accepted Mr Draper 'coming in for a rest', into clinicians who would require him to be detained. The balance between 'convenience of admis-sion process' and 'instability of patient attitude once admitted' had swayed in favour of formal admission. Finally, for a few, offering a deluded reason for accepting admission was an inadequate basis for informal admission, not for pragmatic reasons but because it suggested incapacity, and for them incapaci-tous decisions were ethically inadequate.

Where participants determined that the deluded reason for admission was indicative of incapacity, their ethical attitude varied. Many were in favour of the decision of the House of Lords in *Bournewood*. For them assent was enough. There was therefore no potential for ethically inconsistent thinking between cases such as that of Mr Draper and those of demented elderly patients; neither required formal admission (nor, presumably, the protections afforded by the Act). For a few others, who appeared wedded to capacity as a principle, it would still be necessary to detain the patient, for ethical reasons. For them, however, there often *was* inconsistency of thinking between consideration of the average psychotic patient and the demented patient, since detention was rarely favoured for the latter patient. On questioning it became apparent that the best explana-tion for this was another example of 'learned behaviour'. In particular, it was argued that it has been within the common culture of psycho-geriatric services not to section demented patients (although the same is probably not true in rela-tion to the elderly mentally ill, usually depressed). However, perhaps ultimately what drives decision-making across services in the way that it characteristically occurs is a very broad notion of 'best interests'; that is, incorporating a profes-sional perspective on both clinical and legal best interests.

In summary, therefore, the participants expressed a range of approaches to patients both refusing and accepting admission, both capacitously and not. Most participants were pragmatists of different sorts and with different decision effects, with only a few participants adhering to a capacity-based approach.

4.3 The Use of 'Appropriateness' under Section 3: a Bridge Between Informal and Compulsory Admission?

Under section 3 of the 1983 Act (the section which allows admission for treatment for up to six months) the potential patient's disorder has to be of a nature or degree such as to make it 'appropriate' that the person be admitted to hospital. This concept has been the subject of legal consideration.[21] However, its meaning remains vague, laying the basis for widely differing interpretation. What does the word 'appropriate' mean clinically?

Curiously, in clinical terms, 'the need to be in hospital' may not arise. This is not because the illness *can only* be treated in hospital, but because the patient will not *accept* treatment where he is (in the community). Since the only route by which *compulsory* treatment can be legally achieved is via the Act, and since the Act only allows compulsory treatment *in hospital*, such treatment can only be achieved via admission to hospital. Hence, the person is perceived as needing to be in hospital because of his/her attitude to treatment, which may or may not be determined by the illness itself. Therefore, a quasi-clinical approach to deter-mining 'the need to be in hospital' is adopted. Moreover, the word 'appropriate' is itself driven by the absence of real coercive legal power over patients in the community. Thus, the need for detention, which should be seen as a criterion to be satisfied after it has been determined that the person 'needs to be in hospital', can become conflated with appropriateness.

For many participants, normal clinical practice would be to attempt to per-suade Mr Draper to accept treatment in the community but, in the face of real-isation that this would not be possible, *then* to say that he had an illness 'of a nature or degree which made it appropriate' etc. Whilst illness may generally be seen as being best treated in the community, this can, in practice, manifest itself in two ways. Some clinicians with a libertarian-bent will emphasise the impor-tance of delaying the use of (hospital requiring) powers until all avenues and attempts at persuasion have failed, whilst those with a paternalistic-bent will argue for the need for an extension of legal powers over patients into the com-munity.

---

[21] *R v Canons Park Mental Health Review Tribunal, ex parte A* [1994]; *Reid v Secretary of State for Scotland* [1999].

4.4 Using Compulsion: the Choice of Section 2, Section 3 or Section 4 for Formal Admission

Where a decision was made to use compulsion there was, as already indicated, a professional preference amongst the ASWs for using section 2 (the 28 day provision), whilst the psychiatrists preferred section 3. Section 4 is only appropriate where the patient's urgent need for assessment in hospital outweighs the desirability of waiting for a medical recommendation by a second doctor. Patients admitted under this section are *not* subject to the consent to treatment provisions in Part IV and are therefore in the same position as a voluntary or informal patient insofar as consent to treatment is concerned. Thus, the section has little use where Mr Draper is refusing medication. Whilst there were no joint decisions to use section 4, one ASW and one psychiatrist had section 4 as their first preference after seeing Mr Draper.

Of section 2 or section 3 which, technically, is the 'correct' section to use? In truth, there is no legally correct answer, either to this question or to the preceding one about whether to use compulsion at all. This is because the 1983 Act gives considerable discretion to practitioners so that the question becomes not 'Do I have the power to section?' but 'Do I want to exercise the power?' Since, for all sorts of reasons relating to matters such as bed shortages and hospital conditions, treatment in the community is always likely to be the preferable option, why does hospital based treatment become deemed necessary? And if so, why do practitioners choose one section or another? And, would lawyers understand the problem in the same way?

In Mr Draper's circumstances, section 2 is arguably the most legally appropriate option, if compulsion is to be used. Richard Jones, in his *Mental Health Act Manual* asserts 'The extent of any prior knowledge that might exist about the patient does not deflect from the need to assess the patient's **current** situation'.[22] Jones argues that the intention of Parliament was for section 2 to be used for initial detention, because it provides for assessment, and that section 3 be used if the assessment leads the clinical team to conclude that the patient needs a further period of treatment whilst being detained. Jones makes a number of points to support this view; perhaps the most persuasive is that section 2 and section 3 provide identical powers to treat the patient; section 3 should accordingly only be made if a judgement has been reached that the patient needs to be treated under detention for a period longer than that provided for in section 2. Given Mr Draper's history and the brevity of the assessment, this would appear to be a hard conclusion to reach. Jones further asserts that the use of section 3, without it being preceded by an application under section 2, could be appropriate if, for example, the patient had been the subject of a full multi-disciplinary assessment during a period of in-patient care as an informal patient. Mr

---

[22] Jones 1999:21. Whilst the current edition of Jones is the 2002 edition, reference is made here to the 1999 edition as that would have been the one to which the practitioners could have had access. The ECtHR makes a similar point in the case of *Varbanov v Bulgaria* (2000).

Draper's last period as an in-patient (when he had informal status) was some five years earlier and he had not attended his out-patient appointments for some six weeks.

Similarly, it has been suggested that section 3 should be used for the admission of patients who are 'well known' to services; the Mental Health Act Commission, the body that visits patients detained under the Act, investigates complaints and reviews powers under the Act relating to detained patients,[23] has described the use of section 2 in such circumstances as a 'misuse'.[24] Is Mr Draper well known to services? Whilst he may have a long history of contact with services, does this constitute being well-known? And does the term more properly apply to his current mental state, which might be attributed to a number of causes?

A further distinction between lawyers and non-lawyers is that the former recognise that the law on compulsion was designed to be applied sequentially, with each section needing to be satisfied before moving on to the next. For example, looking at the section 3 criteria (see Appendix 1) it is necessary to be satisfied that the patient is suffering from a disorder that makes it appropriate for him to receive medical treatment in hospital *before* considering whether detention is necessary for the patient's health or safety or for the protection of other persons. This was to ensure that within a health statute, people who were insufficiently disordered, or who did not have a mental health problem at all, were not detained in mental hospitals just because they posed a risk to the safety of others.

So, why do psychiatrists as a group prefer admission under section 3, when section 2 is probably more appropriate? Crudely put, these non-legal practitioners engaged in conflation, making a decision first about whether compulsory admission would be required and then selecting from the criteria whatever seemed necessary to justify admission. Thus, knowledge of risk would colour an assessment of the presence and severity of disorder. Or a desire to commence treatment forthwith would colour the perceived risk, so that the psychological vulnerability of the neighbours would be sufficient to satisfy a 'protection of others' criterion. This mix-and-match approach meant that whatever the facts, their permutations could be sufficient to justify, in a practitioner's mind, any of the range of conceivable outcomes.

This is neither a criticism nor a judgement on practitioners. For practitioners deal with real cases where they will argue that legal niceties are not foremost in their minds; their professional objectivity will also be coloured by knowledge of what outcome they want to achieve (the 'best interests approach' to which so many signed-up) and by the knowledge of the issues that the legal criteria cover. Any practitioner who has used the Act before, or had training in it, will know

---

[23] See s 120 of the 1983 Act which gives the Secretary of State a duty to undertake such functions; this has been delegated to the Mental Health Act Commission. The MHAC also appoints SOADs.
[24] Para 3.1 Sixth Biennial Report 93–95 and DoH/Welsh Office 1993: para 5.3a.

that the protection of others is one of the potentially relevant criteria to be considered when faced with someone who has a mental disorder. So why not ensure that in every case it is given careful consideration? In stark contrast, lawyers come to these situations with the benefit of hindsight and, usually, when the perceived crisis has abated, if not necessarily been resolved.

The difficulty for the non-legal practitioners resides primarily in the distinction between prospective judgements (what might happen) and retrospective judgements (what did happen). And, when assessing whether practitioners have negligently failed to do their duty they can be exposed (in their minds) to professional humiliation and possible annihilation. Whilst inquiries into an event where things went wrong (most prominently in the professionals' minds, inquiries after homicide) have had a focus on whether, had things been done differently, the outcome might have been avoided, cases of negligence require a much higher threshold of foreseeability to be passed. Thus, thinking prospectively, professionals tend to adopt a test of conceivability; of what kinds of harm can I conceive, what risks am I taking? But there is a gulf between what is conceivable, for example, it is within my imagination that I could win £1,000,000, and what is foreseeable, winning a million pounds is not, because it is so unlikely. Yet, time and again the criteria of health, or safety or protection of others were watered down to a conceivability threshold, rather than a foreseeability threshold. In turn, this meant that wherever practitioners were inclined to use compulsion, or felt constrained to do so, there were grounds that they could cite to justify its use.

Finally, there was the natural health professionals' desire 'to rescue'. Unknown to many lawyers, this concept of 'something must be done' fits more readily with a beneficence rather than a non-maleficence approach. It also fits with a desire to be a universal healer; namely, to protect the vulnerable, including at its most broad, Mr Draper's neighbours from psychological distress.

4.5 Health, Safety or the Protection of Others

There are clearly two issues inherent in the tertiary criteria, namely what counts within 'health', 'safety' and 'protection' *and* an estimation of the level of risk of each type of adverse event occurring. Whilst there is no requirement under section 2 or section 3 for the two recommending doctors to agree on the nature of the risk posed, Mr Draper's circumstances demonstrated how readily the criteria can be satisfied and how little risk is required. Indeed, since the sub-sections include the concept of 'health', and the Code of Practice[25] is clear that admission may be justified solely in the interests of a patient's own health (so no 'risk' to others is required at all), the tertiary criteria are arguably so broad as to be almost meaningless.

---

[25] DoH/Welsh Office 1999: para 2.10.

What did practitioners understand the terms to mean? 'Health' includes both physical and mental heath, and would include preventing deterioration in the patient's mental condition. Whilst Mr Draper had allegedly not taken in his milk for some days, and was thought to be drinking alcohol and possibly taking drugs, his physical appearance was good. He had not, as he had previously, lost so much weight that his clothes didn't fit, nor had his personal appearance deteriorated. Indeed, he looked fastidiously well-groomed. So, whilst his 'health' was not regularly used as the sole basis for admission, when it was used it was usually in terms of his mental health. Within mental health, participants obviously, and most often, spoke in terms of reversing the presumed decline in his current health; reference was also made to the potential longer-term disadvantage to his mental health of any failure to treat his current exacerbation or recurrence of illness (for example, because the end state gained after treatment of a recurrence can be less good the longer the recurrence goes untreated and the worse the bottom of the trough experienced). However, no real urgency was expressed in respect of his physical or mental health; for virtually all participants leaving matters over the week-end would have been acceptable were it to be determined by matters of 'health'.

Safety was similarly broadly drawn. Mr Draper's safety was almost uncontentious since he had no history of self-harm (although, of course, suicide is statistically the greatest risk in the mental health arena). However, patient safety was sometimes seen to include the risk of Mr Draper being exposed to the risk of being harmed, through the acts or omissions of others if he was not detained. Many practitioners identified the risk that the elderly male neighbour, who was evidently already under some stress from Mr Draper's perceived behaviour, might provoke Mr Draper into retaliation in a doorstep confrontation. In all probability, Mr Draper would be likely to come out best from this physical confrontation, but the elderly neighbour had already said that he would 'swing for the bastard' if something were not done. Those who highlighted this feature did not also highlight the fact that people often say things they don't mean, or speak metaphorically.

Interpretation of the risk of harming others, and the type of harm concerned, presented far more problems. The 1983 Act does not require serious harm, and probably covers both physical harm and serious emotional harm.[26] Mr Draper's elderly neighbours (about whom Mr Draper had said in the past, when he was off medication and frankly ill, that he would have to do something to stop them from persecuting him) are vulnerable and frail. This vulnerability is both psychological, in terms of their worries about him, and physical, either from an unprovoked attack by Mr Draper or, if he were to retaliate if they took action against him. For some participants, these fears about the potential for violence were seen as having been escalated by the visit of the ASW and the duty psychi-

---

[26] DoH/Welsh Office 1999: para 2.9 where it refers to the risk of 'serious persistent psychological harm' to others.

atrist, since the ASW revealed to Mr Draper that Mr Draper's neighbours have complained about him shouting through their letter-box.

As regards the nature of the harm, most participants did include psychological harm in addition to the more obvious category of physical harm. On close questioning it became evident that whether Mr Draper could be made subject to compulsion under the 1983 Act—in common vernacular, sectioned—might depend not on his mental state and behaviour, but on the degree of vulnerability of those he might harm, or the degree of provocation they might offer to him. Most participants believed that this problem was not a bar to the proper acceptance that 'fear and apprehension', or other forms of psychological distress at least substantially precipitated by the behaviour of the person potentially liable to be sectioned, could be the basis for invoking the 'protection' criterion.

One further issue concerned whether one ought to deal with a victim's vulnerability concretely or abstractly. Thus, how vulnerable is *this* victim, adopting a 'take your victims as you find them' approach, or how vulnerable is the 'average' victim? Should detention *only* be justified if the potential victim with 'reasonable fortitude' would be affected? [27] If so, this would exclude the alternative legal test, used in personal injury law, of the defendant having to take the victim, eggshell skull or personality and all. No practitioner disagreed with the 'reasonable fortitude' interpretation, although in the face of neighbours who are both very vulnerable and vociferous in their complaints the situation is, in practice, likely to be less clear. As ever, hard examples are difficult to ignore through resort to a pre-determined abstract test.

Neighbour disputes are common, particularly those aggravated by noise in poorly insulated flats. Is it an appropriate use of the 1983 Act therefore to resolve such disputes by removal of one party? Answering this question is not easy. For, while the Code of Practice exhorts practitioners to consider whether there are alternative options for managing the risk, what the degree and nature of the risk is and how reliable the evidence is for it,[28] the reasoning of the practitioners would suggest that, in the presence of broadly drawn attributed risk, objectivity is likely to be jeopardised.

As regards the type of violence and harm that might occur, the practitioners varied quite substantially. For some, it was unlikely to go beyond 'fisticuffs', whilst others could envisage something much worse and potentially involving a knife. As regards the circumstances that might precipitate violence, the participants were almost unanimous in suspecting that it would arise from Mr Draper 'having to do something about the neighbours', based either on his similar statement when he was mentally ill in the past or on the belligerent neighbour precipitating violence. Also, when progressive 'increases' in Mr Draper's past

---

[27] This concept derives from criminal law where, in the test for duress, the defendant is expected to show, when faced with threats of serious injury, a degree of fortitude consistent with his or her characteristics. Thus, more would be expected of a young boxer than an elderly teacher; see *R v Howe* [1987].

[28] DoH/Welsh Office 1999: para 2.9.

forensic history were hypothesised so as to include greater violence to others, this ultimately resulted in nearly all participants who had initially determined there to be insufficient risk of harm to others changing their minds, often adjusting their assessment of the nature or degree of his disorder so as to admit and detain him. Only the extent of the increase in past violence and its clarity of association with past psychosis split the participants, some requiring more of each than others.

4.6 *The Balance Between Health, Safety or the Protection of Others*

Whatever types and severities of harm might have been envisaged by the participants, did they tend to alight on one particular harm as critical or did they sum the various types and quantities so as to take a judgement on the overall violence quotient predicted? Most participants looked to one type of harm, almost invariably harm to others, and took any decision on its adequacy (including the probability of its occurrence) for sectioning almost solely on that basis. There was little evidence of weighing, balancing and summing harms in order to determine whether the tertiary basis for detention was met. Rather, what mattered overwhelmingly was harm to others and its potential severity. Moreover, there was little evidence of much serious thought about any required 'thresholds of likelihood' being invoked in order to decide on sectioning.

Many participants expressed themselves in ways that suggested over-prediction of the likelihood of any violence.[29] Again, there is much to suggest that any probability of violence was likely to be inversely associated with the severity of violence and harm predicted. Thus, very serious harm was too awful to risk to any substantial degree. There is evidence in the findings to suggest that, once a decision about the tertiary criteria of harm had been decided upon (often in advance of the primary and secondary criteria relating to the level of mental disorder and the appropriateness of admission), it was very stable. In fact, for one practitioner it was stable even in the face of confrontation with the fact that a previously apparently important determinant of the view was erroneously recalled by the subject (the mythical assault occasioning actual bodily harm conviction). The latter is an illustration of the well known phenomenon in decision theory of 'errors in integrating information'.[30]

There was also evidence from the exercises of the phenomenon of conflation across all of the criteria for admission.

> I've got three parameters here. I've got nature or degree and I've got risk and any one of them can add points onto the score to take me up to my threshold. There has got to be a bit of illness, but if the risks are getting higher, the risks of me not engaging with this man and leaving it are becoming unacceptable. I then have to decide right, if this

---

[29] Bartlett and Phillips 1999:180–82. The relevance of common decision errors is discussed further in ch 3.
[30] Bartlett and Phillips 1999:182.

man is not safe out there where does he need to be? Does he need to be in hospital or does he need to be in custody? . . . If he's not ill then it would be the police. If I am a bit more towards ill then I'd probably go for hospital. With history, I'd go for illness, just because of his history . . . because the Act is couched in such non-specific terms, isn't it? That's all we can do. It does have the potential to be misused. **Psychiatrist, pair 14**

This 'graphic equaliser' approach would suggest that a pure form of preventive detention (ie without illness) would not be acceptable to some practitioners. But, where the risk is merely one that is predicted, there is greater difficulty in the police intervening. As one ASW put it:

I think you'd have to look at that very carefully, because people make threats to other people and indeed carry them out and it has absolutely nothing to do with them being mentally ill. So, is this an issue perhaps for the police if he is making those kinds of threats under the influence of drinking . . . or is this about somebody who is relapsing into a psychotic illness and acting under some kind of delusion or hallucination in some way? **ASW, pair 14**

The study illustrates well how, through experience, decision-makers tend to learn the rules of the game and make their decisions in the light of all of the factors that they might ever be required to consider. Constraining themselves to use only those that legitimately apply to the particular facts of a given case was more problematic.

SUMMARY

Is duo-disciplinary decision-making by non-lawyers better, worse or just different than the kinds of decisions lawyers might take? An answer to this depends upon how one defines good decision-making. If consistency is critical, and the recent case of *Kawka* notes that 'where deprivation of liberty is concerned, it is particularly important that the general principle of legal certainty is satisfied', it necessarily entails the law itself being broadly foreseeable in its application.[31] This study would suggest that whilst there was wide initial variation both within and between professions, so that individual decision-making would militate against consistency, joint decisions did reduce some of that variability by pushing decisions in the direction of those preferred generally by the ASWs. Thus, there was a reduced use of formal compulsion and less use of section 3 over section 2. Historically, of course, this role of the ASW as a brake on or counterweight to the use of compulsory powers by psychiatrists is well recognised. To some extent, a new breed of less authoritarian or paternalistic psychiatrists who have been brought up with the 1983 Act has been thought to somewhat reduce the need for this kind of ASW role.[32] However four points are

[31] *Kawka v Poland* (2001) ECtHR at para 49.
[32] See BASW (2001) at para 2.6.

worth stressing. First, given an identical situation, some ASWs thought compulsion was absolutely necessary, others didn't. Second, that the ASWs were generally less compulsion oriented than the psychiatrists, supporting the basis for the 'brake' theory. Third, that some of these ASWs were able to have an *impact* on compulsion oriented psychiatrists in the paired decisions. And fourth, that within the group decisions there was still real variability in outcome, which might cause one to question the true effectiveness of the ASW role.

The persistence of variability even within group decisions may partly be accounted for by the extent to which these non-lawyers did not feel themselves constrained by the law. Of course, the Act does invest real discretion in practitioners about whether and how to use compulsion; however, lawyers might find surprising the extent to which some non-lawyers were prepared to resort to a 'higher authority' than law, namely their own professional, or more worryingly, personal ethics. Whether lawyers would condone this is uncertain, since a reliance on ethics might take practitioners down a capacity based route (in order to be consistent with other areas of medical practice) or down a beneficence based route, consistent with some aspects of professional ethics. It may come as less of a surprise that practitioners generally were guided by the amorphous concept of 'best interests', although the near universal application of this concept is troubling, particularly since the concept was peculiarly vulnerable to the influence of any perception of risk. And risk itself was fluid, encompassing both clinical-risk based on attributed psychiatric expertise and the risk of harm to others, based on a shifting and malleable factual context.

Perhaps of greater concern was the considerable influence that the impressions practitioners formed before meeting either the patient or their fellow decision-maker had on their ultimate decision. In this context, it is an open question whether true duo-disciplinary decision-making with a merging of expertise can be said to be occurring; in practice, it looks much more like she who argues loudest, argues last.

On the positive side, there was considerable sensitivity in the ways the practitioners intended to deal with Mr Draper and the task was approached with utmost seriousness; they were never cavalier. Although it might cynically be argued that this is an 'experimenter effect', the practitioners did not seem at all hesitant about revealing their own lack of professionalism in other ways, for example, their lack of familiarity with the statutory provisions. Indeed, whilst the emphasis seemed primarily to be on the outcome to be achieved (that is, action justified by a best interests approach), and less on the process and the legality of decision-making,[33] the variability of the strategies adopted by the participants made any particular outcome unpredictable.

Finally, a number of the practitioners were manifestly decision-shy and would have preferred to make no decision at all whilst engaging in the search for more and better information. This is, of course, a tendency prevalent amongst

---

[33] See ch 4 for studies of patients' perceptions of the process of compulsion.

lawyers and it could be argued that the 'better' decision-makers were those who wanted to amass further and better particulars. However, use of the law is also about resolution and a number of participants clearly felt that they had more than enough material to make a decision. Who are the better decision-makers? Again, this is impossible to resolve. Some of those deciding to use compulsion may have had their decisions subject to challenge by a MHRT; others who went down the route of informal admission could equally have found themselves revising their own decisions through resort to in-hospital sectioning. And of those who refused to use the statute to compel admission, some might genuinely have decided that more information was required, or that this was a case that did not require compulsion, or some might have been simply reluctant to make any decision at all. Only a chronological study would reveal these differences. However, the duo-disciplinary approach did, overall, reduce the number of decisions to use compulsion at that point by comparison with the number that would have been made by these practitioners acting alone. In effect, the impact of the individual decisions were diluted, supporting the notion that ASWs can act as a brake on making decisions to invoke the Act.

2

Clive Wright—A Case for Discharge?

RE: CLIVE WRIGHT

REFERRAL LETTER TO SPECIAL HOSPITAL

WOOD PARK HOSPITAL
LONDON N.22

5.2.1986

Dear Dr Hamilton

Re Clive Wright (dob 25.10.1945)

I should be very grateful for your advice in relation to this patient and a view about whether he could be admitted to Broadmoor Hospital. He suffers from a probable diagnosis of schizophrenia. This has been managed by me and my team for some years but recently he set a fire in the hospital and we are now worried about the safety of the staff and other patients. He is also not very bright and has a pre illness history of minor antisocial behaviour.

The easiest way to describe the case to you is to enclose a copy of a medical summary prepared for a recent case conference called to address the risk he posed to the hospital. This represented a lot of careful work by my junior doctor in trawling through all of his past notes and I think it gives all the information which is relevant. The case conference was attended by me as the consultant, the SHO, the nursing key worker, the ward manager, the Director of Nursing for the hospital, the team psychologist and the team social worker. Later on, one of the senior hospital managers attended.

Thank you talking to me today about the patient and agreeing to come to see him next week. I look forward to hearing from you with your view.

Yours sincerely
Dr Gerard
Consultant General Psychiatrist

MEDICAL REPORT FOR CASE CONFERENCE: 2.2.1986
WOOD PARK HOSPITAL
LONDON N. 22

Clive Wright
dob 23.3.45
Status: informal patient until detained under section 3 MHA on 26.1.86
Location: open ward (remained after incident due to absence of locked ward in the hospital)

Personal History
Mr Wright's birth was not entirely normal in that his mother went into premature labour at 33 weeks and he was born by emergency Caesarian section after signs of foetal distress occurred during labour. He then had to spend four weeks in special care, mainly due some respiratory difficulties (presumably because of prematurity and lack of surfactant). However, there is no evidence of developmental delay or of other developmental abnormality (albeit the records of his childhood are scanty and his mother is no longer alive to ask).

He went to a local primary school where, according to his sister, he was popular with others and good at sport. However, he could be somewhat mischievous. He was often in trouble with the teachers. However, there is no known evidence of severe violence, although there is a story that he once hit another child who had to go to casualty. Also, there was a small fire behind a set of bike sheds which, according to his sister, he was suspected of having set. This was when he was 10 years of age. Academically he was at the bottom of the class. His sister said that he never had any special help, although the school was very poorly provided for in this regard. He appeared to gain some popularity from 'acting the fool'. Apparently his reading and writing are still fairly rudimentary.

A similar pattern of academic performance and mildly disruptive behaviour continued at senior school and he was suspended for two short periods because of his behaviour. He eventually left school at the age of 15 years without any exam passes.

Mr Wright gained a job in a hardware store, which he says he enjoyed very much. He said 'I liked all the things it sold and telling people how to use them'. He remained there for several years. However, he was then convicted of getting into a fight and, although he was only placed on probation, he lost his job. He was then unemployed for a further period of two years before he got a job in the stores of a company selling adhesives to industry. This job lasted until he began to show early signs of mental illness, when he again lost his job. He has not worked since then, except in sheltered employment for people with mental health problems.

Social History
Mr Wright has few hobbies or interests, although he says that he used to like collecting things, for example military memorabilia. However, he said that he no longer bothered with this. Otherwise, he likes watching television, especially 'action films'.

Family History
Mr Wright's sister is his only remaining relative. His mother died four years ago from cancer. He said that she was 'a lovely mum' and that she used to 'look after (him)'. She was never violent to him. His father, who died the year before from a heart attack, was a good deal older than his mother. Mr Wright said that he could be violent sometimes and that he was sometimes beaten with a belt. This was usually, however, when Mr Wright 'deserved it'. He was very upset when his mother died but felt less when his father did so. His relationship with his sister is 'a bit up and down', according to the sister. She is married to a middle manager in an insurance company and clearly has had a more 'affluent' and 'socialised' life than Mr Wright.

There is a family history of psychiatric illness in that Mr Wright's mother had a brief puerperal illness after Mr Wright's birth and his maternal uncle spent several years in a psychiatric hospital in his middle years (he is now dead). The diagnosis is unknown. There is no known family history of epilepsy.

Previous Medical History
Apart from his perinatal history the only point of note is that Mr Wright developed temporal lobe epilepsy at the age of five years and he has been treated ever since with anti-convulsives. His epilepsy has been well controlled all his life and he has not now had a fit for over 7 years. His current medication is carbamazepine (fill in dose). He also had an emergency operation for torsion of the left testis but the testis was preserved.

Previous Forensic History
Mr Wright's only conviction is for ABH when he was 24 years of age. He was placed on probation for two years. There are no records available in relation to this period of supervision.

Previous Psychiatric History
Mr Wright was referred once to a child guidance clinic for his disruptive behaviour. There are no records of this. There is also no record of whether his intelligence level was ever tested.

At the age of about 30 years Mr Wright started to become withdrawn and also depressed. He stopped going to work and also accused others of trying to interfere with his work when he was there. There are records from this hospital which describe him as showing paranoid persecutory delusions which related to his sister and brother in law but that these generalised to people on the ward *where he was eventually admitted. He also heard voices describing him as 'very powerful' and 'sent by God to cleanse the world'. On one occasion he threw a chair in outpatients and broke a window because, he said, the staff were 'trying to control (him)'. His grandiose delusions involved believing that he could control the stars and bring about Armageddon. He said he received messages from God which gave him instructions about 'what (he) should do next'. He was treated with neuroleptic medication (although with caution given his history of epilepsy) and gradually his symptoms subsided.*

An EEG was performed and was reported as showing focal abnormalities in both the left and right temporal lobes but also generalised abnormality consistent with the effects of neuroleptics (the EEG was conducted after the drugs were started) No brain scan was conducted. All other haematological and biochemical investigations revealed no abnormalities.

Gradually he improved, and within two to three months he was almost asymptomatic. However, he still maintained that he had had the powers that he had claimed and that others had been trying to harm him.

He was discharged to outpatient care and continued with medication but his behaviour was problematic, in that he was sometimes verbally aggressive, especially to members of his family, and he was also sometimes sexually disinhibited. During this time he was living alone in his own council rented flat.

Over the next few years he remained on medication without apparent complaint but, in 1982, he had a relapse of his symptoms and was again admitted to hospital. The cause is not clear but he may have stopped taking his oral medication. Alternatively, he had found relationships at his sheltered workshop increasingly difficult and this may have triggered a decline in his mental health. He was again treated with neuroleptics and improved, although it became increasingly evident during this admission that he was probably developing some 'negative' symptoms, of declining interest in things, inactivity, social withdrawal and lack of self care. Also, his behaviour became more truculent at times and he sometimes became angry when people tried to engage him, therapeutically or occupationally. The social worker also commented that he was quite difficult to deal with.

On discharge from hospital again he lived in a lightly staffed (non 24 hour) hostel. He seemed to do reasonably well there, although occasionally having altercations and, on one occasion, hitting another resident (who probably provoked him by calling him names).

Thereafter he had several admissions when his 'positive' psychotic symptoms appeared to re-emerge and his behaviour also worsened, apparently without any change in his medication (he was, by now, on depot medication).

History of Present Admission

The current admission was precipitated by a violent episode at the hostel when Mr Wright punched a fellow resident. The circumstances are otherwise somewhat obscure but, on admission, Mr Wright was showing some signs of psychosis similar to those, which he usually experiences (described above). On admission he was showing grandiose delusions and auditory hallucinations, again involving the stars and Armageddon (in fact signs almost identical to those which he showed on his very first admission).

It was within a few days of his admission that a fire occurred on the ward which was, without doubt, started by Mr Wright.

The fire occurred at 8.30pm during the nursing handover. Earlier Mr Wright had been involved in an altercation with another patient in which he had accused the other patient of 'laying traps for (him)'. He had also argued with nursing staff at tea time and had stormed out of an interview room shouting 'you are all in it.' There was no other warning of what might happen. During the handover Mr Wright was observed to be leaving the ward, having told a nurse on the ward that he was going for a walk in the grounds. Some minutes later smoke was seen billowing out of one of the dormitories. The fire brigade were called and a fire which had apparently started in the bedclothes of the patient with whom Mr Wright had had the altercation earlier was quickly put out. However, there was quite severe smoke damage to one end of the dormitory, as well as destruction of the bedclothes. In spite of the smoke alarm in that part of the ward being effective, the fire took hold rapidly, suggesting the possibility that use had been made of an accelerant.

Mr Wright returned to the ward about half an hour after the fire had been discovered. He was, at first, reticent about discussing what had happened but eventually said that it was a pity that 'the whole damn place' did not burn down because it was just there to interfere with people. He did not, however, directly admit that it had been him who had set the fire (the fire brigade said that there was nothing to explain its occurrence accidentally).

Subsequently Mr Wright was 'specialed' with 'one to one' nursing care, with the intention to continue this until a case conference had discussed his care. However, he was very resistant to this and several times tried to leave the ward.

BROADMOOR HOSPITAL ADMISSION CASE CONFERENCE

4.6.1986
Mr John Wright
dob 25.10 1945
Admitted: 4.3.1986
Legal status: Section 3
Legal category: mental illness

Circumstances of Admission

Mr Wright was admitted after a fire occurred on his ward at the hospital where he was an informal patient. He was not charged with any offence (after the police indicated that it would be difficult to prove definitely that he set the fire and, in any event, there was little purpose in prosecution since he was clearly mentally ill and would be sent by the court back to hospital). He was seen by Dr Hamilton from Broadmoor and he recommended admission for further assessment of his dangerousness and treatment of his illness.

Personal History
Social History
Family History
Previous Medical History
Previous Forensic History
Previous Psychiatric History
History of Admission to Local Hospital
See summary in medical report for case conference at local hospital.

Progress Since Admission to Broadmoor
Mr Wright was placed on the Admissions ward and all his medication stopped, in order to establish his 'base line' mental state. This demonstrated almost exactly the same persecutory and grandiose delusions and hallucinations as he exhibited when he first became ill. That is, he described hearing voices which said that he was very powerful and that he had a mission from God to 'cleanse the world'. He said that others interfered with what he wanted to do and sometimes did this by 'crossing (his) thoughts' so that he could not think straight or had to do what others wanted. He also had a delusional belief that he could control the planets and that he could, and would one day, bring about Armageddon. He also said that he was a Christian and he knew that all that he did had the blessing of God.

When questioned about the fire at his local hospital he said that 'they had all deserved to die' but that he was sorry for them now and it was better that they had not died. However, he added that 'no-one should under estimate (his) power for the future'.

Mr Wright was investigated by way of an EEG (given his perinatal history and longstanding history of epilepsy). This demonstrated the same findings as were reported at the local hospital with the exception that there were no evident neuroleptic effects (he was not, of course, on medication, except anti-convulsants, when the EEG was conducted). He has not, so far, had any fits whilst in Broadmoor.

A detailed history was taken from him of his epileptic symptoms in order to investigate whether there might be some overlap with his apparent symptoms of functional mental illness. He described having had 'odd smell', sometimes involving burning, but no visual symptoms of fire, or anything related to fire. He also described visceral sensations at the beginning of fits and a sense of foreboding and fear.

The team psychologist carried out a WAIS-R which demonstrated a full scale IQ of 78, with a verbal/performance difference of 15 (verbal higher than performance)

Interview in the Case Conference
He was interviewed by Dr Hoyle in the conference. This displayed no new features to his illness. Dr Hoyle concluded that the diagnosis was one of **paranoid schizophrenia** plus **epilepsy**. His childhood history also suggested **conduct disorder**, although this was a diagnosis which was difficult to confirm retrospectively in the absence of comprehensive information (which was not available).

As regards his dangerousness, Dr Hoyle believed that he represented a serious danger to the public because of his illness and that he should therefore be detained in Broadmoor for the time being.

He was restarted on neuroleptic medication.

SAMPLE EXTRACTS FROM MENTAL HEALTH TRIBUNAL REPORTS AT BROADMOOR HOSPITAL

1988
Mr Wright was treated with neuroleptics for his illness soon after his admission to Broadmoor and this removed most of his active psychotic symptoms. However, he has always remained suspicious of others and somewhat grandiose at times. He has not shown any particular interest in fire but, at times, he has been verbally, and once physically, aggressive to other patients of whom he is particularly suspicious. He has also started to show negative signs of his illness in the form of poor self hygiene, failure to attend OT, and a generally withdrawn demeanour.

He remains mentally ill and should remain under section for the protection of others and for his own health.

1990
There has been little change in Mr Wright since his last tribunal, except that his negative symptoms have, if anything, worsened. He has also become somewhat disinhibited on occasions and, for example, he will sometimes relieve himself by urinating in the vegetable garden with only moderate care as to whether others are present or can observe him.

He continues to be detainable under the Act for the reasons described in the last tribunal report.

1993
Although Mr Wright shows many negative features of schizophrenia it has become apparent since his last tribunal that his risk to others can no longer be seen in the same terms as it was when he was admitted to Broadmoor. As a result, an attempt was made last year to transfer him to medium security in his local region. Unfortunately, the region concerned is the last in the country to have addressed the need for this level of security and so no bed is available. As a result there is little prospect of moving him on in his rehabilitation in the way

which should occur. This said he is still detainable, and should be detained, under the Act, because of his mental illness, as well as his deteriorated personality. He should be detained for the protection of others and in the interest of his own health.

1995
Mr Wright has been in Broadmoor without serious event now for several years, although the risk that he could set a fire if he stopped his medication or through excessive stress upon his deteriorated personality remains, especially if he had inadequate support. Attempts have been made to move him to medium security but these have again failed. In the circumstances it may be sensible to move him directly into the community from Broadmoor, once a suitable local team has been identified who are willing to take him. Meantime he will have to remain in Broadmoor under the Act (he cannot of course remain here if he is not under the Act).

1996
I am glad to report to the Tribunal that a local CMHT has now agreed to take responsibility for Mr Wright and that he will be moving first to the local hospital for a brief stay so that he can be tried out in much less secure (non secure) conditions, including under some more ordinary life stresses, and then move on hopefully to a highly staffed hostel. Meantime he remains detainable.

WOOD PARK HOSPITAL
LONDON N.22

EXTRACTS FROM VARIOUS DOCUMENTS FROM 1996 ONWARDS

ADMISSION CASE CONFERENCE: 10.8.96
'. . . *Mr Wright, who is under the care of Dr Williams, has remained settled on the ward since his transfer from Broadmoor. He is a rather withdrawn man who shows negative symptoms and few or no positive ones. He is still grandiose in some of his thinking and is also overly suspicious but there is no evidence of the delusions which were associated with his index offence . . . he also shows some mild Parkinsonian side effects of medication, which he does not like and sometimes cause him to resist taking his oral medication . . . His major needs are, however, social . . . and an attempt will be made to place him with his sister, given the great difficulty in finding hostels for such patients*'

DISCHARGE SUMMARY: 10.2.97
'*The main focus of the review prior to discharge related to Mr Wright's social difficulties, which are considerable. An OT assessment demonstrated significant daily living difficulties and the ward staff report related problems, for example*

being very difficult to get up in the morning, difficulty getting him to attend OT sessions and generally "negative" attitudes and behaviour. Although the team had some concerns about the decision, it was thought worth trying him in a group home; albeit Mr Wright would prefer to live with his sister (to which she is really quite resistant. After one or two overnight stays which did not go too badly, given his sometimes difficult behaviours . . . he was sent on leave from his section (not discharged from it) given the slight uncertainty about the success of the placement and the uncertainty about whether he will comply fully with medication (which is now depot) . . . we have to remember that it is a long time since this rather deteriorated man has lived in the community and he is, of course, not under a section 37/41 conditional discharge arrangements as would often happen with such patients who are from Broadmoor.'

CPA REVIEW: 17.8.97
'Although Mr Wright functioned really quite well at the group home he was very unhappy there and constantly talked about going to live with his sister, Mrs Lane. He was adamant that he did not want to remain there, to such an extent that he actually asked to leave and to spend some time back in hospital while attempts were made to review the possibility of him going to his sister's. The staff in charge of the group home also feel that, because of Mr Wright's attitude (not his functioning), he should not remain at the group home. He will therefore be offered a social admission to his old ward in the hospital. He is, of course, still on leave from his section.'

DISCHARGE SUMMARY: 20.10.97
After quite a deal of work having been done with Mrs Lane to overcome her initial resistance, Mr Wright is today going to live with her . . . she was somewhat reassured that, given that we had renewed his section when it expired at the end of August, there would be 'some constraints' (as she put it) on her brother and the possibility of rapid readmission to hospital if the placement should break down.

CPA REVIEW: 5.1.98
'. . . unfortunately things have not been going well at Mr Wright's sister's . . . he has got into altercations with his brother in law and the neighbours complain about his disheveled and somewhat shuffling appearance . . . also, once he urinated over the garden fence and this did not go down well (except into the neighbour's soil!) . . . it looks as if this placement is going to break down . . . but we will keep on trying'

READMISSION CASE CONFERENCE: 28.1.98
'. . . Mr Wright was readmitted after an argument with his sister and brother in law when his sister became unable to cope with essentially his negative symptoms; she reported also that Mr Wright was also showing suspiciousness of the

*neighbours and, at least on admission back to hospital, there was some sugges-
tion that he might be hearing voices again . . . however, overall his state was a
withdrawn one rather than showing of active psychosis . . . He was prepared to
go back to the group home but, unfortunately, there was no place available . . .
We shall attempt to engage him in OT and ask the DRO to become involved
. . . he remains on section of course, having never been discharged from his 'on
leave' status (of course his section was, in fact, renewed just before his original
discharge to the group home). The team social worker will obviously have a key
role to play in any attempts to move him into the community again. Hopefully
we may still be able to renegotiate a place in the same group home in which he
previously seemed to function fairly well.'*

CASE CONFERENCE: 1.5.98

*'. . . unfortunately the group home on which we, and Mr Wright, had all been
placing our hopes for his return to the community has informed us that it is
likely to be full for the foreseeable future and so that is not a realistic option for
discharge . . .'*

SECTION 117 CASE CONFERENCE: 10.8.98

*'. . . given that Mr Wright's section expires now in three weeks time the need to
take a decision about his remaining in hospital or going somewhere in the community is becoming urgent, particularly since he is very keen now to leave hospital . . . however, it will prove difficult to find a placement for Clive since his
sister will clearly need some persuading that he is much better before she would
agree to take him back. He cannot go back to the group . . . ex Broadmoor
patients are never easy to place and arsonists are amongst the most difficult . . .
finding daily occupation for him will be a problem too . . . an OT assessment
shows him still with the manifestations of negative symptoms of his illness, for
example, in needing some prompting to get up and to engage in day time
activities . . . his current mental state still shows no active positive psychotic
symptoms . . . he is fully compliant with medication . . . indeed, he is very pli-
able generally these days. However, Clive is becoming more constructive and is
looking forward to his future outside the hospital, whilst acknowledging that he
may have been his own worst enemy in the past . . . given the lack of resolution
of whether to keep Mr Wright in hospital or to place him in the community, and
where in the community that might be, it was decided that a further Section 117
Meeting would have to be called, and called before the expiry of his section.'*

LETTER FROM HOSTEL TO SOCIAL WORKER

*'. . . we should be very pleased to consider Clive for a place at our hostel, sub-
ject to funding, . . . however, as you know although the hostel does have some
mentally disordered offenders we are always cautious when considering
patients with a history of arson and we should need reassurances from the
CMHT and, ultimately from the consultant, that Clive is now safe . . .'*

Current situation—as portrayed in the video

Clive Wright, a middle aged man in an open necked shirt, and a female nurse, are waiting to see the Local Hospital Consultant, Dr Williams. The nurse suggests they wait in the day room and he agrees, saying he can 'go for a ciggie'. He is seen shuffling along the corridor with her.

The day room is stocked with orange vinyl arm chairs and potted plants. It overlooks a central garden and the room is light and airy. Clive is seen rolling his own cigarette and observes to the nurse that 'smoking is bad for your health', making her smile. She comments on his ability to role the fiddly cigarette and he says he has had 'years of practice—too much practice' and that he started smoking in the Special Hospital. He says that he was there for 12 years, but there was nothing 'special' about the hospital. He tells her that the reason they put him there was because he 'set fire to something', observing without any obvious emotion that 'it's a funny old world'. His speech is slow.

He asks her if she thinks he'll be out in a couple of days or a week; she replies that they should wait to see 'what Dr Williams says' and that there is a lot to sort out—he asks what—and she replies 'like where you are going to live'. Clive retorts that he is going to live with his sister, that she is great and that 'she'll see me right'. The nurse controls, albeit not wholly, her surprise and, in response to his asking again if she thinks it will be soon, says 'maybe—fingers crossed'. Clive attempts to cross his fingers but fails, observing that he can no longer do so and she, in response, crosses the fingers on both of her hands. He smiles warmly, saying 'ta'.

Meanwhile, Mrs Lane, Clive's sister, is with Dr Williams. Mrs Lane appears somewhat younger than Clive, and is well dressed and well coiffured. She is saying 'no' repeatedly and that she can't believe that Dr Williams is seriously thinking of letting Clive out. Her manner is agitated. She says that Clive won't cope and that he is useless and mad. Dr Williams encourages her to sit down, saying that the hospital can't keep him indefinitely and that what they need to do is to begin to plan for his discharge. He stresses that this doesn't mean that Clive would necessarily go to live with Mrs Lane as he could go back to the group home. Mrs Lane retorts 'that's what you said the last time, but when they kicked him out where did he end up . . . .?' She then embarks on an impassioned plea about her life—saying that the time Clive spent in Broadmoor were the best 12 years of her life—peaceful years. She repeatedly questions why he was let out when it was evident to her and her husband when they visited that 'he just wasn't ready' but the 'experts' wouldn't listen to her saying he was alright. She stands and says 'well, I don't call pissing over the fence into my neighbours' garden alright'. She tells Dr Williams that she has children, friends, a decent life and she's not prepared to have Clive ruin all that again. Dr Williams sits impassively.

Clive is sitting in the garden in the sunshine trying to cross his fingers.

Finally, Dr Williams and the nurse meet, with her observing that she has never seen Clive so relaxed. Dr Williams apologises for the morning's delay, saying that his meeting with Mrs Lane had taken longer than he had anticipated. Moreover, he had also just been talking to 'one very angry Hospital Manager' and that it now appeared Clive's progress back into the community might be more complicated. Clive's sister, Mrs Lane, had apparently contacted the Evening Post after her interview with Dr Williams that morning and the Evening Post had, in turn, been phoning the Hospital Manager all afternoon to ask if it was true that they were about to let loose onto the streets a 'psychopathic arsonist'. Judith, the Hospital Manager, has apparently said that she is now very worried about discharging Clive and that she must protect the image of the Trust in the eyes of Joe Public. The nurse retorts ironically, looking out at Clive in the garden with his face uplifted towards the sun 'And of course, Joe Public would be horrified'. Dr Williams concurs.

DECISIONS AND DILEMMAS

T HE MATERIALS PRESENTED above replicate the information available to the professionals taking part in this case study, which concerned the possible discharge of Mr Wright, a long-stay patient, who has been subject to compulsory detention in hospital. Five sections now follow; an analysis of the problems faced by these decision-makers; a synopsis of the decisions they made; an analysis of how those decisions were made; a review of the ethical, legal and clinical issues arising; and finally, a summary of the key findings in this chapter.

Precise details of the methodology adopted for this exercise are set out in Appendix 2, but they are not central to an understanding of what follows. For the professionals who took part in the study, the question posed to them at the end of the exercise, after the video had been shown, was 'what would you do next?' These professionals had first to decide what they individually would have done, and second to agree a joint course of action with their paired colleague, whether that be a section 12(2) psychiatrist or an Approved Social Worker (ASW).

At this point, some readers might want to pause to reflect upon their own actions if they had found themselves facing this situation with Mr Wright. For those who wish just to press on . . .

1. The Nature of the Problem and the Options Arising

The problem Mr Wright's case posed was more acute than might be immediately apparent. He was detained under section 3 for treatment; in his case this provision had to be renewed on an annual basis; yet, the authority for detention was due to expire during the following two weeks. If no further action was taken by Mr Wright's Responsible Medical Officer (RMO), that is the psychiatrist responsible for his medical treatment under the 1983 Act, there would be no legal basis to detain Mr Wright further at the hospital. In these circumstances he would be free to take himself to his sister's house, an arrangement she clearly would not tolerate. It is, of course, possible that Mr Wright might be encouraged to stay at the hospital as a voluntary/informal patient until satisfactory arrangements could be made for his accommodation and/or for out-patient treatment to be organised. But, once the authority to detain him had lapsed, the hospital would not be able to prevent him leaving. However, to renew the section 3 (a process which takes place under section 20 of the Act) Dr Williams, the RMO, needs to be satisfied of a number of factors including, critically, that medical treatment cannot be provided for his mental disorder unless he continues to be detained.

For the practitioners taking part in the study there were a number of options lying between the two extremes of taking no action and renewing the section 3. These options would permit varying degrees of control over Mr Wright's future. They include renewal followed by section 17 leave (as had been tried before with this patient), making an application for guardianship, and the new option of supervised discharge (aftercare in the community under section 25A).[1] However, renewal of section 3 followed by the RMO granting the patient leave in the community still requires satisfaction of the section 20 criteria; and supervised discharge, intended primarily for those with severe mental illness, would require the RMO to satisfy another legal test with three elements (see Appendix 1), critically including that there would be a substantial risk of serious harm or that the patient would be seriously exploited if not in receipt of after-care services. For the practitioners dealing with Mr Wright this posed a further dilemma; to take advantage of the most viable discharge plan (at the 24 hour staffed hostel) the RMO would have to reassure the hostel that Mr Wright was 'safe', an assurance which was hardly compatible with the requirements of section 25A.

There are further imponderables: the RMO is under pressure from the Hospital Manager to be cautious; there is a risk of adverse publicity in the event that Mr Wright leaves the hospital; the patient's sister is resolutely opposed to discharge; Mr Wright seems unrealistic and ill-informed about his sister's views; indeed, Mr Wright's very compliance and passivity, which make him an unlikely candidate for the need to renew the section 3, are likely to increase the risk that he will be exploited outside hospital, given his own inadequacy and the lengthy period he has spent in hospital (at that point over 13 years); there is a history of Mr Wright not coping well in hostel accommodation; and finally, there are questions about the relevance of his recent acceptance of his own prior fire-setting.

The legal options do not nest readily either with notions of 'managed' care or with the idea that there should be some on-going legal restraint on Mr Wright. However, a conventional 'community treatment order'[2] designed primarily to

---

[1] Inserted into the 1983 Act by the *Mental Health (Patients in the Community) Act 1995*.

[2] 'Community treatment orders' (orders made by a court which can be used to compel patients to take medication in the community) cannot be made under the 1983 Act; compulsory medication

secure the compliance of patients with medical treatment, seems ill-apposite in Mr Wright's case, where he has always been treatment compliant.

2. Decision Outcomes

A crude summary of the decisions made indicates considerable variability both within and across the professional groups. In Mr Wright's case, it is the psychiatric views that prevail in the joint decisions; this is perhaps not surprising as the formal authority to renew lies with the RMO, although the RMO is obliged to consult at least one other person who has been professionally concerned with the patient's medical treatment before seeking to renew the section 3 provision.

For the 80 decisions made individually by ASWs and psychiatrists there were:

40 ASWs	*40 Psychiatrists*
—15 to renew under s 20	15 to renew under s 20
—7 to discharge	10 to discharge
—4 to become informal	6 to become informal
—14 other	9 other

For the 40 decisions made jointly by the ASWs and the psychiatrists there were:

—23 decisions to renew under s 20
—3 decisions to discharge into the community
—6 decisions to allow Mr Wright's section to lapse so that he became an informal patient
—8 'others'

However, these formal decisions disguised a range of strategies. Of the 23 decisions to renew the section 3 provision for treatment under section 20 there were:

—5 'straight' renewal decisions
—10 decisions to renew but to send Mr Wright on s 17 leave into the community, either immediately, or rapidly, or more slowly, or once some further possibilities had been explored entailing for example, further assessment or possibly guardianship[3]
—2 decisions to renew but to send Mr Wright to a *hospital* hostel (ie not the one then being offered to him, which would *not* legally have constituted being 'in hospital'). One of these decisions was combined with the imposition of s 25A
—3 decisions to renew but to impose additionally s 25A provisions

under the Act can only be given where a patient is subject to detention in hospital. Such court-based orders are available in other jurisdictions; see section 4.4 in ch 4.

[3] Guardianship (under s 7 of the 1983 Act) is, in practice, an infrequently used option. Jones 2002:61 notes that there were 1,024 cases of guardianship in place on 31 March 2002, with considerable variation between local authorities in their use of this provision. The appointed guardian may be either an individual or the local social services authority; the guardian has powers to determine where the patient lives and so forth, but has no legal power to compel a patient to take medication.

—2 to renew but to arrange guardianship

—1 to renew but to undertake further assessment

Of the 8 'others'

—7 were to allow the section to lapse but to impose a s 25A before its expiry

—1 was to allow the section to lapse but to place Mr Wright under guardianship

One pair also wished to place Mr Wright on the local 'supervision register'.[4]

Again, there were marked shifts in professional preferences after discussion. Whilst renewal was the most popular option for both professional groups at all points (ie after receipt of the papers and after seeing Mr Wright) only 15 ASWs and 15 psychiatrists favoured renewal individually. Thus, whatever took place in the joint discussions it was evident that arguing for renewal either acted as a trump card or the parties talked one another into renewal when neither favoured it pre-discussion. The discharge decision profiles of the two groups demonstrated that the psychiatrists' views prevailed, and prevailed to a degree that reached statistical significance.

Put another way, whilst 62.5 per cent of all participants would have chosen *not* to renew the section had the decision been for them alone, the proportions of psychiatrists and ASWs choosing to renew the section were identical, namely 37.5 per cent. However, interaction between the ASWs and the psychiatrists *increased* the overall proportion of cases where renewal occurred to 57.5 per cent. Again, statistical analysis permitted the null hypothesis, that there is an equal probability of each group prevailing, to be rejected. In this scenario, where formal authority to renew lies with the psychiatrists, they not unsurprisingly prevailed.

Further analysis of the decision shifts shows that in 22 pairs the psychiatrist dominated the outcome; in 6 the ASW prevailed and in 12 pairs neither party did. In the six counter-intuitive outcomes, where the ASW prevailed, he or she favoured renewal in four (where the psychiatrist would have initially preferred to allow the patient to become informal) and in both of the other pairs a more cautious strategy was adopted than the psychiatrist preferred. One exchange between the practitioners illustrates the rapidity with which one or two psychiatrists gave way to a more cautious view:

Clive's section is due to expire, I am actually very reluctant to renew it. **Psychiatrist, pair 20**

Well, I think we haven't got anywhere more suitable for Clive to live. I really think we should take whatever time it takes to find him somewhere which just meets his needs. **ASW, pair 20**

---

[4] The mandatory nature of the supervision register has been abolished, making the register effectively defunct. For further details see Baker 1997, Fennell and Yeates 2002.

Do you think he will be determined to leave if he wasn't detained, even if he didn't have somewhere to go? **Psychiatrist, pair 20**

I think he has built his hopes up to leave hospital, and Clive himself isn't realistic about what he can find in the community. He is not aware of his sister's—I wouldn't say animosity towards him—but his sister's placing of her and her family's needs before Clive's. It's not fair to expect an unqualified person to look after somebody like Clive and I am aware it is difficult to find places for people with Clive's history. They do exist, but they are expensive and with his wanting to leave hospital immediately, he might be back in two weeks time. **ASW, pair 20**

The psychiatrist went on to agree to renewal.

Thus, an ASW favouring renewal could trump the psychiatrist; but a psychiatrist favouring renewal was never trumped by the ASW. Clearly, renewal was the safety option and this corresponded with either party arguing in its favour being more likely to dominate the decision. Even if neither party was initially in favour of renewal, it might nonetheless emerge as the chosen option during a discussion where neither party had been confidently in favour of their other individually preferred outcome. This occurred in four pairs. Thus, an ASW who has no formal role in this process *can* successfully impose their view if it favours caution, but they will not necessarily succeed against a firm psychiatrist who is not so cautious. Put another way, it appeared that caution as an attitude was at least as important as who holds formal legal power.

The overall confidence levels are also of note. On average, the psychiatrists gained in confidence from the discussion (perhaps reflecting either their tendency as a group to 'get their way' or that Mr Wright's situation seemed to make them feel initially more troubled than that of Mr Draper). ASWs grew in confidence as they gained more information, but this growth was not as marked as it had been for Mr Draper, again perhaps reflecting the fact that they did not 'get their way' as frequently in this case.

The *ALCESTE* analysis (see Appendix 2) of the professional discourses in Mr Wright's case was notably more striking than for the discussion of Mr Draper's circumstances. For Mr Wright, the psychiatrists were again concerned with his current condition, but references to questions of risk were also dominant. In contrast, the ASWs' speech patterns were more concerned with general discharge issues and how the case should be managed if Mr Wright were to be discharged.

3. Decision Analysis

3.1 Conflict Resolution

Whilst direct conflict arose in Mr Wright's case as infrequently as it had done in Mr Draper's case, the discussions about Mr Wright tended to be somewhat shorter. This was because although those ASWs who disagreed with their psychiatrist could bring moral pressure to bear as a means of encouraging the psychiatrist to renew (often along the lines of 'we owe this man more after all this time than another opportunity to fail'; or 'what will happen if he doesn't like it at the hostel—it's really not fair to expect his sister to take him in?'; or 'isn't he likely to start more fires if he breaks down again . . . ?'), ultimately they would withdraw with a 'well, doctor, renewal is really a matter for you'. Equally, the psychiatrists would often make it plain that they had no intention of not renewing, regardless of how strongly the ASW held the view that this was inappropriate. Unlike the situation with Mr Draper, where the psychiatrists could present their opinions about clinical risk or risk *per se* with a degree of professional authority, it was harder for the ASWs' views to be imbued with the necessary 'exclusive' expertise, when their arguments seemed to be based on issues of appropriateness and best practice. Similarly, when faced with an intransigent psychiatrist who was planning to renew, drawing on arguments about the questionable legality of so doing, appeared equally unsuccessful.

The stability of decisions given increasing amounts of information reveals, on a crude analysis, a similar pattern as for Mr Draper. For 30 ASWs sustained their first preference and 10 changed their view, whilst 26 psychiatrists sustained their first preference and 14 changed their view. Given the degree of initial variability within professions, this again suggests that, whatever may be the first position adopted, there was a tendency for individuals to stick with that choice. This was particularly noticeable given that the ASWs have no formal responsibility in this process.

In eight pairs there was a marked drop in confidence on the part of the ASW.[5] This would occur where the psychiatrist had failed to persuade the ASW of the appropriateness of their chosen course of action and the ASW remained unhappy with the final decision. For example, in pair 18, the ASW wanted Mr Wright to have his section renewed so that he would have the security of being on a section whilst at the same time protecting his rights. The psychiatrist, who had no intention of renewing, intended to place Mr Wright on a section 25A and to send him to the available hostel place, saying to the hostel staff whatever was required to get him accepted. In pair 30 the roles were reversed, with the ASW arguing for section 25A and to place Mr Wright on the local supervision register; the psychiatrist revealed that nothing could convince her that Mr Wright was 'safe' and so she wished to use renewal under the Act as a form of desensitisation for herself. As she stated:

> He hasn't had a structured pattern of leave or been integrated into the community with supervised leaves. And just to expect him to go straight from the hospital to the community . . . it's really nerve wracking. In fact, I wouldn't do it. **Psychiatrist, pair 30**

In pair 37, whilst both the ASW and the psychiatrist agreed that Mr Wright had a serious mental disorder, the ASW did not believe that he needed treatment

---

[5] Pairs 1, 3, 18, 25, 28, 29, 30 and 37.

under compulsion in hospital and favoured allowing him to become an informal patient and encouraging him to take more responsibility for his own life. The psychiatrist intended to renew with a view to imposing a section 25A and moving Mr Wright to the hostel; she intended to use the law to ensure that he was compliant with a required place of residence. Thus, one professional wished for a hands-off policy and the other for a very hands-on approach, using the law as a framework for a package of care. Again, since it was the psychiatrist who enjoyed formal power, in all these pairs the psychiatrists imposed their view against the wishes of their ASW colleagues.

3.2 Conflict Resolution Between Cases

Whilst situations of conflict between the pairs in Mr Wright's case could have been preceded by conflict in Mr Draper's case (since the professional pairs remained identical) this was not invariably the case. Some participants approached the second discussion clearly having learnt from the first that the interaction needed to be approached cautiously. Others, in contrast, seemed more combative in Mr Wright's case, particularly if they had not 'got their way' in the first case. Clearly, these effects are likely to be magnified where parties work regularly together, and are aware that they need to go on working together. Independence of mind can be softened by the knowledge of past and future interactions. In other fields where parties have an on-going (if intermittent) relationship, for example, those between tribunal advocates and tribunal members, a form of coded language develops so that an advocate will not necessarily press their case in the strongest of terms where they recognise an application to be hopeless.[6] There is nothing unusual about this. What is surprising in this study is that such effects were observable even over the space of two interactions between former strangers, and between strangers who were not going to have an on-going relationship.

Looking at the paired outcomes across the cases of Mr Draper and Mr Wright it was evident that the factors in play between the parties had a variable impact depending upon the particular pair in question. Thus, for nine pairs there was one decision maker—either the psychiatrist or the ASW—who dominated both decisions regardless of whether they were the professional with the statutory formal edge in the decision-making. Hence, six psychiatrists and three ASWs effectively determined the outcome in both the cases of Mr Draper and Mr Wright. In contrast, for 11 pairs the decision-making followed the format that might have been expected solely on the basis of which discipline has the ultimate authority. Thus, in these eleven pairs the ASW dominated the decision about Mr Draper and the psychiatrist the decision about Mr Wright. One pair, pair 20, followed a wholly unconventional route, with the psychiatrist dominating the

⁶ Peay 1989.

decision for Mr Draper and the ASW the decision for Mr Wright; perhaps this is an example of a pair where there had been a truely persuasive exchange of views (or perhaps, an ASW on the 'rebound'?). For the remaining 19 decisions there appeared to be reasonable agreement in respect of either the case of Mr Draper or the case of Mr Wright or both.

What this would seem to imply is that whilst the formal structure imposed by the law has an impact in some pairs, in others, the personal factors associated with the individuals who make the decisions are more important. And for the remainder, about half of the cases, neither factor is clearly consistently dominant. Of these 19 cases, a number can be explained on the basis that both parties agreed from the start that there was only 'one' viable course of action; others have been influenced by the fusing of best interests reasoning and, for the remainder, all of the factors, including some element of give and take, seem to be at work. What is clear though, is that the law has not played a determining role in most decisions.

4. Legal, Ethical and Clinical Issues

As with Mr Draper, the conflicting responsibilities and uncertainties faced by the professionals produced a situation of complex interacting dilemmas. Thus:

> I think the other confusion is what your responsibilities are, to whom and what the balance is to him, his sister and the community. The Mental Health Act in a way applies to all of them. He becomes the subject of it, he is the one who gets persecuted by the Mental Health Act but actually, once you start taking account of other views, which you have to, I think the ethics of it automatically are dubious. No, they are not dubious, they are just very difficult. If I was a psychiatrist maybe 50 years ago, I had no community team, I had an office and you didn't care what your public thought. But now, because I have to interact with so many more people the network is more complicated, but the ethics I think have become more complicated. . . . ultimately we need to decide what this guy needs, and if we come to a decision, roughly about what the parameters of those needs are. If he doesn't agree with it we have to take a decision about whether it is acceptable for us just to say, you don't have to accept these decisions. I actually don't think we can do that any more. **Psychiatrist, pair 14**

4.1 *The Section 20 Renewal Criteria*

Participants found the decision about whether or not to renew Mr Wright's section 3 to be amongst the most 'legally' difficult they faced. Where a patient is detained on a section 3 the RMO has a continuing responsibility to discharge the patient (under section 23) where continued detention would no longer be lawful. However, the Act provides no statutory criteria governing the exercise of this power. Discharge from the section does not, of course, necessarily mean discharge from the hospital. Moreover, official guidance makes plain that, when a patient is discharged from detention, it should be explained to him or her that they may either leave hospital or stay on as an informal/voluntary patient.[7]

Jones takes the view that the RMO should adopt the approach in *ex parte Huzzey,* a case concerning the basis on which Hospital Managers should exercise their powers to discharge, where the nearest relative requests discharge and the RMO issues a barring certificate under section 25.[8] Latham J observed 'If the criteria for admission no longer exist, I cannot see how any decision by managers not to discharge could be other than perverse . . .' Accordingly Jones argues that, if any of the criteria that would be required to be satisfied for a decision to admit no longer pertain, then the patient should be discharged. In brief, these criteria would require Mr Wright to be:

—suffering from a mental disorder
—of a nature or degree which makes treatment in hospital appropriate; and
—that such treatment is likely to alleviate or prevent a deterioration in his condition *or* that the patient, if discharged, would be unlikely to be able to care for himself, to obtain the care which he needs or to guard himself against serious exploitation; and for
—detention in a hospital still to be necessary in the interests of the patient's own health or safety or for the protection of others.

Furthermore, section 20(4)(c), makes plain that renewal requires the psychiatrist to be satisfied that the necessary treatment 'cannot be provided unless [the patient] continues to be detained'.

One or two participants expressed the view that they had no choice about what to do since Mr Wright did not satisfy these criteria and he should be discharged *forthwith*; hence, the duration of authority for his detention could not merely be allowed to lapse. However, most participants were content to see the decision they faced in the context of 'renewal or not?'. But, the circumstances of his case caused a dilemma. The majority of the practitioners felt that he no longer needed to be in hospital but nonetheless wanted to maintain some control over him. This stemmed primarily from the fear that Mr Wright's inadequacy and unrealistic expectations about his sister's continuing preparedness to house him were likely to cause any alternative community placement to break down unless some protective legal mechanism were in place. Participants were thus particularly keen to maintain control over his place of residence. Curiously, in some pairs this uncomfortable choice was resolved by arguing that renewal gave Mr Wright more rights (an argument which few had adopted in the case of Mr Draper).

Like yourself, I don't feel comfortable about section 3 being renewed, but, it may be what we need to do, so that he has got some rights while he is in hospital to call a tri-

---
[7] Para 301 of the Memorandum.
[8] *R v Riverside Mental Health Trust ex parte Huzzey* (1998). See also Jones 1999:114.

bunal which he wouldn't have as an informal patient. It also gives us powers if we do find somewhere that he can go on leave, but we can recall him as and when necessary. **ASW, pair 17**

Of course, such a strategy needs to be assessed in the light of what it was believed that tribunals would do. And many took the view that tribunals, faced with these difficult choices, would be as pragmatic as the practitioners,

Hopefully, it's morally defensible. Yes, I must say that in my experience I think the tribunal will probably uphold, whether or not they are right in doing it in law I don't know, but I think they probably use the same line of reasoning as us—this is a chap who is a pretty serious risk and he needs to be closely supervised—and perhaps one would hope that they might not be so strict about the rigid letter of the law. I don't know. **Psychiatrist, pair 35**

How this dilemma was variously resolved reveals some intriguing strategies. There were, of course, some psychiatrists who took the view that Mr Wright did not satisfy one of the necessary legal criteria and that, come what may, his section could not be renewed.

Yes, section 25, I think that is a possibility. But I am just wondering, could we start off by asking should we be detaining him in hospital against his wishes at the moment? I am not sure if I have the evidence to sign a recommendation. **Psychiatrist, pair 14**

Some of these were prompted by a general sense that he had been in hospital far too long and needed to be in the community, even if heavily supported. Some stumbled at 'nature or degree which makes it appropriate for him to receive medical treatment *in a hospital*' arguing that his compliance with medication and/or the offer of a hostel place made treatment 'in a hospital' unnecessary. Others, whilst feeling that medical treatment in hospital was not 'inappropriate', could not in all conscience argue that his treatment could *only* be provided if he continued to be detained.

However, the majority appeared to start from the premise that Mr Wright was owed a successful placement and that, as caring professionals, they could not permit another community placement to break down; they therefore needed to renew, even if only to buy some time for themselves to sort things out.

For some, the conflict between their ethics and a pragmatic solution was all too apparent, but resolvable by adopting a cautious approach.

I think ethically the more justifiable thing would be not to renew it and to say the problem is one of resources, not one which can be solved with the use of the Mental Health Act. I've been at a tribunal where a patient of mine was discharged on the basis that the tribunal felt she could be managed at home safely providing there was a community psychiatric nurse visiting twice a day over a period of two or three weeks. We endeavoured to do this in that individual case by withdrawing resources from other clients, so in the end it was an economic decision which probably is possible in theory. Taking each case in isolation you could manage a lot of people at home if you could put in sufficient resources. But if you can't, then the safest option is to detain. . . . I might be inclined to renew with misgivings. **Psychiatrist, pair 36**

Some of these participants also looked for a strategy that would enable Mr Wright to be out in the community on the equivalent of a 'long-leash'.[9] For some this meant renewal followed by section 17 leave per se.

> It seems a shame that one is having to renew a section 3 just to allow a period of leave of absence down the line. But given his history, I think there will be a risk if he went out without any legal structure around him. Also, I think he is getting restless and very frustrated, although he is not trying to abscond at this point in time. Once he realises he could leave, I am not sure that he would stay and he may make his way to his sister's and cause problems there. **Psychiatrist, pair 17**

The terminology of constraint was also evident here.

> It's difficult to place people with this sort of history and his combination of needs. So I feel my hands are tied really . . . renewal on a section 3, but I would welcome him appealing against it. It's one of those sections where I feel unhappy about it. **Psychiatrist, pair 17**

There has been some confusion in recent years about the relationship between renewal and section 17 leave.[10] This has been clarified by *ex parte Barker* which makes plain that a patient's detention can be renewed even if they are on leave under section 17 provided that the patient's medical treatment, viewed as a whole, involved some treatment as an in-patient.[11] Whether it would be lawful to renew under section 20 with the explicit intention of sending a patient on leave, in order to reside at a 'non-hospital' hostel, *and* with the primary intention of being able to recall the patient to hospital should the placement break down, was not, at that point in time, clear. However, this was what many participants wished and chose to do, even though it meant, even in their terms, applying the criteria creatively. Notably, the case of *ex parte DR* (2002)[12] has now largely provided judicial authority for this arguably aberrant professional practice; judicial sympathy with the plight of practitioners seemingly struggling with the demands of mental health legislation is not uncommon. Lawyers are clearly not immune from the dilemmas posed by the need to reconcile the perceived demands of particular cases and the strictures of the law; and, if the cases of *B v Croyden* and *Thameside* are not atypical, lawyers' solutions to these dilemmas are not so dissimilar to those of the practitioners.[13]

---

[9] For the derivation of this terminology see ch 5.

[10] See *R v Hallstrom, ex parte W (no 2)*; *R v Gardner, ex parte L* [1986] and Peay 1986.

[11] *B v Barking Havering and Brentwood Community Healthcare NHS Trust, ex parte Barker* [1999].

[12] The recent case of *R (on the application of DR) v Mersey Care NHS Trust* (2002) does help to clarify the situation by asserting that a proposed leave of absence can properly be regarded as part of a treatment plan since it would preserve a patient's links with the community, reduce stress caused by hospital surroundings, help build a relationship of trust between patient and doctor, and thereby engender dialogue and insight on the patient's behalf.

[13] See also, for example, *Thameside and Glossop Acute Services NHS Trust v CH (A Patient)* [1996] and *B v Croyden Health Authority* [1995]; both of these cases deal with the difficult issue of what constitutes medical treatment for mental disorder.

What is curious about these discussions is that there was so little airing given to the possible use of guardianship under section 7 of the 1983 Act. Arranging guardianship is never straightforward, and clearly, in Mr Wright's case, his sister would probably not have wanted to take on the role of guardian. Yet, the local social services authority could have become the formal guardian, and this would have permitted residence requirements to be maintained over Mr Wright. Since Mr Wright was medication compliant, one of the perceived limitations of guardianship, that it does not give the guardian the power to compel the taking of medication in the community, would be less pertinent in his case. It is accordingly hard to ascertain why so few practitioners saw this as a viable option. It is possible that the relatively infrequent use of guardianship in practice (see above) contributes to its invisibility. But, supervised discharge, to which the discussion now turns, was at the time of the exercise a similarly rarely used option, and it did attract considerable discussion between the practitioners.[14]

4.2 *Supervised Discharge/After-care Under Supervision—Section 25A*

Section 25A[15] was inserted into the Act by the Mental Health (Patients in the Community) Act 1995. It was designed to help ensure that the patient receives after-care services which are anyway to be provided under section 117 of the Act. It is available for patients suffering from any of the four forms of mental disorder in the Act (mental illness, psychopathic disorder, mental impairment and severe mental impairment) but is primarily intended for those with severe mental illness.[16] The criteria require the RMO to be satisfied in respect of three elements. First, if the patient were to leave hospital, that the after-care services which should routinely be provided to all discharged patients under section 117 would not be received. Second, that there would, as a result, be 'a substantial risk of serious harm to the health or safety of the patient or the safety of other persons or of the patient being seriously exploited'. And third, that being subject to supervised discharge would be likely to help secure the patient's receipt of after-care services, that is, the legal provision would make a difference. It was a popular choice amongst the pairs dealing with Mr Wright, but why? And how did practitioners justify its imposition?

Jones asserts that the provision was intended for revolving door patients, who have a history of defaulting on medication where, in the past, this has led to them again becoming sufficiently ill to trigger compulsory admission.[17] In support he cites Baroness Cumberlege who had explained in Parliament that the Government were 'trying to identify a small group of mentally disordered patients whose care in the community is less effective than it should be because

---

[14] For a discussion of the comparative merits of guardianship and supervised discharge, see Hadfield *et al* 2001.

[15] See Appendix 1.

[16] Code of Practice 1999: para 28.2.

[17] 1999:126.

of a repeating pattern . . .'[18] Mr Wright is neither a revolving door patient, nor has he defaulted on medication.

An application for supervised discharge has to be made when a patient remains 'liable to be detained'; it is accordingly available both for patients subject to section 17 leave (coming into force once the period of leave expires) *and* for patients detained in hospital for whom the legal authority for the use of compulsory treatment is about to lapse. However, just because it would be permissible for a section 25A to follow on from a section 3 (so that the clinicians could choose to use section 25A rather than another section 3) it is not clear whether it was the intention of the legislature that section 25A should be used for those patients where a section 3 *could not* be renewed. For this, arguably, would take it lower down the scale of compulsion than might be implied for provisions intended primarily for those with severe mental illness. The participants however, viewed section 25A as a form of legal panacea, albeit that some of them recognised that it had very few teeth.[19] Some even acknowledged that its use for Mr Wright would be aimed primarily at engineering his compliance with a specified place of residence, thereby discouraging him from returning to his sister's, where he was evidently not wanted. Thus, whilst renewal of the section 3 was perceived by some practitioners as a means of facilitating discharge, even those who would not readily adopt this position were seemingly content to attempt to use section 25A in order to achieve a successful discharge.

The reasons the practitioners gave for wanting to use a section 25A were varied and illustrate its apparent malleability. Thus:

> To me the only use of Section 25 is that it heightens the awareness of all the agencies concerned with providing care and it guarantees that the person gets a service. It may be a misuse of the Act. **ASW, pair 20**

> A supervised discharge pragmatically sounds better to most people than guardianship. **Psychiatrist, pair 35**

It was also difficult to ascertain when someone should be taken off section 25A since, like being subject to guardianship, all the time it was securing compliance it was perceived as 'working'. But, if matters were going smoothly, was there a need for the legal provision any more? It was a paradoxical dilemma.

> But you don't know whether that is working because he is likely to be detainable under the Act. That was what happened with Andrew Robinson [*a patient who was subject to an inquiry after homicide*] wasn't it? The only time that there was a period of stability was when he was actually on guardianship, but because it was working it seemed like there was no need for it any more. You can't tell. **ASW, pair 40**

---

[18] *Hansard* HL vol 563 col 108.
[19] Whilst s 25A contains a power to 'take and convey' patients who are non-compliant with medication back to hospital, even there, if negotiation fails, there is no power to impose medication without the imposition of s 2 or s 3.

Whilst section 25A was felt preferable to guardianship since it had 'a little more teeth', practitioners also recognised that the enforceability of both were limited.[20] But this was not a reason for not using a section 25A. Thus:

> ... neither of them have really got any teeth, but it might be that if he feels he is under some sort of Mental Health Act section he might respond to it ... **Psychiatrist, pair 14**

However, this psychiatrist, who had experience of successfully maintaining three psychotic young men on section 25A in the community, recognised that using supervised discharge raised an ethical dilemma:

> I think the trouble with it is the lack of ethics around being completely open with people about what it actually means. To be perfectly honest, this section 25 is a piece of paper and it means nothing. You say 'these are the conditions, do you agree to them?' Well they say 'alright then' and I am going to renew it and I have renewed all three of them and it has worked and they have perceived a legal framework, and it is dodgy, I think morally dodgy but in the end, this is an end that justifies the means. They stayed out of hospital, they stayed well and they are starting to work and doing all sorts of things. **Psychiatrist, pair 14**

However, the dilemma for this psychiatrist was acute for, when challenged about whether he told his patients that medication could not be enforced in the community, he responded:

> Yes ... and I told them the truth, obviously in a sort of whisper.

4.2.1 'Substantial Risk of Serious Harm' Under Section 25A

Here, Jones notes that a *risk* of harm would not be sufficient.[21] What makes the risk substantial is the history of repeated breakdown. However, the harm contemplated might be either to the patient's mental or physical health, or of serious psychological harm to a potential carer of the patient. In all cases though, the harm predicted has to be serious.

Is there a difference between 'substantial' and 'significant'? Lawyers (and presumably parliamentary draftsmen) attach considerable meaning to the choice of one word over another. Whether lay people, or indeed mental health practitioners, share these views is quite another matter. A thesaurus check indicates that the two words are not synonyms. *The Concise Oxford Dictionary* includes for 'significant', 'of considerable amount or effect or importance, not insignificant or negligible'; for 'substantial', it describes as 'of real importance or value, of considerable amount'.[22] The 1983 Act uses 'significant' in section 1, thereby distinguishing between a slight impairment, a significant impairment and a severe impairment. Section 25A uses 'substantial' and was written after it was held in *Lloyd* that 'substantial' ... 'does not mean total ... but at the other end of the scale it does not mean trivial or minimal'.[23] Of course, section 1 is using

---

[20] See also Hadfield *et al* 2001, Pinfold *et al* 2002.
[21] 1999:126; see also *AG v English(David)* [1983].
[22] 1950 ed.
[23] See *R v Lloyd* [1967] which concerns diminished responsibility.

the term significant to describe the degree of impairment; section 25A is using substantial as an index of the probability of a risk materialising. However, the use of the two words was explored with the professionals since reforms to the Mental Health Act have variously canvassed the use of both terms.[24]

At face, substantial seems to imply more than significant. To the participants the relationship between the two was variable and often obscure:

> I think because I'm hesitating, I can't think of a good reason why it's different, I think it probably means the same. **Psychiatrist, pair 40**

Some felt they were interchangeable; others rated a substantial risk as low as a 10 per cent chance of the predicted event occurring during the six months period of a section 3; and some as high as 70 per cent. There was, therefore, considerable tolerance in use of terms.

However, the practitioners largely all appreciated the particular conundrum the exercise posed. For, in order to secure the place on offer at the staffed hostel, the consultant was going to have to reassure the hostel that '. . . Clive is now safe'. And, whilst virtually all of the psychiatrists said it was impossible to give a guarantee that the patient was completely safe, most did accept that 'a substantial risk' was not compatible with 'safe'. Thus, they could either have the hostel place, or they could have the section 25A, although they perceived the two as reinforcing of one another in safety and care terms. Yet, having both was problematic unless they were prepared to dissemble. Most were. In the clash between legal integrity and clinical outcome, the former was manifestly more vulnerable.

Thus, some of the best illustrations of post-hoc rationalisations emerged in respect of this use of supervised discharge, where practitioners opted for this as a means of control, but then had to resort to stretching their justifications of the patient's perceived level of risk (which they had previously cast as low in order to gain access to the hostel place) in order to bring them within the section 25A criteria.

The psychiatrist in pair 35 was perhaps the most open about her preparedness to engage in what she described as 'morally indefensible, but professionally acceptable' decision-making in order to achieve control over Mr Wright in the community. She started from the position that there was no impediment arising from Mr Wright's psychiatric condition to letting him leave the hospital to go to the hostel place, as soon as all the practical arrangements could be organised. Indeed, she asserted that he should go 'as soon as possible'. However, she and the ASW both agreed that renewal of the section 3 was necessary. When challenged about how it was possible to satisfy the section 3 criteria (and, in particular, that it was 'appropriate for him to receive medical treatment in hos-

---

[24] See ch 5.

pital') when she was intending to send him forthwith to a non-hospital hostel she remarked:

> Ah, I didn't know that . . . I have never come across that before. I don't know how I would get around that . . . well, in that case I will renew it and then I'll send him on leave after he has been renewed. **Psychiatrist, pair 35**

When challenged that this would effectively entail twisting her clinical opinion to fit the Act, she was fully prepared to do this.

> . . . pragmatically, if it gets me to the position where I have him on a section 3, then I can work towards the supervised discharge and try him out in a hostel. I would rather be in that position, than let him go. **Psychiatrist, pair 35**

And finally, there was an honest admission of what lay behind this strategy of manipulating the 1983 Act in order to achieve a particular objective; it was not, as she had earlier asserted, to prevent him from relapsing and returning to Broadmoor, but rather:

> It's really there for our protection, I think. I think the Mental Health Act is there for the protection of patients, but it is very obviously there for the protection of medical practitioners as well. I admit that. I think that your personal experience exposes you to the crucifixion of other doctors; there was a major incident where they allowed a schizophrenic chap to go home, he stabbed his sister-in-law to death, two years ago. It made the front page of the Yorkshire press. As a result, you can feel them breathing down your neck. It does change your view. **Psychiatrist, pair 35**

4.2.2 'Serious Exploitation'

Whilst the participants were most immediately worried about Mr Wright's latent preponderance to set fires, some were attracted to the alternative section 25A criterion of 'serious exploitation'. In the debates in the House of Lords prior to the introduction of this section, Baroness Cumberlege had included in 'the risk of serious exploitation' the notion that the patient might be lured into prostitution or that they might be exposed to the risks of drug abuse. Jones prophetically adds the risk of economic exploitation.[25] It is this latter risk that practitioners most frequently identified when adverting to serious exploitation as the basis for imposing section 25A. Yet, they were prepared to apply it to a level of risk that was so low that it would almost certainly not be upheld by the courts. Similar distortions occurred in respect of questions concerning the patient's vulnerability and risk of exploitation, as had occurred for the notion of a 'substantial risk or causing serious harm'.

4.3 The Translation of Legal Theory into Non-legal Practice: the Case of 'Nature or Degree'

In order to renew section 3 or to admit a patient to hospital under compulsion it is necessary for the professionals to be satisfied that the patient's mental disorder

---

[25] 1996:115.

is of a 'nature or degree' which 'warrants' (section 2) or makes 'appropriate' (section 3) the detention or renewal. The term 'nature or degree' is thus of central importance both to the case of Mr Draper[26] and of Mr Wright.

The meaning of 'nature or degree' was considered by Popplewell J in *ex parte Smith*.[27] It was acknowledged that whilst 'nature or degree' is *disjunctive* (that is the test could be satisfied on grounds of either the nature of the patient's disorder or its current degree), in very many cases the two terms are inevitably bound-up together. Broadly, the word 'nature' refers to the particular mental disorder from which the patient has been diagnosed as suffering, its chronicity, its prognosis, and the patient's previous response to receiving treatment for the disorder; and 'degree' refers to the current manifestation of the patient's disorder.

Participants' understanding of 'nature or degree' was problematic. Many had difficulty understanding the term as a technical legal concept and others difficulty in applying it to the clinical data. When asked to rate the seriousness of the disorder of both Mr Draper and Mr Wright, the majority view favoured the more serious end of the presenting conditions (see Appendix 3). But, a notable minority was not satisfied that the patients were significantly 'unwell'. These differences persisted whether participants were asked to assess 'nature or degree' conjunctively or disjunctively.

On average, both ASWs and psychiatrists saw Mr Draper as having a disorder that was slightly more serious in its historical nature than its current degree, with the psychiatrists finding the difference between historical nature and current degree to be even more marginal. Similarly for Mr Wright, the ASWs saw his historical nature as markedly more serious than current degree and the psychiatrists agreed.

Was there, however, enough evidence to justify admission for Mr Draper or renewal for Mr Wright? From a clinical perspective, for both patients the nature of their past disorders was fully documented in the case papers. The issue therefore turned, for Mr Draper, on whether this was another manifestation of the same disorder, or whether it was something different altogether (for example, a grief reaction to his mother's death), or whether it was not even a mental disorder at all. For Mr Wright, a clearly institutionalised man, one important issue concerned whether 'negative' symptoms can properly be regarded as current 'degree' or whether they are really part of the nature of his on-going illness.[28] Whilst negative symptoms can be a manifestation of chronic psychiatric disorder, they can also be associated with institutionalisation; and institutionalisation was a product not solely of his diagnosed disorder, but also of a long-term professional response as to how to manage Mr Wright generally. In addition to this confusion, there remained the question of whether he remained vulnerable

---

[26] See ch 1.

[27] *R v MHRT for the South Thames Region, ex p. Smith* (1998).

[28] Psychiatrists use the term negative symptoms to include emotional apathy, slowness of thought and movement, under-activity, lack of drive, poverty of speech and social withdrawal. They can all impede effective rehabilitation.

to positive symptoms of deterioration. It was thus evident that for some types of patient and some types of disorder the legal distinction between nature and degree fell apart in the clinician's hands. However, this may not be a clinical shortcoming, but rather the law's inability fully to reflect clinical constructs.[29]

Clearly, assessing current degree depends partly on what is observed of the patient directly. Mr Draper's behaviour and speech suggested possible positive symptoms but did not do so unequivocally. Mr Wright displayed apparent negative symptoms (but no positive ones) and, for seemingly the first time, he had accepted his involvement in the fire that the notes repeatedly allege that he set some 13 years previously.

However, current nature can be inferred where there is recognition of a past history of deterioration plus a recurrence, evident from the notes, of factors previously associated with such deterioration; for example, cessation of medication, disengagement with professionals or changes in behaviour may not in themselves directly demonstrate mental deterioration, but may be shown to have been associated with such deterioration in the past. Indeed, most of the psychiatrists did adopt this 'history repeating itself' approach, and did so by interpreting the current information (both from the notes and on seeing the patient) within a medical or disease model.

> In practice it is very difficult for people with his history to escape from that, because there is a disease called 'been to a psychiatric hospital'. You can never actually get away from it. **Psychiatrist, pair 19**

Yet many ASWs interpreted the same information solely or largely within a social model; alternatively, they started from the presumption that a social explanation was at least tenable. This required greater amounts of data consistent with deterioration within a disease model to overturn their assumption. The psychiatrists started from the opposite assumption and their chosen model required data that was inconsistent with making the diagnosis of deterioration in order to refute their presumed conclusion. Hence, it was not the data that was different but rather the presumptive interpretative model. The burden of proof of disease therefore fell in different directions, according to the practitioner's style of decision-making. Although there were some ASWs whose style was 'medical' and some psychiatrists whose style was 'social', the congruent association of style with professional status was more common.

Jones explains the situation thus:

> The course of a patient's mental illness is never entirely predictable and this Act requires the professionals involved in assessing a patient for possible compulsory admission to exercise their judgment to determine whether the patient's condition and situation at the time of the assessment meet the statutory criteria for admission. If it is the case that a mere failure to continue with medication would be sufficient to satisfy the statutory criteria with respect to a patient who has a history of admissions

---

[29] Eastman and Peay (eds) 1999: ch 13.

subsequent to previous failures to continue with medication, this would lead to the personal examination of the patient by the recommending doctors under s.12(2) and the interviewing of the patient by the approved social worker under s.13(2) becoming sterile exercises. One of the objectives of the examinations and interview of such a patient would be to identify whether there is any evidence (apart from the cessation of the medication) to suggest that history is beginning to repeat itself by the reappearance of a deterioration in the patient's mental health. If there is such evidence the 'nature' of the patient's mental disorder could lead professionals to conclude that detention in hospital is either 'appropriate' or 'warranted', even though the current manifestation of the disorder (the 'degree') could not be used to justify such a conclusion.[30]

Clearly, where the patient is known personally to the doctors and the ASW (not so in Mr Draper's case), or where they have good knowledge of the patient's psychiatric history from the papers, then it may be easier to determine when to intervene in the case of a deteriorating patient. Subtle signals will mean more and can be more relied upon. With revolving door patients who have ceased to take medication, the role of the professionals will be partly to assess the patient's response to its loss. Where there are no signs of mental disorder it would be very difficult to satisfy the criteria for admission solely on the basis of 'nature'; but, where the professionals identify some evidence of deterioration in the patient's mental health, then admission could be justified.

Yet, the participants demonstrated the fallacy behind this approach. Current degree was capable of infinite flexibility of attribution, depending on what the professional wished to achieve. Did the degree drive the response or the response drive the assessment of degree? The information in the papers on historical nature was clear for both patients, but was the current manifestation in Mr Draper's case a recurrence of the previous pattern, a new manifestation, or not a mental disorder at all? And, in Mr Draper's case, why did so many of the psychiatrists stick with their initial assessment based on the case papers when what could be gleaned from the video was more ambivalent in respect of his current condition?

This raises an important point concerning the type of data used by practitioners in determining particularly the current degree of illness. There was a tendency for some participants, most commonly ASWs, to utilise only direct current data, that is the observed mental state or its recent documentation. However, many psychiatrists determined the likely mental state by way of a combination of direct current information and inference based on known patterns and associations of relapse in the past. Indeed, psychiatrists who decided to recommend detention of Mr Draper would argue that his mental state could not reasonably be determined solely on the basis of their observations.

I don't think the social worker and the consultant were in the flat long enough really to establish whether he had got proper delusions. **Psychiatrist, pair 37**

---

[30]   1999:28; see also MHAC 1998 and Blom-Cooper *et al* 1995.

Of course this combination of inference and current observations fits better with a 'medical' than a 'social' model, since it is the repetition of pattern *as pattern* that nourishes the method of inference.

A final confounding tendency of some participants, especially of psychiatrists, was to incorporate behaviour that was not, of itself, suggestive of mental disorder into the 'nature' or 'degree' of illness. This applied specifically in relation to behaviour that was dangerous to others. Hence, in pair 40 for Mr Draper the psychiatrist drew conclusions about his behaviour as indicative of relapsing illness. This might be seen as an aspect of current 'degree'. However, since the basis for concluding that the behaviour suggested illness-relapse was its coincidence with relapse in the past, it thereby became part of the characteristic long-term nature of the person's illness. This type of reasoning allows violent behaviour, or even its threat, to have double application in the Act. It can serve to justify both perceiving the presence of illness (of a nature *and* degree) and the need for detention for the protection of others. Looked at another way, there is an in-built conflation of the more properly separate and sequential criteria for detention; in all of the confusion over terms, this way of operating may not even be readily apparent to practitioners.

SUMMARY

A number of the themes evident in chapter one re-emerge here. First, that there is considerable variability in terms of what the professionals would want to do, and a variability which is even wider in terms of their creative use of the law in order to achieve outcomes regarded as being in the patient's best interests. Second, that the profession with the formal power, in this situation the psychiatrists, dominates the outcomes of the discussions where conflict was evident. And third, that the cautious strategy, to renew the provisions to authorise the use of compulsion with Mr Wright, could trump against the formal power of psychiatrists who either felt themselves legally bound to do otherwise or whose first choice would have been to have moved Mr Wright into the community through a strategy negotiated with him.

Generally, the desire to retain control over Mr Wright, through resort to some form of legal strategy, was most evident. Given this imperative, the almost total absence of any discussion about the use of guardianship is curious. Unlike supervised discharge, which came into being after the passage of the Mental Health (Patients in the Community) Act 1995, guardianship has been an option in broadly its current format since the introduction of the Mental Health Act 1959. Yet its visibility has remained low. Perhaps it is the fascination with all things 'new' that leads to a focus on supervised discharge rather than guardianship. Or perhaps it is another illustration of the influence of common cognitive errors, discussed in chapter 3, and, in particular, of the tendency of decision-makers to focus on one option as being the only option. However, guardianship would have permitted some, albeit limited, legal control over Mr Wright; yet seemingly, only section 25A was perceived in this potentially attractive light.

Indeed, participants were keen to use section 25A even though they recognised that it had few teeth and even once they realised that they would have to bend their clinical assessments if they were to bring Mr Wright within the section 25A critieria. In weighing what were regarded as the potential benefits of section 25A (of which few had direct experience) against the need to compromise on either their ethical principles or their perception of what the law required, outcomes triumphed. Preventing a further *failed* placement of Mr Wright in the community seemed to be the most important consideration. This was, in many respects, another manifestation of the best interests reasoning which had emerged in the case of Mr Draper.

In this context, of turning a blind eye to the law's constraints and restraints on the use of compulsion under section 25A, it is perhaps not surprising that the professionals displayed little common understanding of a key phrase in the Act, namely 'nature and degree'.[31] As this was progressively unpacked, it became evident that the term was so malleable and so at odds with clinical constructs that its legal impact was barely discernable. Similarly, the language of 'significant' and 'substantial' seemed not to impact on the practitioners in any meaningful or consistent manner.

The law, with its emphasis on consistency, predictability and appropriateness of application, thus seems to have a marginal impact when lined up against the powerful forces of 'best interests', clinical imperatives and, most tellingly, fear of failure. And, as emerged from the analysis of decisions across the two cases of Mr Draper and Mr Wright, it appeared that the presence of a dominant personality in the decision-making pair had as much impact on outcome as the 'ever present' presence of the law with its statutory favouring of one discipline over another. Is it then possible to design a law that effectively meets and reconciles all of these objectives? This question will be returned to in the final chapter.

---

[31] See also Perkins 2002. Her research on MHRT members is discussed in ch 4.

3

Hazel Robinson—A Case for Compulsory Treatment?

RE: HAZEL ROBINSON

Letters in General Practice File

From: Dr Williams, Consultant Psychiatrist, Wood Park Hospital, N22

1.3.88

Dear Dr Jones

Re Hazel Robinson (dob 15.2.1972)

Thank you for referring this 16 year old young woman to me. As you described in your letter, she has been greatly distressed by the death of her father recently after a fairly long illness. She gave a history of frequent tearfulness, some loss of appetite, sleep disturbance (but without early morning wakening), difficulty in concentrating on school work, some social withdrawal and also feelings of guilt (perhaps arising from her father's death at a time when there would be the normal tensions with parents which go with adolescence).

There is no history of childhood disturbance per se, although I noted that her mother pointed out that she had always been a sensitive child who needed to be looked after carefully. The mother also remarked that she had been concerned that, when Hazel was coping with her father's illness, she was becoming 'too involved' with her current boy friend, as a source of comfort (although it was not clear to me what she meant by this).

Although she has obviously taken her father's death very badly, and indeed does have some depressive symptoms, I did no think that the balance of advantage was in favour of prescribing an anti-depressant. This was mainly because I am always cautious in prescribing to someone as young as her and it did also seem to me that she might feel even more 'different' at school if she had not only lost her father but was also having to take medication. She was in agreement with this, indeed she said that she was innately rather opposed to seeing such difficulties as 'illness' and was also against medication.

I have arranged to see her again in six weeks time. She seemed entirely happy to agree with this way of doing things.

Yours sincerely

Dr Williams
Consultant Psychiatrist

16.4.88

From: Dr Williams, Consultant Psychiatrist, Wood Park Hospital, N22

Dear Dr Jones
I saw Hazel again (this time without her mother). She seemed a little better and certainly was managing her school activities better than she had been. She was also not as isolated and was crying less. However, she said that she still thought about her father a good deal and also still felt guilty for some things she had said to him during his illness and this evidently continued to trouble her. I remain concerned that she is a rather unhappy young woman whose reaction to her father's death is somewhat beyond the usual and that this probably suggests some unresolved problems. However, it may well be that this is all part of an unfortunate intermingling of normal adolescent turmoil with the sad loss of her father (a case of terrible timing).

With these various cautions, I think that there is probably not much to be gained from me continuing to see her. However, please have a low threshold for re-referring her should you be at all concerned in the future that she needs specialist psychiatric help.

Yours sincerely
Dr Williams
Consultant Psychiatrist

From: Student Health Service, University of Leeds.

3.3.1992

Dear Dr Jones, Re Hazel Robinson, Second Year Undergraduate
I am writing to you about your patient who has been under my care during term time since she came up to university 18 months ago. Although she coped quite well with her studies in her first year at Leeds, this year she has had some major problems. In particular, after a few problems in her studies last term, which she weathered, she has become very depressed indeed in the last few weeks.

Almost certainly the depression was precipitated by her deciding to have an abortion just after returning from the Christmas vacation (which she had spent in fear of her mother's reaction if she were to tell her that she was pregnant, which in the end she did not do). Soon after the termination her boy friend ended the relationship (I think not because he did not want to stay with her but because she did not discuss with him aborting his child). She is now very tearful, not eating properly, not sleeping and also has thoughts of harming herself (although she has not laid any plans or done anything else to suggest that she might be at real risk of suicide). Above all, she is guilt ridden about what she has done, and this has been made much worse by the reason which her boy friend has given to her for his abandonment of her, as well as by links which she makes in her mind between the child's death and recollections which she has of feeling guilt for the way in which her father died without her being able fully to repair all the damage which she perceives she did to him through disputes with him during her adolescence.

I have told her that I am sure she should not continue with her studies this year and I have ensured with the University authorities that she will be able to repeat her second year in the autumn of this year. She will be coming to see you in a day or so, after returning home.

If there is anything I can do to help her back into her studies, hopefully in October, then please let me know. She is a nice young woman who has had a somewhat raw deal in life already in various ways and who deserves all the help we can give her.

Yours sincerely
Dr Young
General Practitioner
Student Health Centre.

From: Dr Williams, Wood Park Hospital, N22

15.5.1992

Dear Dr Jones,

Re Hazel Robinson (admitted 17.3.92, discharged 22.5.92)

I am enclosing a discharge summary prepared by my SHO in relation to Hazel's admission. As you will see, she is a good deal better, although she will need careful monitoring and continuing treatment with an anti-depressant in order for her progress not to be reversed. She clearly has some major difficulties which, almost certainly, predisposed her to the quite severe depressive illness which she has just gone through, and it will be important to ensure that she is watched carefully through any further major stress periods in her life.

My SHO will continue to see her in outpatients for the time being, at least until she (hopefully) returns to university in the autumn. Thereafter she will obviously be the responsibility of what appears to be a very good student health service (I do no think that it would add much for me to refer her to a consultant colleague in Leeds). If, when she comes back for vacations, you have any concerns about Hazel which would warrant re-referring her then please do not hesitate to do so.

I will copy this letter and the Discharge Summary to the GP in the Student Health Centre who initially wrote to you when Hazel became unwell.

Yours sincerely
Dr Williams
Consultant Psychiatrist.

DISCHARGE SUMMARY

Name: Hazel Robinson (dob 15.2.1972)
Admitted: 7.3.92
Discharged: 22.5.92
Diagnosis: moderately severe depressive illness
Legal Status: Section 2, then informal.

History of Presenting Illness

Hazel described changes in her as 'just to do with the abortion' and seemed to believe that what she was experiencing was a 'normal reaction', adding that she was just upset that she had had to tell her mother about the abortion after her return from university. Indeed, she was reluctant to describe changes in her, appearing to be concerned that doing so would result in us 'giving (her) pills'. She had even been reluctant to come to see us and had essentially been 'brought' by her mother after the GP had telephoned Dr Williams concerned. However, she did also say that she deserved to be punished for what she had done to the baby and that it was 'murder'. She said that she just wanted to be left alone and other people should not be concerned about her. Asked whether she felt badly enough about herself to harm herself she said that that was nothing to do with anyone else and that '(her) life was (her) own'.

Her mother described frequent tearfulness which then gave way to constantly appearing depressed, but without actually crying. She also said that Hazel had lost weight, to such an extent that her clothes no longer fitted her and she looked lost in them; she also was not sleeping and, when she did sleep, woke up early in the morning (she heard her get up and walk around the house). She said that she was withdrawn, would not talk, would not go out, and ate very little. Also, she was not bothering with her appearance. Her mother said that, when she tried to ask Hazel what was the matter, all that she ever seemed prepared to talk about was her father and what she had done to him by being so cross with him before he died. Her mother said that she thought that, in fact, all the problems had been caused by her getting to know the wrong sort of boy at university who had irresponsibly made her pregnant (it seemed to us that there had been a good deal of conflict between Hazel and her mother over the abortion, since Hazel had returned from university and had been forced to tell her mother about it).

Past Psychiatric History

Hazel experienced some depressive symptoms after the death of her father when she was 16 years of age. She went to her GP with symptoms of sleep disturbance, frequent crying, social withdrawal and difficulty keeping up with her school work, which persisted for some months after her father's death and which ultimately resulted in her being seen by Dr Williams. He felt that, although she had symptoms which might have responded to an anti-depressant, it was not indi-

cated in her case, particularly given her age and the fact that what she was experiencing could be a manifestation of a combination of adolescent turmoil and coping with her father's death where there had been some conflict between the two of them. In the event her symptoms seemed gradually to resolve and she was discharged quickly back to the GP, although her mother gives a history of her being abnormally moody right up until the time when she went to university. She herself describes still continuing to be somewhat preoccupied with thoughts of her father even after she went to Leeds.

Otherwise, there is no history of earlier childhood disturbance.

Family History

Hazel's father was a bank manager who died when she was only 16 years of illness from cancer of the lung. She described him as a good father who 'always looked after (her)'; she said that she had been close to him but that there had been difficulties in their relationship in the last two or so years before his death. She described feeling very guilty for what '(she) had done to him during his illness', saying that she had been very angry and rebellious towards him and that that had made him ill. This was a preoccupying theme of her thoughts (see below). Her mother, who used to be a teacher, she described as someone to whom she had not been very close until her father's death, when they had somewhat clung together. However, she seemed also to find her mother rather intrusive in her life, particularly as regards boy friends. She said that her mother's marriage had not been happy and that there had been frequent rows, including about Hazel herself. She described feeling caught in the middle somewhat between her parents in the latter years of her father's life. She also said that she felt angry with her mother for not being nicer to her father when he was dying, although she also said that her mother 'had not helped (her) with (her) feelings about her father, either before or during his illness' (this seemed rather unexplained and may have merely been as reflection of her depressive illness). Hazel has no siblings, although her mother had another child (a daughter) two years after Hazel's birth who died at only a few days of age. Hazel says that she wishes that she had had a sister and often thinks about her dead sister (although this too might be a reflection of her illness).

There is a family history of mental illness in that Hazel's father had suffered a depressive illness when Hazel was about 14 years of age and had been admitted to this hospital for several weeks and treated ultimately with ECT. He recovered only partially and was soon thereafter diagnosed with cancer of the lung.

Personal History

Hazel was born by Caesarian section after foetal distress, and went to a special care baby unit for the first week of her life. There were also problems establishing breast feeding and so she was soon bottle fed (history from her mother), although otherwise she then developed normally. She was described by her mother as a happy child, although Hazel herself said that she was someone who had always had only one or two close friends and who was rather shy. She went to a local primary school (where her mother in fact taught for a while, whilst Hazel was there). She then went to the local comprehensive, where she initially did well (partly through additional assistance from her mother, as her mother described it). However, her performance fell away somewhat in her teens, and particularly so after her father became ill and eventually died (at this point she was referred to a psychiatrist, see below). She said she just scraped into university (Leeds) and went there to read geography. He first year went reasonably well but then she had difficulties in a relationship (see below) and this appears to have precipitated her illness (again, see below).

Previous Medical History
Hazel has no significant medical history except for a termination of pregnancy 6 weeks ago (see below)

Alcohol and Drugs History
Hazel tried cannabis once just after she went to university but did not like it. She says that now she does not approve of drugs, because they interfere with you body and 'make you into who you are not'. She has never drunk much alcohol.

Psychosexual History
Hazel has had only one sexual partner. In fact it was difficulties in that relationship, which started immediately after she arrived at university, which seemed partly to precipitate her illness. She became pregnant very soon after her first experience of sexual intercourse and became very worried particularly about the likely reaction of her mother. She felt she could not tell her mother and then, soon after her return from the Christmas vacation, had a termination. Her boy friend became angry at this, saying that she had aborted 'his' child and he terminated the relationship.

Personality
Hazel described herself as someone who was not at all successful and who only just scraped through things in life (for example, getting into university). She said that she preferred to have one or two close friends and had never liked 'crowds'. Her mother said that her 'just scraping through' was not how things were and, for example, in spite of her father's death she had got into university with more than the grades she had needed. Otherwise, she described Hazel as a shy girl who had never found mixing with people easy and who had preferred to plough her own furrow. She said that she was perfectionistic and intolerant of failure in herself, tending to drive herself too hard at times. Sometimes she became 'a bit obsessional' about things.

Mental State Examination
Hazel presented in appearance and behaviour as a rather thin young woman whose facial expression varied not very much but who, when discussing the

abortion or her father, cried quietly (tears just rolling down her face without any other change in her depressed facial expression); she looked a little uncared for and her clothes were somewhat dishevelled. Her speech lacked normal spontaneity and she gave only short answers to questions put to her (not initiating conversation); however, there were no abnormalities of the form of her speech. Her thoughts were preoccupied with morbid subjects, and particularly with the abortion and with the loss of her father; she described guilt and killing the baby and at having hurt her father so much, so that she had 'made him ill' and he had eventually died; when pressed she seemed not fully to accept that she could not have caused his cancer but kept coming back to the fact that he had become ill after she had shouted at him and got cross with him; she also described believing that she ought to be punished for the bad things she had done, although she did not say how this ought to occur; these various beliefs were held on the border of being delusional. Her perceptions were normal and she did not, for example, describe (or display) auditory, or other, hallucinations. Her mood was unvaryingly depressed, without features of agitation. As regards insight she could be pressed to accept briefly that, for example, cancer cannot be caused by disagreements, but then kept coming back to the same concern; she did not see herself as ill but, rather, as responding understandably to her abortion and to the other bad things she had done in her life.

Treatment and Progress

Hazel was admitted informally. However, on the second day of her admission she said that she no longer needed to be in hospital and started to pack her bag. As a result she was placed initially on a section 5(2), which was then converted to a section 2 (the GP doing the second medical recommendation), based on concern that she needed both further observation and concern that she could be at risk from herself. She was observed on the ward for a further two days without any specific therapeutic intervention. However, at the ward round it was decided that she clearly suffered from a depressive illness and was asked to start medication. She immediately became concerned that we were going to move on from medication eventually to give her ECT (which was not intended and which had not been raised by the team). (In fact, her mother said that her father had once received ECT which had affected his memory for a time and that both she and her daughter had always been opposed to that form of treatment). Under some persuasion Hazel agreed to take medication (amitriptyline) at a rising dose to 175mg per day. Gradually, her mood improved and she became more involved with activities on the ward and, after about four weeks, her mood disorder appeared to have resolved almost completely (her mother confirmed that she was, indeed, back to her normal self). However, she continued to talk a good deal about the abortion and the fact that she should not have had it; she also talked about thinking that she had been unkind to her father. Her key worker spent some time discussing these issues with her and they did, after a while, seem to be seen by Hazel more in perspective, although the key worker still felt that there was more work to be done (which Hazel did not want to pursue, saying that it was all too personal to discuss with others).

After increasing periods of leave, she was discharged home to her mother's house, to be followed up in outpatients by Dr Williams, still on the same dose of amitriptyline.

5.7.92

From: Dr Williams, Wood Park Hospital

Dear Dr Jones

I am writing to summarise my outpatient care of Hazel since she was discharged from hospital (I am copying my letter to the Student Health Service at her university). Hazel has done fairly well and there has been no resurgence of her depressive symptoms per se. She remains on her anti-depressant, although somewhat reluctantly (such reluctance being supported, I think, by her mother who, at times can seem intrusive and 'taking over' rather than just caring, which I believe she is). Hazel has kept her appointments, usually accompanied by her mother (although I have tried to see Hazel on her own as much as possible). I remain just a little concerned, however, that Hazel's mood is fragile and that she could break down again in the future. I have little on which to base this concern, except perhaps that she always seems over-introspective and a bit unwilling to talk about the things that concern her (for example, her relationship with her father). In any event, I think she is well enough to have another shot at university and, to that end, I have talked to the very sensible doctor there who initially referred her back to you when she gave up her second year course. We agreed that she could re-start and Hazel is keen to do so, saying that she must prove herself (mainly to her mother I think).

I will give her an appointment to see me during the Christmas vacation.

Yours sincerely
Dr Williams
Consultant Psychiatrist

3.12.92

From: Dr Young, Leeds University Student Health Centre

Dear Dr Williams

In Strict Confidence

I am pleased to tell you that Hazel has had a fairly successful first term back at Leeds. As you know, she was still somewhat fragile at the end of the summer but we felt that she could, with sufficient support, manage to start back, and that optimism has largely proved well founded. She continues to take her amitriptyline and I am sure that that is important, although she is rather reluctant about it and says that 'being sad is not being ill'. We have spent a number of sessions discussing some of the things in her past which might make her particularly vulnerable to 'being sad' (or perhaps 'becoming ill', in our terms) and that seems to have proved helpful. Indeed, she seems much more willing to accept and use a more psychotherapeutic than a pharmacological approach to helping herself.

Although she was initially reticent about letting me tell you about one of the likely causes of her vulnerability, she eventually agreed that I might do so (I explained that it was important that a doctor who could be more 'permanent' in her life should be aware of such an important background factor). Specifically, she told me (with great difficulty and gradually over several sessions) that her father had sometimes acted sexually 'inappropriately' with her when she was about 13 years of age. In fact, it seems to have gone further than that since she eventually said that, on two occasions, he tried to climb into her bed with her when her mother was away at a teaching conference, saying to her that he was very unhappy in the marriage and was lonely. I think that it is likely from some of her answers to questions I put to her that things went a little further even than this and that there was some sexual touching on both sides, perhaps born out of genuine love and concern for her father, although obviously she will have been highly ambivalent about anything she allowed herself to consent to. All of this appears to have occurred before her father became ill but it obviously had a major effect on the way in which Hazel coped (or rather did not cope) with her father's illness and death. It seems likely that it is the guilt from these events which at least is partly at the heart of Hazel's vulnerability to depression.

I will obviously keep you informed about anything else which seems important, albeit within sensible bounds of confidentiality (given that I think Hazel sees me as something of a psychotherapist, which I am not!).

Yours sincerely
Dr Young
General Practitioner
Student Health Centre

15.6.93

From: Dr Young

Dear Dr Williams
I am pleased to tell you that Hazel has finished the year successfully, although she did apparently have one 'narrow squeak' in her exams. She seems to be coping fairly well with things social and, although she has not ventured into having another relationship, she seems reasonably content. She is going to Greece with a girl friend for a short holiday but, otherwise, intends to spend the summer at home with her mother.

She has stopped taking her amitriptyline but, touch wood, has remained reasonably well. I still think that she is rather vulnerable to relapse though.

Thank you for speaking to me on the phone last week. We agreed, I think, that I would continue to see her and that it would probably not add much for you to continue to give her appointments during the vacations.

With best wishes.

Yours sincerely
Dr Young
General Practitioner
Student Health Centre

5.3.94

From: Dr Young, Leeds University Health Centre

Dear Dr Jones
This is intended as a brief update on Hazel, who is now coming to the end of her final year at Leeds. Although she is not a young woman who ever brims over with enjoyment of life she has coped fairly well with the rest of her course and, as she prepares to take her finals in May and June, can expect to do reasonably well. Since I last wrote to you Hazel and I have had regular sessions and she has also seen one of the counsellors in the Centre on a regular basis. Obviously a good deal of what she has discussed has been influenced by her disclosure about her father's behaviour towards her, although she has always been reluctant to discuss its effect on her in direct and explicit terms. I suspect that it will always haunt her in some sort of way although, hopefully, its influence over her will diminish with time.

I will write to you after her exams are over in order to (so to speak) sign her off, and back to your direct care (if she decides to return home initially, which I suspect she will do).

Yours sincerely,
Dr Young
General Practitioner, Student Health Centre

18.6.94

From: Student Health Centre, Leeds University

Dear Dr Jones
I am writing to let you know that, Hazel completed her finals successfully and was awarded a 2.2 degree. She was a little disappointed with this, as you would expect given the high standards she sets for herself. However, she intends, I think, to return home for the summer before going to London University to do a PGCE and then embark on a career in teaching.

I hope that things go well for her. She has struggled against a tendency towards depression throughout her university career and has done well to finish successfully.

With best wishes.

Yours sincerely
Dr Young
General Practitioner, Student Health Centre

Extracts from General Practice Notes

1.11.94: Came to see me complaining of feeling depressed. No biological symptoms. Discussed anti-depressants with her but she was reluctant. See in 4 weeks.

3.13.94: Little change but seems to be coping with her course; still adamant that she will not take medication, says that she has talked to her mother about it and she is of the same view.

19.3.95: Is a little better and getting out a bit more. Course seems to be going ok.

1.10.95: Passed her course and has started probation teaching year at a local comprehensive; social life still rather restricted. No biological features of depression, although she never seems particularly happy.

14.10.96: Passed her probationary year and has been confirmed at the same school as a permanent member of staff. Her life seems a little insular, still living at home, but things seem generally ok.

12.12.96: Is finding things difficult, particularly keeping discipline at school; is staying in all the time when not working and is not eating very well; sleep also rather poor. Again discussed anti-depressants, in view of all of her history but she is still very reluctant.

12.3.97: Came asking for contraception; has met a young man who seems to be cheering her up, although her relationship with mother is more difficult, mother doesn't approve of the boy friend; given advice about different forms, prescribed Minovlar.

5.6.97: Has set up home with Peter, seems a good deal happier, repeat Minovlar (as before).

[GP has retired in the interim, new GP Dr Alison Hussain]

1.8.98: Stopped taking the pill and has done pregnancy test, which was positive; confirmed here; wants shared care (letter written to St Charles Hospital), edd 3.3.99.

17.11.98: Seems just ok but the gloss seems to have worn off things a bit, boy friend apparently finding her tendency towards depression not always easy, pregnancy progressing normally.

3.1.99: A bit tearful sometimes but coping ok. Stopped working at Christmas to take maternity leave, not sure if she will want to go back after the baby.

1.2.99: A little better, although anxious about whether she will cope with the baby.

15.2.99: About the same; head engaged, no proteinuria, bp 130/80.

29.2.99: All well.

13.3.99: Had full term normal delivery 10.3.99 of a boy, Ben, breast feeding established satisfactorily; has 'baby blues', although in a young woman with her history she needs to be watched carefully for depression; community midwife visiting according to usual schedule; I will see every week in the surgery to check her mood.

20.3.99: Midwife reports that Hazel is doing well and coping well with breast feeding; she is no longer tearful; partner happy with things; bonding well.

27.3.99: Everything ok; enjoying the baby, partner well engaged with everything.

7.4.99: No problems.

16.4.99: Anniversary of father's death; worrying about this and feeling guilty; also feeling guilty about her much earlier termination of pregnancy; she needs watching closely.

20.4.99: Is clearly depressed; discussed anti-depressant with her but she says that she does not need it.

25.4.99: Really no better, not going out very much and worried that she is going to be a bad mother, still unwilling to consider anti-depressants; partner promised to keep in touch; he cannot understand because she had said how much she wanted a baby.

29.4.99: Has agreed to take an SSRI, which I explained are a new type of anti-depressant; has, in any event, stopped breast feeding, prescribed Prozac in increasing dosage.

17.4.99: Seems to be taking the tablets but her relationship with the baby and functioning generally are deteriorating; mother has offered to come and stay to help, but Hazel wants to try to succeed on her own.

24.4.99: Partner worried that she may not be taking her tablets, although she says she is; condition no better, partner considering taking time off work to help with Ben.

3.5.99: Seen, she looks very depressed, is not going out, has lost some weight and is not sleeping well (?early morning wakening), partner has spoken to Hazel's mother because he cannot take any more time off work, she will come and stay to help with Ben; Hazel maintains that she is taking the Prozac but there is now some doubt, especially given that she is getting worse rather than better.

14.5.99: Seen, looks very depressed, depressed expression, little speech except when spoken to, marked weight loss, not going out at all, not looking after the baby at all (this done by partner and mother, who is now staying), irritable, not eating, fatigued and not sleeping, very poor self care and little or no home care, talking about being a bad person who didn't deserve to have a baby, morbid thoughts also about her father and her guilt for his death, as well as about her previous abortion, thinks she should be punished for all the bad things she has done and for being a failure. It is now clear that she has not been taking her Prozac (partner found loose tablets hidden in a cupboard); will not re-start them. Some disagreement between partner and mother about how to handle the situation, mother wants to take her 'back home' (that is, to mother's home). Diagnosis, moderate to severe depressive illness, must see a psychiatrist. I will speak to Dr. Williams today for advice and a domicilliary visit.

15.5.99: Clinical state even worse than yesterday, not taken much fluid since yes-terday, hardly speaking, not caring for, or about the baby, everything being done by Peter and by mother; not eating, not going out, morbid thoughts if any-thing worse; says she will not take medication, 'because it will not help'. Spoke to Dr Williams yesterday and today, he will visit later today.

Situation as portrayed by video

Ben can be heard crying upstairs as Dr Williams comes down to speak to Peter, Hazel's partner. They sit at a table covered with plates, uneaten food and the baby's rattle and napkins. Dr Williams explains that the GP is to visit as well and they must wait. Peter says, with some irritation, that he does not understand Hazel's condition since he thought that having the baby would make Hazel happy, as that's what she said she wanted. Dr Williams refers to her long history of depression. Peter becomes more agitated and frustrated as he gives details of her current failure to eat or drink, or to take care of herself or the baby. He says angrily that she is tired all the time, but she doesn't sleep, yet she mopes around all day and most of the night and doesn't go out of the house. He is doing all of the shopping. He complains that she won't even clean herself up and that he can't remember the last time she had a bath. He picks up a framed photograph in which the glass is smashed and says 'She just won't talk to me. She threw this at me . . . I was holding Ben at the time'. He continues 'Doctor, I don't think she loves him. Sometimes when he cries and she just can't stand it she shouts at him to 'shut up' and well, he doesn't understand . . . he's just a ten week old baby . . . so he just keeps on crying and yesterday she well [he makes a shaking move-ment twice with both hands as if Hazel were holding and shaking the baby] . . . well, that's not Hazel, not the Hazel I love'. Dr Williams explains that Hazel needs his love, now more than ever.

At this point Hazel's mother enters saying to Peter and Dr Williams that 'Hazel and the little one are asleep', so she suggests that they keep their voices down. She leaves the room.

Peter says that both Hazel's mother and the health visitor blame him, and he asks if Hazel will need to go to hospital. Dr Williams says 'almost certainly yes'. Peter asks about Ben and Dr Williams responds that Ben could go to hospital with her. Peter baulks at this saying that he's not having his son 'in a place like that' asserting that he will keep them at home and find a way to 'make Hazel take her medication'. Dr Williams explains that medication may take too long and that they may be able to get her back on her food if they gave her a short course of ECT.

At this point Hazel's mother returns saying that 'there is no way my daughter is going to be wired up to those bloody machines—she's always been opposed to it and so have I, long before you came on the scene' (looking at Peter). Peter tries to retort 'the doctor says . . . '. And she replies that the doctors had their chance years ago and that her daughter was fine living with her. Finally she says, again directed at Peter 'in the two years she's been with you she's gone steadily downhill—if you love her why don't you take better care of her—you didn't even have the decency to marry her.' In a raised voice, she continues 'do either of you have any idea what she's been through or what she feels?' Peter gets to his feet, turning on her and shouting ' I'll tell you why she moved in with me, it was to get away from you'. Hazel's mother stands there aghast and the sound of baby Ben crying upstairs filters into the room.

Later that day Hazel Robinson, who notably does not appear in the video, is admitted to hospital as a detained patient under section 3 of the Mental Health Act 1983. Set out below are her hospital notes following admission.

HAZEL ROBINSON

CASE FILE

Wood Park Hospital, N 22

ADMISSION SUMMARY

Date of Admission: 15.5.99
Legal Status: *Section 3 Mental Health Act (mental illness).*

History of Presenting Illness
History taken mainly from partner, Peter. Hazel had an uneventful (planned) pregnancy, healthy boy, Ben. Baby blues at 3–4 days but went away. Doing well until anniversary of her father's death, when she started to ruminate about him and to feel guilty; also started to feel guilty about a much earlier termination of pregnancy; initially resistant to antidepressants but then agreed. However, gradually increasing depression, up to current state where she has almost no appetite, substantial weight loss, not drinking spontaneously more than sips (although more with some encouragement), housebound, not caring for self, the house or the baby, irritable (once shook they baby in front of Peter), says she feels nothing for Peter or Ben, morbid thoughts about her father (who may have, in fact, abused her, see below), expressing guilty feelings about being a bad mother and not being worthy generally. Refused to come into hospital, partner (nearest relative) initially unwilling (said Ben needed his mother and would not allow Ben to come into hospital with Hazel, into the Mother and Baby Unit) but then agreed to admission under section if Ben stayed at home (2 medical recommendations by Dr Williams and Dr Hussain, social worker in full agreement). ECT discussed with partner, very reticent at first but prepared to accept at least as an option; mother adamantly opposed and says her daughter has always been opposed to it as a form of treatment (that is, even when fully well).

Past Psychiatric History
Depressive symptoms after father died, eventually resolved (not given any treatment, although considered). Moderately severe depressive illness during second

year at university, admitted this hospital under section 2 then informal, treated with anti-depressant, in hospital for 6–8 weeks, resolved and returned to university (see earlier Discharge Summary). Regular counselling sessions by Student Health GP and counsellor throughout rest of university career which uncovered history of some sexual abuse by father, about which Hazel felt guilty (her thoughts being made worse when he got cancer and then died). This likely to be one cause of her depressive tendency. Gained degree and trained as a secondary school teacher, coped without medication eventually (she has always been reticent about this anyway).

Family History
See previous summary.

Personal History
See previous history up to 2nd year at university. Thereafter, qualified as a teacher. Worked in comprehensive school until December last year (left for maternity leave).

Social History
One or two close friends; enjoys music and reading.

Alcohol and Drugs History
As previous summary, no change.

Previous Medical History
As previous summary.

Psycho-sexual History
Had one previous boy friend before current partner; at university. Became pregnant and had a termination. The father would not accept what she had done and ended the relationship (this being the precipitant of her previous depressive illness, see above). Met Peter two years ago, formed a sexual relationship but Hazel was a little reluctant initially (history from partner, who seems, perhaps, a bit overbearing and insensitive). Sexually satisfactory relationship. Happy together, but Hazel apparently always tending towards the depressed. Planned pregnancy. Normal pregnancy and delivery. Breast fed but tailed off as became mentally ill. Ben at home, looked after by mother (partner has had to return to work).

Mental State Examination
Obvious weight loss and also dehydration, depressed facies, little variation of expression, speech lacking spontaneity (but will reply if spoken to); mood depressed; thoughts preoccupied with feeling valueless and guilty (about her father, her previous abortion and Ben, also for causing conflict between her

mother and her partner); a bit evasive about questions concerning self harm or suicide; no obvious abnormal perceptions; cognitively oriented in all modalities.

EXTRACTS FROM HOSPITAL MEDICAL NOTES

16.5.99: Refusing suggested oral medication (reinstatement of Prozac); pushes away staff who try to give it involuntarily, no success in giving her medication so far. Blood count normal; electrolytes and urea just ok, but some concern that could go into renal failure if does not start taking substantially more fluids. Attempts to achieve more oral fluids so far rather inconsistent in results, often pushed away by Hazel. Showing little concern about the baby at home.

16.5.99: At interview with the consultant she appeared not to be actively seeking suicide merely wanted to be left alone; her thoughts are capable of interpretation in terms of her understandably unresolved feelings about her father's abuse of her and her feelings about her earlier abortion which have both been thrown up by her own new status as a parent. The suggestion of possible treatment with ECT are met with objections based on what she understands about transient memory disturbance, in relation to which she says 'I have spent a long time forgetting my father and the abortion and now I want to be able to think about them so that I can work out what I should really think'. However, she still persists with inappropriate guilt, especially in relation to her abusive father.

DECISIONS AND DILEMMAS

T HE MATERIALS PRESENTED above replicate the information available to the professionals taking part in this case study of the possible imposition of compulsory treatment on Hazel Robinson. Five sections now follow; an analysis of the problems faced by these decision-makers; a synopsis of the decisions they made; an analysis of how those decisions were made; a review of the ethical, legal and clinical issues arising; and finally, a summary of the key findings in this chapter.

Precise details of the methodology adopted for this exercise are set out in Appendix 2, but they are not central to an understanding of what follows. For those professionals who took part in the study, the question posed to them at the end of the exercise, after the video had been shown, was 'what would you do next, both clinically and/or legally?' These professionals had to decide first what they individually would have done, and second to agree a joint course of action with their paired colleague, whether that be a section 12(2) psychiatrist or a Second Opinion Appointed Doctor (SOAD).

As with the earlier two chapters some readers might want to pause at this point to reflect upon their own actions if they found themselves facing this situation with Hazel Robinson.[1] For those who wish just to press on . . .

---

[1] Notably, in this case the register in which the patient is discussed changed. Hazel Robinson, unlike Mr Draper and Mr Wright, was primarily referred to by her first name both in the case notes

1. The Nature of the Problem and the Options Arising

The professional pairs in Hazel Robinson's case comprised a consultant psychiatrist adopting the role of her responsible medical officer (RMO) and a psychiatrist from the Mental Health Act Commission's list of Second Opinion Appointed Doctors (SOADs). This psychiatrist played the role of the SOAD. SOADs provide 'second opinions' where the RMO wishes to give certain forms of treatment under section 57 and section 58 of the 1983 Act. Hazel's case specifically raised the issue of giving electro-convulsive therapy (ect) without her consent. In a non-emergency situation, this would require the authorisation of a SOAD. ASWs have no formal role in this decision about compulsory treatment in hospital.[2]

The courses of action the participants had to consider for this detained patient included both clinical options and the legal options to support those clinical choices.

—Should the RMO pursue any compulsory treatment and if so, what: medication, rehydration, ect?
—And if ect, should this be on an emergency basis under section 62 which permits the RMO to authorise the treatment in certain life threatening circumstances without a second opinion?
—Or should a SOAD visit be requested with a view to authorising ect under section 58 (see below)?

Other questions arise for the decision-makers if no compulsory treatment were to be imposed.

—How long can the RMO wait whilst pursuing a policy of negotiation, monitoring and engagement?
—At what point in an attempt to gain Hazel's agreement to take fluids or medication does the doctor's desire to explain the consequences of a failure to agree become a form of coercion? Thus, if the RMO says to Hazel 'I can't do nothing' or 'If you don't take fluids you will deteriorate and then I will have to consider using ect' is any consent forthcoming from her invalid?

Resolving these issues required the RMO to address both Hazel's immediate medical needs (was her life threatened by her failure to eat or drink?) and her expressed wishes (were they a valid reflection of her views?). If some practitioners thought

---

and by the practitioners, perhaps reflecting both a more paternal approach by all involved and the fact that her case history dates back to when she was 16. The discussion below tries to remain true to this usage.

  [2] However, an ASW may be consulted as one of the 'two other persons who have been professionally concerned with the patient's medical treatment' (s 57(3) 1983 Act) with whom the SOAD has to consult before certifying treatment under s 57 or s 58 of the Act. Fennell 1996:208 notably questions the practical value of this multi-disciplinary exercise where consultation has been seen as a 'tiresome formality'.

that they would be able to negotiate the administration of ect with Hazel, did they also believe that she had the capacity to consent to ect?

There were also questions about the validity and relevance of her prior expressed wishes; it was known, for example, that she had been opposed to ect. Furthermore, was there any risk to the baby (in terms of her continuing failure to bond with Ben) and issues concerning the separation of Ben and his mother during her detention and treatment? How should Ben's interests and rights be weighed against those of his mother's perceived need for treatment? And, in respect of the views of Hazel's partner Peter and her mother, which should be accorded the greater weight, and in respect of what are their views relevant? Legally, Peter, who has lived with Hazel as her 'husband' for more than six months takes precedence under the 1983 Act as Hazel's 'nearest relative'; but are Hazel's mother's views therefore of no importance?[3] Finally, the RMO may well wish to consider the likely consequences of using compulsory treatment as an interim measure with a patient who was likely (given her history) to require long-term, if intermittent, psychiatric care.

In the Hazel Robinson case the legal issues were perhaps more straightforward than for Mr Draper and Mr Wright. However, the issues were complicated for some doctors by the ethical desire to respect a patient's prior expressed capacitous choices, even though such choices would not be legally binding for a detained patient. The clinical issues were less clear-cut. Was giving ect in these circumstances in line with good medical practice?[4] Moreover, clinical and legal issues interacted: thus, just because a doctor had the legal power to impose the treatment that s/he felt to be in the patient's best short-term interests, would that clinically be a preferable option to identifying a treatment which may be less successful in the short-term, but more acceptable to the patient? How important was maintaining a therapeutic alliance with the patient?

Thus, the strategic possibilities in this case are complex. Ultimately, the issues were made to turn on whether the RMO wishes to give ect and, if so whether s/he wishes to invoke section 58, the provision of the Act which permits certain treatments (including ect) to be given only where specified criteria are met. These criteria require:

—either the patient's consent (which has to be documented), or
—a second opinion from the SOAD certifying that the patient is either not capable of understanding the nature, purpose and likely effects of the treatment (and therefore cannot give valid consent), or
—if the patient has refused to give consent, treatment may be given nonetheless if the SOAD certifies that, having regard to the likelihood of its alleviating or

---

[3]   S 26(6) 1983 Act.

[4]   There is no clear-cut answer to this question because Hazel's circumstances do not remain static during the exercise. As will emerge below, the participants were pushed into the position of having to consider the clinical relevance of ect because, as the exercise progressed, other treatment strategies they might have wanted to pursue were characterised as failing.

preventing a deterioration in the patient's condition, the treatment should be given

Alternatively or additionally,

—the RMO may wish to give ect under section 62 (which provides for 'urgent' treatment and requires neither consent nor a second opinion).

Thus, assessments of a patient's capacity have a bearing on whether the patient can consent to treatment, but not on whether they may refuse treatment. This is a feature of the 1983 Act, in that it permits compulsory treatment against the express capacitous wishes of detained patients. However, since the professional pairs dealing with the case of Hazel Robinson never directly see her, it would have been inappropriate to make the case turn upon the issue of capacity; it does not. Hazel is presumed to retain her capacity to make decisions, but for her detained status.

Other possible options include the administration of medication without consent under section 63, or compulsory re-hydration, also under section 63. Section 63 provides a general authority to treat without consent where the medical treatment is for the patient's mental disorder; however, in respect of medication, this can only be given under the authority of section 63 for a period of 3 months. Thereafter, the administration of medication to a detained patient falls within section 58 and accordingly requires consent or a second opinion (see Appendix 1).

2. Decision Outcomes

The case study required both doctors to record their clinical strategy and legal decision in the first instance *as if* they had been the RMO. Then, the member of the pair who was the qualified SOAD was required to adopt the role of SOAD (should this be necessary) and decide whether or not to approve the other doctor's decision (acting as the RMO) as constituting a reasonable course of action.[5]

The 27 decisions made individually by the RMO, and SOAD acting as RMO, were as follows (one SOAD is missing; see Appendix 3):

	14 RMOs	*13 SOADs*
no immediate compulsory treatment	3	2
re-hydration under s 63	3	2
medication under s 63	2	3
emergency ect under s 62	1	3
ect under s 58 with SOAD	3	3
other	2	

[5] That is, the SOAD must be of the view that the treatment is in accordance with a practice accepted at the time by a responsible body of medical opinion skilled in the particular form of treatment in question *Bolam v Friern Hospital Management Committee* [1957].

The joint decisions following 'the visit' of the SOAD were constrained so as to reflect either the administration of ect, or a decision either not to request it, or if requested, not to authorise it. Ultimately, ect was authorised in 11 of the 14 pairs. This figure is not, however, directly comparable with the earlier figures since, in the process of discussing Hazel Robinson's case, further hypothetical time elapsed and other treatment strategies were characterised as failing. Thus, it would probably be more appropriate to note that in three of the 14 pairs ect was not authorised (or requested) whatever the patient's circumstances.

The joint decisions thus comprised:

—3 decisions not to authorise (or request) ect;
—11 decisions to authorise ect under s 58;

Of the decisions where ect would have been administered under section 58, individually one RMO and 3 SOADs (acting as RMOs) would also have given prior emergency ect under section 62.

Curiously, the individual decisions indicate that the SOADs, when adopting the position of an RMO, were somewhat more likely to select ect as their first preference than were the RMOs. Following receipt of the papers, 6 SOADs had ect (either under the section 62 'emergency/urgent' provisions or under section 58 where a second opinion would be required) as their first option, whereas only 4 RMOs put these options first. Similarly, after viewing the video, 7 SOADs had ect as their first option, with only 4 RMOs placing ect first. The confidence levels between the two groups also indicated the SOADs to be marginally more certain about their first preference; the SOADs' average confidence varied from 78 per cent (receipt of papers) to 85 per cent (after video) to 80 per cent (in the joint decision). The RMOs were 75 per cent confident throughout the three decision points.

Generally, SOADs are likely to have more experience of ect, since their role as a SOAD will necessarily bring them into contact with this treatment; yet, many of the RMOs had either not used ect, or not used it for many years. Even those who had used it, did so infrequently. Also, the SOADs were markedly older than the RMO group, with a number being retired practitioners. Their confidence levels may generally have been higher in all that they did; certainly, as a group, they were much less ethically disturbed, for example, about overruling a capacitously made advance directive refusing ect in all circumstances (see below). They were also marginally less likely to change their initial views, given increasing amounts of information, than were the RMOs.

3. Decision Analysis

1. Confidence and Conflict Resolution

Apart from pair 1, where both parties' confidence in the final decision (not to pursue ect) dropped markedly, for most of the paired decisions there was a reasonable level of confidence in the agreed decision. This should not imply that there was never disagreement between the professionals; pair 2 encapsulates the kind of conflict that occurred. Here, the RMO did not initially want to give ect, preferring to push fluids and anti-depressants. He took the view that the patient was safe in hospital, was not at risk of harming the baby and was not overtly suicidal. Moreover, he was uncertain whether her depression was 'clearly bio-logical'. His reluctance to give ect also stemmed from his belief that he would have to continue with Hazel's treatment in the long-term and he wanted to have 'the best co-operation that I can have from this girl, including perhaps help to look after her baby'. In contrast, the SOAD, expressing what he would have done had he been the RMO, wanted to administer ect as quickly as possible, in order to shorten the duration of her illness and 'because the relationship will break down with her partner as well as with the baby'. Thus, the medical short-term approach found itself in direct conflict with the more socially oriented long-term approach.

Yet, the meaning that should be attached to the individual responses is hard to discern. For example, in pair 1 the discussion between them indicated it was likely that the low levels of confidence expressed by both parties reflected not a desire to do something else at that point, but rather a low level of confidence that what they had chosen to do would prove successful. Generally, Hazel Robinson's case was regarded as clinically difficult.

Of course, in real life, disagreement between the parties would rarely be man-ifest, let alone be recorded or measured. In this sense, the hypothetical approach adopted here did permit both disclosure of and some evaluation of that sense of discomfort or regret practitioners must sometimes have when walking away from a decision with which they have seemingly agreed. Had an attempt been made only to record the preferred individual decision of each professional after the discussion, it might well have shown that both parties were in broad agree-ment with the joint outcome. Indeed, having been exposed to the views of the other party and aired or tested their own views against that party, their adher-ence to their own previously unexpressed view may well have genuinely moder-ated. Hence, the method adopted in the study permitted unease to be documented, whereas an observational method might well have focussed exclu-sively on the fact of 'agreement'. As it stands, the 1983 Act is only interested in agreed outcomes. However, there would have been implications arising from individual decision-making if the Draft Mental Health Bill 2000 had been enacted in its then form (see p 135).

3.2 Common Decision Errors

The notion of 'good decision-making' embodies two elements; first, how the decision is made, for example whether appropriate factors are taken into account and irrelevant ones excluded, and second, whether the outcome is itself correct. Less emphasis is placed here on the latter because, as stressed earlier, in most of the decisions the practitioners were required to take there were no inherently right or wrong answers. However, the process by which decisions are made is subject to critique; indeed, the theoretical terrain of decision-making has shown generally that how people make judgements and consider uncertainty is subject to a number of common flaws.[6] These decision errors have been examined in the context of mental health decision-making by Bartlett and Phillips;[7] here, four of their common decision errors emerged in the participants' various cognitive strategies in respect to the application of mental health law.

The first relevant error is frame constriction; this may be thought of as the tendency for decision-makers to adopt a single narrow perspective. This is illustrated by the marked difference between the SOADs and the RMOs. Despite asking the former in the first instance to adopt the role of RMO, more of them than the RMOs opted for ect as the treatment of choice. Was this because, arising out of their real life experiences as SOADs where they would be called upon not infrequently to give second opinions on the use of ect, they perceived Hazel's case in terms of 'ect or not?'

Second, there was the 'single option fallacy'. Elsewhere, this has been referred to as 'the terminology of constraint'; namely, the perception by the decision-maker that he or she has no choice but to follow a particular course of action. Since not all practitioners either developed the same clinical plan or resorted to the same legal options, clearly there was room for manoeuvre within the facts of Hazel's circumstances. However, it was also evident that a number of the practitioners took decisions under pressure and with what they perceived to be little or no choice. Doing nothing beyond observing Hazel and continuing to push fluids was, for some practitioners, not an option. Yet, for others, opting for ect was equally problematic.

> I haven't been able to find in the history any evidence of true psychotic symptoms, she has some preoccupation with guilt over her father but from my reading of the records, that is fairly long-standing and is perhaps related to the sexual abuse that is alluded to . . . my own view is that it would be reasonable in the light of her wishes not to have ect and the family's, to actually try a little longer. **SOAD, pair 12**

This SOAD was volunteering to the RMO that she would return to the hospital at very short notice should Hazel deteriorate (which the RMO described as 'a fabulous service'). Under questioning, the SOAD explained that she saw Hazel's problems as being more neurotic than psychotic, 'and I have never had any success when I give ect to people who are neurotic'. The RMO agreed, but only in a qualified fashion:

> we haven't got accurately documented psychotic symptoms, but I have got a very strong hunch that she does have a lot of psychotic symptoms. **RMO, pair 12**

---

[6] Baron 1994; Dawes 1988; Russo and Schoemaker 1989.
[7] Bartlett and Phillips 1999.

It is, of course, fascinating that, even with a hypothetical case, a psychiatrist can have 'a very strong hunch'. Equally interesting was the SOAD's response to the RMO's assertion of psychotic symptoms.

> I'm not convinced about that . . . when you talk to women who have had terminations, and when the next baby comes they get very mixed up between the baby they have lost and this baby and I think it is really more of a psychological problem. **SOAD, pair 12**

What all of the other psychiatrists who proposed ect for Hazel would make of this aetiology would itself be fascinating. In any event, it does demonstrate that there was diagnostically more than one way of classifying the case, and thus, more than one way of treating Hazel. In this context, which might be the correct approach is not the key issue; for clearly practitioners who either wholly discounted ect or who perceived it as the only option were both falling into the error of potentially unjustifiably restricting their decision options.

The third example of a common decision error evident in the discussions was over confidence; that is, people are generally too sure of themselves when assessing probabilities.[8] It has been a common finding between all three cases that generally the practitioners assigned high confidence levels to their individual decision-choices. In Hazel's case, the SOADs were somewhat more confident in their original decisions than were the RMOs; yet both parties could become uncomfortable and defensive about their reasoning processes when an attempt was made to explore them during the interview phase of the study. Perhaps their original confidence in their own decisions could not be readily justified.

A final decision theme of relevance concerns that of 'ignoring your track record' (or giving spurious credence to your successes). A number of practitioners remarked, when questioned about their successes with using ect with non-compliant patients, that, in their experience, patients were frequently grateful afterwards to have been given the treatment. However, this is inconsistent with those practitioners who, on giving ect to Hazel, albeit reluctantly, remarked that this would not jeopardise their long-term relationship with her, since they did not anticipate that she would be prepared subsequently to return to them for voluntary treatment. In essence, they were prepared to take on the role of the 'bad doctor' in order, in their view, to save her life, in the knowledge that it would be open to her to commence a relationship with a more 'understanding' psychiatrist once she had recovered from this acute crisis. What this implicitly acknowledged was that patients have long-term psychiatric careers as well as histories, and that a patient like Hazel Robinson was most likely to continue to need to draw on the mental health services. Whilst her relationship with services was, on this occasion, under section, it had largely not been so in the past and was likely not to be so in the future. This line of reasoning also acknowledged that patients can switch between doctors, and only establish long-term relationships with some of them. Thus, it is entirely conceivable that those

---

[8] See generally, Gigerenzer 2002.

practitioners who remarked that they had experienced patients who had been grateful for ect (in real life) were merely drawing on their successes; they may have had no knowledge of those patients who were not grateful and who accordingly had avoided all further contact with them. Thus can a spurious confidence in the beneficial effects of a particular treatment be sustained.

4. Legal, Ethical and Clinical Dilemmas

In Hazel Robinson's case the individual elements of the Act which had to be dealt with under sections 58, 62 and 63 were fewer in number and the ethico-legal issues are more conveniently dealt with on an issue-by-issue basis. In fact, the practitioners involved in this case seemed to engage generally in somewhat more sophisticated reasoning. This may be because the case involved complex clinical issues that laid the basis for such reasoning since, once back on legal or ethical ground, many of the common hesitancies in their reasoning emerged.

4.1 Capacity and Consent

Whilst the Robinson case broadly concerns the issue of consent to treatment, whether Hazel is capable of giving consent to any treatment is not the primary issue. Indeed, as she never 'appears' it would have been unfair to ask partici-pants to judge her capacity to consent directly. However, a number of features in respect of her views about ect were evident from the written materials and the video. First, she had expressed concern when she had been ill previously about the possibility of her being given ect. In this earlier instance she had subse-quently been persuaded to take medication. Her opposition was seemingly based on her father's experience of the treatment; namely, that it had affected his memory. Her most recently expressed views about ect were recorded in the case notes:

> met with objections based on what she understands about transient memory distur-bance, in relation to which she says 'I have spent a long time forgetting my father and the abortion and now I want to be able to think about them so that I can work out what I should really think'.

Hazel is undoubtedly seriously depressed, although its causes are not self-evident. Her mother (who is Hazel's next of kin, but who does not fulfil the cri-teria for the technical role of 'nearest relative'[9] for the purposes of the Act) has expressed both her own and Hazel's long-standing opposition to ect; Hazel's

---

[9] See s 26 (1) and s 26(6) of the 1983 Act. The patient's nearest relative enjoys certain powers under the Act; for example, he or she can authorise an application for admission to hospital of the patient (although this role is usually performed by the ASW) and, if the RMO does not take steps to prevent this, the nearest relative can also have the patient discharged from detention under both s 2 and s 3.

partner, Peter, who is her nearest relative (having lived with her as 'man and wife' for more than six months), is initially opposed to ect but appears more compliant as the case progresses. In law, as her 'nearest relative', he would be the individual with the right to discharge Hazel from the section 3 provisions.[10] In that sense he is the person who needs to be persuaded that ect is the best treatment for Hazel, since he is the only person with the power to interfere (even if not permanently) with any doctor's desire to give ect.

Hazel may or may not be capable of consenting to ect, but she clearly was not doing so. The test of capacity, which was established in the High Court case *Re C*,[11] entails three elements in respect of the patient's ability to engage in the decision-making process: 'first, comprehending and retaining treatment information, second, believing it, and third, weighing it in the balance to arrive at a choice'. Applying this test, the presumption that she retains the right of self-determination has probably not been displaced. However, the case turns on whether ect will be given against her will and what weight should be attached to her prior known views.

Whilst many participants took account of Hazel's current refusal to have ect, only a small number were persuaded that it was necessary (whether ethically justified or not) to respect that refusal. This position was explained thus:

> If she was my patient, and I knew her really well and I could understand why she didn't want it, and I did not think it was part of some disorder, then I would respect it . . . whether it is a blood transfusion or ect, if the patient doesn't want it, and they regard that as sacrosanct, then I would not break that. If I thought it was part of a whole series of overvalued ideas etc, then I would say I am sorry, and I would override it.
> **SOAD, pair 4**

There is a strong argument that if compulsory treatment is necessary, that the doctor ought to select the method of treatment least objectionable to the patient.[12] This would be consistent both with the Code of Practice's notion that for urgent treatment, the treatment given ought to be that which represents the minimum necessary response to avert danger to the patient or others, and with the World Health Organization's Principles of Mental Health Care Law.[13] To Hazel, the least objectionable treatment would not be ect.

The whole issue of capacity and consent was one with which the practitioners understandably struggled. Some were swayed by the idea of needing to maintain a therapeutic relationship over many years with Hazel. Others, for example

---

[10] This right to discharge is subject to the RMO's power to issue a barring certificate under s 25; if the RMO is of the view that the patient 'if discharged, would be likely to act in a manner dangerous to other persons or to himself' then a restriction can be placed on the nearest relative's 'right to discharge'.

[11] *Re C (Adult: Refusal of Medical Treatment)* [1994] affirmed by the Court of Appeal in *Re MB (Medical Treatment)* [1997]. See also the case of *Re B (Consent to Treatment: Capacity)* [2002] discussed in ch 5.

[12] DHSS *et al* 1978 para 6.18.

[13] See WHO 1996 Principle 4.

the RMO in pair 2, thought that her situation, although acute, was brought on by 'a lot of social circumstances which aren't favourable . . . and that my feeling would be that she would still be able to be persuaded'. However, the SOAD in this pair asserted:

> usually the insight is retained for a long long time in depression, unlike other psychotic conditions . . . and they don't want our ect treatment. In this case it's so difficult because she's refusing all medications, so in that case I would go along with a lack of insight. It's not just the ect she's refusing. **SOAD, pair 2**

The RMO in pair 10 accepted that Hazel wasn't keen on ect even before she became depressed, because of her father's experiences, but went on to illustrate the classic 'capacity shift'; namely, that greater capacity is required on behalf of the patient to refuse treatment, than to accept it on the doctor's recommendation. Thus:

> I suspect her capacity to make decisions is limited by her depression, or is coloured by her depression. She has feelings of worthlessness and she has said 'nothing is going to work, nothing is going to make me feel better'. So I think you could say that perhaps her capacity is a bit limited but, if she'd agreed to have the ect, I think I would have accepted that. **RMO, pair 10**

In contrast, the RMO in pair 2 started from the position that he wanted to try and treat her without ect. He explained his reasons:

> she has longstanding opposition to ect; it predates her illness and is very much part of herself, she likes to be in control of things—it is part of her personality; she doesn't even like to smoke cannabis because she likes her mind to be her own; she's never really even wanted to take medication. In circumstances like that I hesitate to impose something that somebody is strongly opposed to. I can see that it is quite possibly going to happen, but I will try to avoid it. **RMO, pair 2**

Here, Hazel's opposition to medication was seen not as a general lack of insight, but as part of her enduring personality; it presumably would need to be taken into account when determining what her true choice would have been, uncorrupted by her disorder. Isolating a person's true choice is accordingly particularly problematic where the diagnosed disorder is essentially a disorder of personality, that is, a disorder that is integrated with one's whole persona, rather than being some kind of unwelcome add-on which could potentially be excised. However, this was an RMO who took the patient's right to refuse as his starting point. When it was pointed out that the 1983 Act allowed him not to respect the patient's view he responded

> I am not concerned about the Act. The Act is a framework in which we are allowed to practise. It is looking at myself in the mirror that is my mental health act and the other one comes second. **RMO, pair 2**

This was thus another example of an ethical approach being injected into or taking precedence over what the statute permits, but does not require.

Whilst some opted for absent or reduced capacity as a reason for summoning the SOAD (skating over any analysis of whether her current refusal was capacitous, since section 58 and section 62 permit capacitous refusal to be overridden) most practitioners seemed to welcome the reassurance of an outside view, given that the treatment was so clearly against the wishes of her mother and of herself. Thus, the SOAD's function appeared primarily to be a safety-net for the RMO, rather than for the patient, as might otherwise have been perceived by those looking at the structure of the Act.

Notably, since the study was conducted the role of the SOAD has been subject to judicial review.[14] In *R(Wooder)*, the Court of Appeal has held that where a decision is made to give medical treatment to a competent non-consenting adult patient fairness requires that reasons be given for the decision. It reached this conclusion on the basis that the common law implies a duty to give reasons as of right where the subject matter is an interest, like personal liberty, which is so highly regarded by the law that fairness requires reasons. And, whilst SOADs will not be required to dot every 'i' and cross every 't', they will be required to give reasons clearly on what they reasonably regard as the substantial points on which they formed their clinical judgement.[15] Indeed, Lord Justice Sedley made explicit reference to the notion that the SOAD's opinion carried with it clinical, legal and moral dimensions which, if necessary, were the Court's business. Moreover,

> the impact of the decision is so invasive of physical integrity and moral dignity that it calls without more for disclosure of the reasons for it in a form and at a time which allow the individual to understand and respond to them.[16]

In reaching this judgment, the Court of Appeal effectively shored-up the role of the SOAD; and, whilst recognising that this role is only to consider and certify the reasonableness of the RMO's proposed treatment, the Court has concluded that SOADs' independent judgements should nonetheless be accessible to patients (unless disclosure would cause serious harm to the physical or mental health of the patient or any other person). Moreover, in its reasoning the Court made additional reference to the notion that implementation of a statutory duty to give reasons led to a higher quality of decision-making.[17] Expressing reasons for decisions is then to acquire a new prominence.

4.2. Advance Statement of Refusal

Hazel Robinson's case also permitted an examination of the influence on participants of a capacitously expressed advance refusal of a specified form of psy-

---

[14] *R (on the application of Wooder) v Feggetter* [2002]; *R (on the application of Wilkinson) v Broadmoor Hospital [2001]*.

[15] *R (on the application of Wooder)* [2002] at para 29.

[16] *R (on the application of Wooder)* [2002] at para 37.

[17] The Court of Appeal cited the work of Sir Patrick Neill QC 1998: 163–4, and his reference to a review of Australian practice.

chiatric treatment, that is, Hazel's previously expressed desire not to be treated with ect. Although currently such advance refusals are legally binding in relation to treatment for physical disorder,[18] they cannot override the 1983 Act. That is, an advance refusal cannot bind practitioners not to invoke the Act at some future date, even if the terms of the patient's refusal of future intervention are highly specific and even if the circumstances contemplated are clearly and unambiguously defined. In the case notes there was clear evidence that in the past Hazel had said that she did not want to be treated with ect. Participants varied greatly in their responses to this capacitously-made oral advance refusal, albeit a common aspect was that many were unaware of its exact legal status. This doubt related both to someone detained under the Act and specifically in relation to Part IV of the Act, which concerns consent to treatment.

In order to further explore this conundrum, of the legal weight of an advance refusal, participants were then faced in the study with the production of a written advance refusal of ect. It was suggested that this had been made when Hazel was capacitous when she was pregnant, and in the full knowledge that she might become depressed after the birth (and authenticated as such by both her GP and a solicitor). Combining these aspects of the advance directive with evidence that it was made after a comprehensive reading of all of the available literature on ect published by the Royal College of Psychiatrists, many practitioners began to feel increasingly uncomfortable. Although such an advance refusal currently has no authority in law, few participants felt confident about their knowledge of the law. Perhaps equally worrying, was the range of ethical positions propounded.

Why should practitioners be more worried about ignoring a written advance refusal than overriding a current capacitous refusal by a detained patient? First, the practitioners were aware that the authority of the law was clearly present in the latter situation. But, it was also evident that, given the potentially life-threatening consequences to Hazel of refusal, many practitioners were prepared to conclude that her capacity was insufficient for the decision to be made (that is, capacity in relation to treatment of mental disorder was distinguished from capacity in relation to physical disorder, even though those suffering from physical disorders may make their decisions in a state of considerable stress or emotional turmoil[19]). For example, the SOAD in pair 10 argued that it was likely that Hazel suffered from a form of 'sub-clinical incompetence' that had been present all of her life because of her low self-esteem. Indeed, he argued that a refusal by someone with mental disorder made whilst they were capacitous could be distinguished from that made by someone suffering from physical disorder because in the former case the refusal would be almost bound to be tied in with the patient's psycho-social history. This preparedness to find some way of undermining a capacitous advance refusal made by someone who subsequently

[18] See the House of Lords in *Airedale NHS Trust v Bland* [1993], and subsequently, *Re C (Adult: Refusal of Medical Treatment)* [1994].

[19] In practice, the difference in competence of those with physical and mental disorder to make treatment decisions is nothing like as great as is commonly assumed, Appelbaum and Grisso 1995.

went on to develop a mental disorder was common. Indeed, in the recent case of *Ms B*, similar arguments were made (unsuccessfully) in an attempt to rebut her right to refuse treatment. Ultimately the court reaffirmed (for the logic of the law was clear) the right of a capacitous patient to refuse medical treatment, even if that refusal will result in their death.[20] Interestingly, even the SOAD in pair 10 would have, albeit very reluctantly, respected the capacitous written witnessed advance refusal (even though legally there was no obligation so to do).

Secondly, the spurious legal authority of the advance refusal clearly unsettled some and made them more ready to resort to an exhorted ethical position. Those who did not reason in this way nonetheless attempted to undermine the validity of the advance refusal with a series of strategies such as 'how could she possibly know what it would be like or how she would feel once she had the baby?' Others, who advanced a stronger ethical line in the first instance, seemed prepared to allow the law on advance refusals to trump their ethical position once they realised it was lawful for them to do what they therapeutically wanted to, even if this conflicted with their ethics. Yet others simply did not understand the law.

> I think I am bound to respect her competent opinion if given when she was competent. I don't think we have any option really. **RMO, pair 14**

In short, the position was fluctuating and muddled and many participants metaphorically wriggled; it was not uncommon for both parties to be confused about the legal position, or as one SOAD put it, 'I'm in a minefield here.'

The desire for some legal coherence was also evident. Whilst most seemed to prefer bringing the law for the mentally disordered into line with that for the physically disordered (that is, a capacitous refusal would be respected), more than one wished for the opportunity to treat the person with capacity for a physical disorder against their will, but in their best interests (reference was made both to the Hippocratic Oath and to the various ways and means by which capacitous refusal was overridden, ignored or outmanoeuvred; for example, giving Jehovah's Witnesses their own blood products or arguing that their refusal was based on duress). The doctor's desire to treat, even with an intervention that many rarely used, was presented as an imperative, well before the situation had become life threatening.

4.3. Clinical Issues and the Use of ECT

What constituted good (or even acceptable) clinical practice varied: when pressed as to why anti-depressants were not being pursued in preference to ect one RMO remarked:

> Yes, but she is refusing most emphatically, this is the problem, and there is a hope and indeed it often is the case when, once you give ect, then they become more amenable. **RMO, pair 5**

[20] *B v An NHS Hospital Trust* [2002].

Whether this constitutes, from a patient's perspective, the use of ect as 'an exercise of disciplinary power'[21] is a debatable point, but this RMO further remarked 'I'm not going to have patients dictating or making bargains with me about treatment'. This was in marked contrast to many of the other psychiatrists who talked broadly about the need to negotiate or establish a therapeutic alliance with the patient through dialogue. Even the word 'barter' was used by the SOAD in pair 6. It would be unwise to place too much stress on the actions of one or two arguably aberrant doctors, save for the fact that the SOAD system acts non-prescriptively. Their role is merely to authorise treatment and their ability to refuse such authorisation is based not on what they would do as doctors, but on whether what was being proposed met the *Bolam* test of being in accordance with accepted practice by a responsible body of medical opinion skilled in the particular form of treatment in question.[22] Thus, as some of the participants saw Hazel's situation as life threatening, they moved much more quickly to a course of ect (with the SOAD's authorisation under section 58 that, whilst Hazel had refused consent, the treatment should nonetheless be given having regard to the likelihood of its alleviating or preventing a deterioration of her condition). Others saw her position as one that needed to be monitored and attributed the life threatening aspects to her poor intake of fluids; this was a matter that could be managed medically if necessary. Preserving her life in the short-term could thus be achieved whilst also assessing her underlying mental condition without immediate resort to ect.

The SOAD in pair 6 was concerned that there was no way of being certain whether other SOADs would agree with the proposed course of action.

> Just like most consultants act autonomously, where you don't really know what your colleagues are doing, likewise with SOADs. SOADs act by themselves. We get together for training days and we might let off steam about how difficult it is to arrange second opinions and all sorts of mechanics but I don't know if we actually discuss ethics . . . we're asked to give an opinion on somebody else's treatment plan and there has to be a line between what is acceptable and what is unacceptable. **SOAD, pair 6**

Whilst there was considerable disagreement amongst the RMOs there was only limited disagreement amongst the SOADs. Exceptionally, one SOAD refused the RMO's request for authorisation of ect because the SOAD adopted the view that ect was a treatment of

> last resort, but not as a first choice of treatment, not at this stage . . . I don't think we can give ect for dehydration . . . we should keep it as a last resort because she is not happy, the boyfriend is not happy, and her mother is not happy, and she herself is not keen at all. I think, give the medication a chance *[the RMO was proposing an initial course of anxyiolytics—drugs to reduce anxiety—to allow the patient to mellow and*

---

[21] Fennell 1996:7.
[22] *Bolam v Friern Hospital Management Committee* [1957].

gain confidence in herself]. You are monitoring her very closely. I think she will improve. I don't think you should panic. **SOAD, pair 7**

It was also possible for a firm clinical refusal by the SOAD to be undermined by subsequent emergency administration of ect under section 62. Section 62 permits the RMO to give ect in urgent situations, for example in order to save the patient's life, without first obtaining the authorisation of the SOAD. Despite the absence of any evidence of clinical effectiveness based on the administration of one treatment with ect, where an RMO adopts this route, it effectively forecloses on a SOAD's objections, arguably rendering them impotent. The participants' decisions provided illustrations where section 62 would be used to administer ect in what were clearly non-emergency situations. Indeed, the RMO in pair 6 who took this course of action even acknowledged that there would be time to contact the SOAD and use section 58, that is, to employ the safeguard of the second opinion authorising ect. Where a SOAD would have refused to authorise ect and yet it was given on this one-off urgent basis under section 62 because the RMO either failed to understand the true purpose of section 62 as an emergency measure, or failed appropriately to constrain its use, the 'safeguard' which the SOAD represents becomes spurious. And SOADs notably were not happy about having their role attenuated by the non-emergency use of 'emergency' ect. As a SOAD remarked:

> obviously I would not be very happy about it. It should not have happened . . . but even if the RMO has been a little bit overcautious and has administered ect, then I would rather continue giving it. Basically, it is no use just giving it once, there is no magic in one ect. **SOAD, pair 7**

Conversely, where the patient's situation is regarded as so precarious that ect is being used primarily as a life-saving measure, the role of the SOAD becomes technically superfluous, since the recommended course of treatment could hardly be regarded as not falling within what would constitute reasonable practice. It is therefore arguable that the threshold for the SOAD's role may currently be set too low.[23]

4.4. Professional Concerns

As with the earlier cases of Mr Draper and Mr Wright, there was evidence in the practitioners' thinking that their concern about the consequences of their decision-making also extended to a professional concern about their own position. However, in the case of Hazel Robinson, the fear was not so much about whether she might harm others, but how they might explain themselves were Hazel to die. How to deal with the conflicting views of the relatives and the advance directive attracted this response:

---

[23] See also Richardson 1999; and *R (on the application of Wilkinson) v Broadmoor Hospital* [2001].

the whole thing with this one is a real minefield, but I would want to approach them separately just to check out that she really was competent when she made the advance directive and ask them what they want me to do. I'm afraid these days, more and more you're thinking, how is this going to look in court? What is this going to look like at the inquest, if you take the worst-case scenario? What is the coroner going to say, when I say to the coroner 'yes, I let her down'? **SOAD, pair 11**

The desire to share the responsibility for these difficult decisions was evident.

I'm very hesitant on this because I don't know what I would really do. In reality I may well say I would rather have somebody else participate in the decision or take the decision, and say go ahead, do this. **RMO, pair 11**

I believe I ought to respect the advance directive but would find it extremely difficult to do so and I would probably try to park the responsibility with the SOAD. **RMO, pair 13**

To which the SOAD responded:

To be honest with you, I would phone the Mental Health Act Commission and try to chew it over with somebody legal, as I am honestly not sure of the position. **SOAD, pair 13**

Another strategy was to take the responsibility for treating, either by casting Hazel into the role of someone who was incapacitious (or not fully competent when the advance directive was made). Thus, when faced with the situation where Hazel had apparently made a rational decision and given rational reasons for not wanting ect the response was elicited:

I would have to decide how rational that was. She may be giving rational reasons but in my view they are not or it may be a semblance of rationality when in actual fact it is mental illness that is talking. **RMO, pair 8**

This response reflects two possible positions: (a) the doctor's view of what is rational for the patient should prevail; and (b) the doctor believes that the patient's views are a product of the illness which do not reflect her true views. The first is ethically problematic; the second reflects a genuine debate about what should be the basis of a capacity test (should the true-choice approach discussed above apply?). And, even though capacity does not have a formal role under the 1983 Act, some clinicians were prepared to imply it into the Act in some circumstances. Thus, in pair 4 above, the SOAD would have overriden a capacitously made refusal if he considered it to be 'part of a whole series of over-valued ideas etc'. But, in other circumstances he would have respected her wishes, even though the 1983 Act would allow the treating doctor to disregard her current wishes, regardless of whether she was capacitous or not.[24] Thus, this clinician was impliedly introducing an incapacity test into the way in which he

---

[24] Although, as a SOAD, the clinician would have to have regard under the 1983 Act to the likelihood of the ect alleviating or preventing a deterioration in her condition, see s 58(3)(b).

chose to operate the Act, illustrating the way in which the Act gives a power to treat, but it does not impose a duty to treat regardless.

An alternative approach was simply to apply the principle of beneficence:

> I find it cruel to let somebody die who I feel I could treat. **RMO, pair 11**

This was also expressed as:

> this girl has a treatable illness and when I took my Hippocratic Oath I said that I would try and help, do everything I could to help my patients. It's very different when someone makes an advance directive about something like cancer, but she is likely to improve. Then if she wants to take her own life after she has recovered from her mental illness, she is at liberty to do that. But personally, as her doctor, I would feel extremely uncomfortable about allowing her to continue to deteriorate. I think realistically she probably would get better eventually. **RMO, pair 12**

It is, of course, curious that this doctor would respect (in prospect) Hazel's right to take her own life but would not respect (in retrospect) her advance directive.

The same RMO was also aware of the possibility that any conversation with Hazel about treatment might be perceived as one that used ect as a threat to get her to take another form of treatment, and this was recognised to be unethical. However, in describing how the meeting with the patient might unfold if a decision about ect had to be taken the RMO remarked:

> I would go in as non-threatening a manner as possible to talk to her to try to understand where she is at, and what she wants. Having read the notes I don't think I am going to get very far. But it is always possible and worth giving it a try, and I would probably go with a number of nursing staff, but I wouldn't want any of the family there. **RMO, pair 12**

Would it be too harsh to suggest that this is a psychiatrist who can apply the veneer of negotiating with a patient, but who has not fully understood that true negotiation entails a preparedness to reach decisions that can leave practitioners with an uncomfortable degree of ambivalence about the outcome? For the remarks read as if the RMO would strive to obtain the desired outcome through a form of subtle manipulation and not through a genuine desire to understand Hazel. Indeed, this psychiatrist had previously made it clear that any advance directive would be rejected.

It also contrasts markedly with an alternative approach to Hazel's negative attitude to ect.

> I don't fancy myself being able to talk her out of it. And I think the more one does that, the more one is imposing a stress upon a patient, which, if you are not going to act on it immediately is just burdening them more, so I think it is just unkind. I would have one discussion and that would be it . . . I wouldn't keep labouring it. **RMO, pair 4**

In pair 11 the critical difference in legal knowledge between the RMO and the SOAD was also highlighted; indeed, the RMO's lack of knowledge about the legal situation merely exacerbated the dilemma perceived. Hence, when discussing the involvement of the relatives in treatment:

> I think I would have to say to the relatives, at the point at which I feel she really needs ect, I would have to say to them that if they can't agree then it's better that we take the decision. I wouldn't want to force relatives into feeling they had agreed to something that they really can't agree to because of their beliefs. There is already enough conflict and friction between the mother and the husband . . . in terms of future relationships within the family, it might be quite detrimental to them if one of them agreed to her having ect and the other one opposed it. **RMO, pair 11**

And later, from the SOAD: 'The relatives have no standing and as the SOAD it's not my problem.' Or as the SOAD in pair 12 put it: 'I have the Mental Health Act.'

The advantage of calling a SOAD is self-evident in this case; they at least were largely aware of the legal position, even if they recognised that the threshold for the SOAD's agreement was low. Thus, 'my job is to make sure that the Act is being adhered to, and it is, and I have to say what the RMO is doing is legal and reasonable . . .' (namely, did the proposed treatment satisfy a *Bolam* test of being in accordance with accepted practice by a responsible body of medical opinion skilled in the particular form of treatment in question?). However, what would have happened if consent had been forthcoming from the patient, but had been obtained by coercion; or, if the RMO believed that obtaining consent from one of the relatives was enough to obviate the Act's procedures? Here, a misapprehension by an RMO about the nature of the law would, in effect, deny a patient access to a safeguard to which they were otherwise entitled. In short, obtaining consent from a patient to the administration of ect obviates the need ever to call upon the services of a SOAD; yet that patient's consent may in itself be invalid if obtained under inappropriate circumstances. Whilst the RMO would still have to certify in writing that the patient had given consent, this potential scenario nonetheless represents a worrying practical lacunae in the 1983 Act.

SUMMARY

The case of Hazel Robinson highlights a number of features already evident from the earlier cases. Lack of detailed knowledge of the law was apparent; for example, the confusion in pair 8 (replicated elsewhere) about the identity of the nearest relative, and confusion between this concept (a specialised role under the Act) and that of next-of-kin (which has a common medical and legal usage). There were also examples where confusion about even the most basic aspects of the law was rife. For example, in pair 5 the RMO was under the impression that he could give ect both under section 62, which does permit the emergency administration of ect *and* under section 63. In law, there are no circumstances under which ect could be given under section 63 since ect is a treatment regulated by section 58 (ie one requiring consent or a second opinion).[25] This RMO was further confused about the relationship between SOADs and the Commission. He also seemed very hazy about why he would be unable to give blood to a competent refusing Jehovah's witness, remarking 'well, this is a special case—it has gone to the courts already'; in this he failed to understand that this was the established common law position for all treatment for all competent patients except those under section under the 1983 Act in respect of treatment for their mental disorder. And, whilst this RMO may have been exceptional in his lack of understanding of the law (or exceptionally frank about it), the profusion of clinico-ethico-legal fudges that occurred amongst the pairs and in the subsequent discussions was striking.

On a somewhat more positive note, what emerged most strongly from these encounters, almost without exception, was a desire to help Hazel.[26] However, this was combined with their sense of clinical and legal confusion. Doctors would ask for someone to 'hold their hand' or 'to share the responsibility' or they would be phoning 'the Commission', 'the Trust solicitor' or their 'Medical Protection Society' at any point when they were confronted with an area of law they found problematic (this was particularly true in respect of the advance directive). Thus, recognising that they were on uncertain terrain, many said they would have sought further advice.

However, some were curiously similarly confounded by the notion of the capacitous mentally disordered individual. One SOAD explained the dilemma eloquently:

> Because mental illnesses are so varied in type, onset, severity, some people, yes, they do retain capacity. A demented person who has lost his memory and logic and reasoning, you can't expect rational answers from him. But a person who is mildly neurotic, biting her fingernails etc, she can give rational answers to whatever you ask about her, including her phobias and her anxiety. So, it is not the illness itself, it is the severity and type. And that is where the problem lies, this is what needs looking at and this is where we need some sort of consensus of opinion amongst ourselves, which we haven't got. **SOAD, pair 7**

As will be discussed in chapter five, this anxiety about assessing the capacity of those with mental disorder emerged also in the processes of formal consultation over the various and varied proposals concerning the direction law reform should take. What is curious about this is that assessing capacity is something that psychiatrists must already do on a daily basis when treating those with mental disorder on a consensual basis. Indeed, the 'capacitous mentally

---

[25] The Secretary of State has specified that ect is a form of treatment which falls under s 58(1)(a): Reg 16 of the *Mental Health (Hospital, Guardianship and Consent to Treatment) Regulations 1983*.

[26] The absence of much discussion by the clinicians about Ben's rights and interests, is telling. Whilst lawyers might perceive the legal interests of mother and child to be bound together (see Art 8 of the ECHR), the clinician's focus is narrower. The potential failure of mother and child to bond was raised by one or two participants, but was readily outweighed by Hazel's perceived pressing medical needs.

disordered' individual must constitute the bulk of a psychiatrist's practice when not acting under the authority of the 1983 Act. Perhaps the distinction does lie in the nature of the task. For consensual treatment, assessments of capacity are presumably implicit in the manner of the practice of psychiatry; for detained patients, assessments of capacity, if such a requirement were embodied in legislation, would have to be explicit and potentially sufficiently robust to rebut any legal challenge.

4

Decision-making Research: Context and Content

L EGAL DECISION-MAKING HAS been subject to considerable research. The decisions of judges, lay jurors, magistrates and other personnel in both the criminal and civil justice systems have been scrutinised by lawyers, psychologists, philosophers, economists and others.[1] What has been less frequently researched has been the decisions of non-lawyers about the law in non-court-based fora. And research into the decisions of non-lawyers in multi- or duo-disciplinary contexts in mental health law is positively sparse. This chapter reviews some of that literature and draws out the main lessons for understanding how such practitioners apply law. It also questions what has emerged from the current study that adds to that literature, and finally asks whether the findings have any relevance for those who would seek to achieve greater effectiveness in law. However, the chapter first establishes why it is important to undertake this task.

1. THE IMPORTANCE OF RESEARCH

Whether its purpose is for punishment, protection or treatment, use of the deprivation of liberty should be tightly constrained. Reflecting this notion of a 'right to liberty' all international Human Rights Treaties embody and protect the right to liberty except in very specific cases. Notably, under the European Convention on Human Rights, the only article to attract automatic compensation for its breach is Article 5, which deals with the 'right to liberty and security of person'.[2] Since the application of mental health law authorises intrusions of the utmost gravity, including intrusions on freedom of movement, on the freedom from non-consensual medical treatment and on the right to privacy, it might be expected that its application would be similarly tightly constrained. Indeed, the principle of legal certainty, discussed further in the following two chapters, would demand no less.

The legal provisions which govern the detention (and subsequent treatment) of those suffering from mental disorder have been characterised by one judge as fulfilling this criterion. Thus,

---

[1] For a recent review see McEwan 2000.
[2] See ECHR Art 5(5). The ECHR is now incorporated into UK domestic law by the Human Rights Act 1998.

... the circumstances in which the mentally ill may be detained are very carefully prescribed by statute. Action may be taken only if there is clear evidence that the medical condition of a patient justifies such action ... [3]

Yet, detailed analysis of the wording of the 1983 Act reveals a body of law that is inherently discretionary and highly reliant upon the interpretation and judgement of the practitioners who are required to apply it.[4] In many situations, practitioners face a real choice as to whether to use the Act, and if so, which section or sections to use. Moreover, the failure of the statute to define many of its key terms (for example 'mental illness') together with its use of vague and circular language reinforces the scope for variation in practice.[5] Thus, the very application of the law, and whether it is applied consistently and fairly, will depend in large part upon those who apply it and their knowledge and attitudes towards it.

This assertion is not novel. It has long been recognised in the field of legal decision-making that the practical effect of law is dependent not only on its substance, or even on the nature and quality of the services to which it applies,[6] but also on the knowledge, attitudes and decision processes of the practitioners by whom it is applied.[7] Mental health law is peculiarly vulnerable to these individual influences not just because of its discretionary nature, but because its discretionary nature is subject to little effective review.[8]

Given this acceptance of the importance of the knowledge and attitudes of those who apply the law it is not surprising that there has been a growing concern about the lack of formal training of practitioners in the relevant law. Whilst ASWs undergo extensive training in the law,[9] the same does not apply to psychiatrists; even section 12(2) approved psychiatrists can be certified on the basis of as little as two days training in law.[10] This period of training compares poorly even with that given to trainee police officers, who represent the other major body of non-legal decision-makers given the power to detain people.[11] As Professor Robert Kendell, a recent President of the Royal College of Psychiatrists, observed:

> In some cases ... both senior and junior psychiatrists have not been as knowledgeable about the Mental Health Act 1983 as they should be. Concern has also been expressed

---

[3] Sir Thomas Bingham MR in *Re S-C (Mental Patient: Habeas Corpus)* [1996] at 535.

[4] Eastman and Peay (eds) 1999; Hoggett 1996.

[5] Richardson and Thorold 1999.

[6] See, for example, Bindman *et al* 2002 who note that whilst variation in compulsory admission is related to social deprivation and to the functioning of local mental health services, unexplained variation remains.

[7] Hawkins 1986; Hogarth 1971.

[8] See generally ch 1 in Eastman and Peay (eds) 1999; Peay *et al* 2001; Roberts *et al* 2002.

[9] Approximately three months training in mental health, including mental health law, is required; CCETSW 1992.

[10] NHS Executive 1996.

[11] Trainee police officers receive approximately 17 weeks of training in all aspects of a constable's powers.

from some quarters about the lack of a formal examination of psychiatrists' knowledge of the legislation . . .[12]

This represents a change in attitude both as to what psychiatrists should know, and how such insights might be acquired.[13] Notably, calls for more, and more relevant, training have also been evident in other fields, for example for Mental Health Review Tribunal members.[14] Even though the MHRT always includes a legally qualified member and hears representations from lawyers, such calls for training of its multi-disciplinary membership persist. This may be in part attributable to recognition of the importance of its role in acting as a safeguard for patients against unjustified detention, but it is also in large part due to the power of research to demonstrate its functional shortcomings.[15]

It is also apparent that critical decisions about whether to admit patients under compulsion to hospital and treat them thereafter, possibly without their consent, together with decisions about the length of time patients should remain liable to this regime, have been entrusted to those who have been acknowledged to be inadequately trained. Moreover, there has been little attempt to ensure that such decisions are made consistently. Instead, the Act adopts an approach of checks and balances; it presumes that one profession will counterbalance another (as in the process of admission) or that the knowledge base of one group will be supplemented by the knowledge base of another, simply by requiring decisions to be made in a group context. However, neither of these may be true. Indeed, the relative knowledge levels of various groups of mental health professionals have recently been subject to assessment via a national survey, and knowledge levels were found to vary widely, both within and across professions.[16] Perhaps of some comfort was the finding that higher knowledge levels were associated with more frequent use of the Act. Yet professions who played a key role in the use of compulsion, for example GPs, were nonetheless found to have worryingly low levels of knowledge about the relevant law. Equally, research on MHRTs has questioned the extent to which knowledge amplification occurs as a result of mere exposure to those from another discipline; this suggests that a multi-disciplinary approach may not per se lead to consensus decision-making based on knowledge maximisation.[17]

When the Department of Health decided in the late 1990s that the 1983 Act required reform, it is perhaps not surprising that they discovered a dearth of research and statistical knowledge about the Act that might otherwise have helped them better to understand how the Act was then being applied. This recognition of a lacuna in knowledge led the Department to establishing a major

---

[12] RCP 1997.

[13] Caldicott and Mann 1994.

[14] Perkins 2002. Historically, MHRT members have been less well-trained and supported than many other tribunal members.

[15] Perkins 2002a.

[16] Peay *et al* 2001.

[17] Peay 1981.

programme of research into the operation of mental health law; a programme that included the current study and the national survey of knowledge referred to above.[18] To what extent the current proposals for reform of the law are based on an understanding of the 1983 Act's operation is another matter. This is discussed further below.

How one sets about studying decision-making will vary, depending on a number of factors, but often being influenced by the extent to which the questions to be examined concern the outcome of decisions (what is decided and by whom; what variability is there between different decision-makers?) or the process by which decisions are made, the 'how' of decision-making. One example of each will suffice to demonstrate the range. In the former category lies a Swedish study looking at the practices and attitudes among Swedish psychiatrists regarding the ethics of compulsory treatment.[19] Conducted in 1996, the study used a questionnaire which contained demographic items, attitudinal items and three brief case-vignettes in an effort to examine the situations in which psychiatrists recommended compulsory interventions in various clinical situations. The results, based on responses from 214 psychiatrists, showed that whilst there was good agreement in respect of the cases of patients with paranoid psychosis and depression, the third vignette, which had been constructed as a non-psychiatric case, still elicited a psychiatric diagnosis from 65 per cent of the respondents, with in-treatment being recommended by 42 per cent. Such an outcome reflects the well-documented tendency for people to find the things for which they are primed to look. Equally interesting, there was a divergence between the attitudes the psychiatrists expressed in response to the questionnaire, namely that 37 per cent of them would regard it as unethical to force electro-convulsive therapy (ect) on a patient 'who could benefit from it and refuses', and their response to the clinical vignette, where 74 per cent would recommend ect if the patient were continuously suicidal. As the authors observe 'This discrepancy merely illustrates the gap between what we consider our ethical beliefs to be, and what clinical experience dictates in practice'.[20]

In the latter category, of studies looking at the 'how' of decision-making, lies Quirk *et al*'s research into twenty assessments under the 1983 Act.[21] Eleven section 2 and nine section 3 assessments were observed. The process of assessment was charted from 'build up' through 'assessment' to the 'aftermath' together with the strategies, processes and perceptions of the mental health teams, including ASWs. This was done as best as was possible in an observational

---

[18] DoH 2000; see also the DoH National Research Register at www.doh.gov.uk/.
[19] Kullgren *et al* 1996.
[20] 1996: 395.
[21] Quirk *et al* 2000. For a seminal study, see Bean 1980.

study, supplemented by interviews with key parties. A number of other assessments were aborted and many seemingly extraneous variables had an impact on the outcome. Conversely, there was very little reference to the law throughout by anybody; sub-headings to the research revealingly include those of 'deception', 'pragmatism', 'planning for transport' and 'tensions between roles'. One key issue that emerged concerned the unavailability of doctors who might have provided the second medical assessment required for the use of compulsory powers; accordingly there was a worrying reliance on particular second opinion doctors who could be guaranteed to come out to the assessment (and section). At the end of the study, the reader has learnt a great deal about the process and has an in-depth impression of what really goes on in some assessments. Similarly, the reader will likely share the authors' concerns about the true independence of the three parties involved in the assessments. However, one is left wondering to what extent these findings are fortuitous or replicable in other parts of the country? Yet, on the basis of even this small sample, it is clear that the professionals' view of the process is not, in reality, necessarily or even regularly *ad idem* with that of the person subject to assessment (see below).

Finally, some studies adopt a 'how many' approach to decision-making; examples of these would be those that look only at the outcome of decisions and, through statistical analysis, attempt to tease out significant factors that must have preceded these outcomes. Such studies have a statistical power not replicated in the more fine-grain analysis of either the *in vivo* or *in vitro* studies discussed below. They can, nonetheless, provide important insights. For example Audini and Lelliott's study on the use of Part II of the 1983 Act, a study which analysed data on more than 31,000 cases of admission, provides authoritative evidence of the demographic variables associated with the use of compulsion.[22] The study's most striking finding was the overrepresentation of black people and those from ethnic minorities amongst those admitted under compulsion; indeed, black people were about six times more likely to be sectioned under Part II of the 1983 Act than white people.[23] Of equal interest, although more of an interpretation than a finding, the authors concluded that the increase in the use of compulsory admissions during the 1990s may reflect a more risk averse culture;[24] with a greater presentation by young men of co-morbid mental health and drug misuse problems the use of compulsion becomes an attractive option to those conscious of perceived heightened risk.

---

[22] Audini and Lelliott 2000. See also the work of Middleton *et al* (in DoH 2000) on the various activities of the Mental Health Act Commission.

[23] Part II deals with the compulsory admission of non-offender patients to hospital and guardianship.

[24] The use of compulsion increased by over 60% during this period DOH/National Statistics 2002.

3. *IN VIVO* VERSUS *IN VITRO* STUDIES

Another way of thinking about decision-making studies is reflected by a fundamental division in decision-making research, namely, that between *in vivo* and *in vitro* studies. In essence, this constitutes the difference between those conducted in life and those in the laboratory. Both have their obvious limitations, but both types are evident in the mental health field.

The major review of research under the Mental Health Act 1983 included a number of *in vivo* studies which examined use of the Act in different situations.[25] Yet studying decision-making *in vivo* implies a range of methodological and ethical problems, including their cost in time, resources and money. Participants may frequently be difficult to contact; the relevant 'decision-process' may be both infrequent and intermittent, whilst also being routinely aborted; it is not always convenient to interview participants immediately after important decision points, and accordingly their recollections and explanations of why they did what they did may be distorted; some research is barred by statute (jury research being the most notable example of this) or barred in practice by problems of access; finally, the unsystematic nature of *in vivo* studies means that data collection frequently has to be extensive in order to control for the many exogenous variables which complicate such studies.

Whilst *in vitro* studies (also known as vignette or simulation studies) have their own limitations,[26] they do provide an opportunity to study decision-making under relatively controlled conditions. For the purposes of this study's objectives an *in vitro* study crucially permitted examination of the extent to which the Act is *capable* of being applied consistently, by different professionals and by combinations of professionals of different backgrounds. Indeed, such studies may be the preferred approach to the study of particular participants; for example,

> when behaviour is largely governed by formal legal rules, procedures or strong social norms, then research should and does rely less on artificial or simulation methods and more on field methods . . . In contrast, when there are few formal rules that specify behavioural expectations, then more highly controlled and hence artificial methods may and have been employed.[27]

The field of psycho-legal research has been peppered with vignette studies of various kinds; for example, studies of sentencing decisions based on written materials;[28] role playing exercises which involve parties reproducing their official roles, amongst the most innovative of which was the McCabe and Purves 'shadow jury research' which studied the decision-making of members of the

---

[25] Wall *et al* 1999.
[26] Helpfully summarised by Corkery 1992:255.
[27] Corkery, citing Bray and Kerr 1982:294.
[28] Hood 1972; Corbett 1987; Moxon *et al* 1992.

jury panel who sat through real trials as a mock jury receiving all the information heard by the real jury, whilst being excluded from those parts of the trial from which the real jury were excluded;[29] and audio-visual taped re-enactments of trials.[30] Other jurisdictions have also employed the vignette as a tool to study decision-making.[31]

Depending on their objectives, these studies have ranged across a spectrum from those where the situation was highly artificial and a limited amount of selected information was presented, to those which attempted to reproduce, insofar as is possible, the real life decision-making situation. Indeed, where full information was given, decisions in vignette studies have been shown to mirror accurately decision-makers' real decisions.[32] Many of the studies have been experimental, in that they attempted to manipulate key pieces of information (for example, the gender or race of the defendant) whilst holding all other factors constant, in order to assess the specific impact made by the chosen variable(s). Other simulation studies have been designed more as a means of making accessible, and thereby examining, reasoning processes, on the assumption that these would remain relatively robust if sufficient external reality could be achieved.

4. STUDIES OF DECISION-MAKING AND DECISION PROCESSES IN MENTAL HEALTH LAW

4.1 Research on MHRTs

My own work on Mental Health Review Tribunals in the late 1970s was the first to examine decision outcomes and processes of (real) mental health tribunal members dealing with a hypothetical case under the Mental Health Act 1959.[33] This research coincidentally looked at the impact which members' legal knowledge and attitudes towards the law had on their decisions about the continued compulsory detention of patients. It examined members' actual decision-making practices, their decisions in a hypothetical case (using written and audio-visual materials within a role-play exercise), and their knowledge and attitudes. Since tribunal members are drawn from lawyers, psychiatrists and lay people, the research enabled comparisons to be drawn between these groups. The findings demonstrated that even though tribunal decisions are made by three people acting together, members' individual 'track-records' of real decision-making and their decisions in the hypothetical case were related to their knowledge, attitudes and conceptualisation of their role. Thus, individual

---

[29] 1974.
[30] Block 1991.
[31] For example, Simon 1967; Hogarth 1971; Jacoby *et al* 1982; Potas and Rickwood 1984.
[32] Corkery 1992:266 citing Hood 1972.
[33] Peay 1980, 1981.

factors, namely a member's knowledge, attitudes and past experience of reaching decisions, were shown to be crucial to understanding the lack of consistency in tribunal decision-making.

It is notable that this research was conducted in an era before there was any meaningful training of MHRT members in their roles. With this caveat in mind, my vignette study specifically illustrated considerable variation in decision outcomes, both on an individual basis and between tribunals, given identical information.[34] Associated with these varying decision outcomes were very high levels of expressed confidence in the decisions reached. Decision outcomes were best predicted by the member's initial response to the written materials, and remained so despite the presentation of new evidence. What this suggested was that members arrived at the tribunal with relatively fixed ideas about the case, and that all subsequent information was selectively interpreted as supporting that initial view (whether it was to discharge or not). The robustness of an individual's original view of evidence has also been replicated in simulated jury research, where decisions following group discussion largely mirror the original juror's views; and even where a juror changes their vote in order to be consistent with the majority view the possibility remains that they have done just that, changed their vote and not their view.[35] Also, in my research the relevant legal criteria were not well understood; assessments of the patient's diagnosis, seriousness of disorder and dangerousness were fluid; and some members stressed the importance of reaching a decision that was in the patient's best interests, rather than adhering strictly to legal criteria. Thus, much of this was consistent with Fennell's assertion that tribunal decisions were influenced more by common-sense factors than by legal criteria and that the legal concepts formed no more than 'shorthand reference points', providing only organising boundaries within which 'a number of subordinate, non-legal conceptual categories are indexed'.[36]

One further finding emerges from my earlier research which is pertinent to the multi-disciplinary context applicable to decisions to admit, discharge and treat patients without their consent under the 1983 Act; namely, that group decisions rarely represent an 'average' of those of the parties concerned. This used to be known as the 'risky shift phenomenon' since it was thought that groups would take riskier decisions than any of the parties alone would have tolerated. However, in practice the effect is somewhat more subtle. My research indicated that the group decision was more extreme than that of the individuals concerned, but that its nature could be either more risky or, notably, much more cautious. A group decision was thus not a consensus decision, but reflected the views of its most dominant member and the effect of taking the decision in a group could be to enhance that individual's view, and not to ameliorate it.

[34] 1981:178–82.
[35] Arce *et al* 1996.
[36] Fennell 1977.

Much more recently, Perkins observed 61 tribunal hearings of section 2 or section 3 applications of whom five patients were discharged; she observed that the most striking characteristic of the tribunals was the variation in the procedures and processes adopted.[37] Whilst many of her findings replicate those of my second study[38] (which was both quaintly reassuring and deeply frustrating in that so little had changed in well over a decade), her observations about the statutory criteria were telling. She argued that their complex wording led to enormous variation in their interpretation; tribunal members (who include a legal member who chairs the proceedings) particularly struggled with the concept of 'nature or degree' (a concept that it is proposed will survive in new legislation).[39] The legal members were heavily guided by what the medical experts said, whilst those medical experts were themselves unsure about the meaning to be attached to these quasi-legal terms. As Perkins noted:

> In the absence of any clear and consistent interpretations of the discharge criteria, tribunal members substituted their own criteria. These were the presence or absence of symptoms, of insight, of compliance and co-operation and of risk and danger to the patient and other people.[40]

This substitution in turn involved members in balancing liberty against maximising therapeutic outcome, and balancing the patient's rights against the protection of the public. Both of these exercises entailed a degree of predicting future outcomes, rather than focussing, as the criteria emphasise, on the patient's current status. Where the future is inherently uncertain, caution prevails.

Her observations, consistent with my own, included noting MHRTs' preferential reliance on medical evidence (where psychiatrists are assumed to have the patient's best interests at heart, but patients are generally viewed as less credible), the rapidity with which decisions were made, the relative lack of discussion either of the outcome or of the way in which the evidence might support or refute it, the tendency for consensus to emerge 'by osmosis' and for whatever differences of opinion there were to be resolved easily and amicably. It might be suggested that the process of decision-making at tribunals, which does not require members to reach prior individual decisions, will most likely facilitate this emergence of a consensual decision. That only five patients were discharged similarly adds weight to the notion that decisions to discharge (the riskier option) were less likely to emerge through this process of group decision-making.

Whilst here is not the place for a critique of the tribunal system, and it is anyway to be overhauled by the process of law reform, it is worth noting that there

---

[37] Perkins 2002.
[38] Peay 1989.
[39] Perkins 2002a: 7–10.
[40] Perkins 2002a:10.

has been a recent significant investment in the training of tribunal members in an attempt to ensure greater uniformity of practice.

4.2 Does Good Decision-making and Due Process Go Hand in Hand?

Another theme which comes out of the tribunal research, but which is mirrored in the work concerning compulsory admission to hospital, is the extent to which the outcome of the decision may not be the most important factor from the perspective of the individual who experiences the process. Rather their 'assessment of the fairness of the case disposition process' may be the most critical factor.[41] Clearly, patients who recognise that they have little or no chance of being discharged might value more highly the manner in which they are treated by the tribunal and the opportunity it provides them to express their views and seek explanations for their continuing treatment and detention.[42] Yet, this argument does not apply so forcefully to civil patients, where it might be expected that the prospects of release are higher than for those patients on restriction orders[43] detained in the Special Hospitals.[44] Nonetheless, more recent research does confirm the fundamental gap between the perceptions of the tribunal members and those of the patients whose cases they review.[45] Patients were significantly less likely to agree that the tribunal was fair.

Why is this important? Aside from the obvious answer that legal safeguards ought not only to operate fairly, but also to be seen to operate fairly if those for whose benefit they are in place are to have any confidence in the system, there is another and more subtle argument. And it is this. Is it possible that patients who have very negative responses to their experience at the tribunal become more treatment resistant?

This possibility is raised because of other research that has been conducted in respect of the admission process. Work in both the United States and the Nordic countries has demonstrated that there is no ready correlation between patients' legal status (that is, whether they were admitted to hospital under statute or entered voluntarily) and their beliefs about whether or not they had been coerced into hospital.[46] Thus, in the Nordic study of 863 admitted patients, 13 per cent in Denmark, 8 per cent in Finland, 17 per cent in Norway and 5 per cent in Sweden believed that they had come to hospital involuntarily, whereas they were in fact voluntary patients. Similarly, of the formally committed 6 per cent in Denmark, 33 per cent in Finland, 47 per cent in Norway and 19 per cent in

---

[41] Tyler 1996.

[42] See generally Peay 1989.

[43] Such orders restricting discharge to either the MHRT or the Home Secretary can be imposed by the Crown Court when sentencing offenders where it is thought 'necessary for the protection of the public from serious harm' s 41(1) 1983 Act.

[44] Nor does it apply to the process of admission, where the outcome may be crucial.

[45] Ferencz and McGuire 2000.

[46] Monahan *et al* 1999; Kjellin *et al* 2001.

Sweden reported that they had come into hospital voluntarily. Process variables here were the best predictors of perceived coercion. In the US MacArthur study a similar significant minority of those who had gone into hospital as voluntary patients, believed that they had been coerced; here it was found that negative pressures, such as threats and force, engendered feelings of coercion, whereas positive pressures, such as persuasion and inducements, did not. Moreover, the amount of coercion a patient experienced was strongly related to his or her beliefs about the justice of the process by which they were admitted. As the authors observe:

> a patient's beliefs that others acted out of genuine concern, treated the patients respectfully and in good faith, and afforded the patient a chance to tell his or her side of the story, are associated with low levels of experienced coercion.[47]

Thus, procedural justice was critical for the patient's perceptions of their legal status. But, the question remains (and is likely to remain unanswered because of the empirical difficulties of testing the notion) as to whether patients who believe that they have engaged willingly in hospital admission are more likely to respond to the treatment offered; and conversely, whether those who believe they are under compulsion will be treatment resistant.[48] Logically, if a positive placebo effect exists (and this is well-documented) why should there not also be a negative placebo effect (that is, treatment is less effective because the patient is not fully compliant)?

One study in South East London has attempted to shed light on this issue.[49] Whilst endorsing the above findings on coerced admissions (with over one third of voluntary patients feeling highly coerced, and process exclusion and perceived pressure being strongly associated with perceived coercion) the study failed to find any association between perceived coercion and subsequent engagement with follow-up. However, as the authors note, events at the time of admission may have a relatively small impact on engagement with follow-up compared with factors related to the patient's relationship with community services after discharge; equally, patients may well be aware that there are limits to the use of compulsion in the community. However, Bindman *et al* also suggest an additional explanation; namely that patients may be coerced into maintaining contact for fear of readmission. In this context, it would have been interesting, if ethically and methodologically problematic, to have examined treatment compliance during the period of admission following coercion or the perception of coercion.

Both of the overseas studies of patients' perceptions of coercion form part of larger research enterprises. The MacArthur study, a research initiative dating back to the 1980s, has other major elements looking at the relationship between mental disorder and violence, and at the use of coercion in the community, in

---

[47] Monahan *et al* 1999.
[48] Wertheimer 1993.
[49] Bindman *et al* 2001.

essence a study of out-patient commitment. The study on various aspects of the admission process also goes well beyond that adverted to above. The Nordic Study on 'Paternalism and Autonomy', which started in the mid 1990s, uses a three-pronged methodology. It looked not only at patients' perceptions of the process, but also charted 6,162 admissions across five Nordic countries in an attempt to establish the reliability and validity of public statistics on involuntary hospitalisation, whilst also examining the legal basis for such admissions under the five jurisdictions.[50] Both the MacArthur and the Nordic initiatives have produced a wealth of data, far beyond the more limited interests of the study reported here.

One final aspect of the South East London study is of interest. Whilst patients may be aware of the limits of compulsion in the community, they seem all too aware of the possibility of the use of compulsion in hospital, even if they enter voluntarily. This may itself contribute to the experience of coercion patients report even though their legal status on admission may be that of 'voluntary'. In the sample of 100 admissions in one mental health sector, 19 were under section on admission, but a further 20 were sectioned during their index admission. The national statistics mirror this reality. Statistics for the year 2000–01 of patients formally detained under the Act reflect both Bindman *et al's* findings and the outcome of the current study.[51] Thus, of 25,159 civil admissions (a figure which has remained broadly constant since its dramatic increase between 1990/91 and 1994/5)[52] there were 13,349 section 2 admissions for assessment (for up to 28 days), 9,714 section 3 admissions for treatment (for up to 6 months) and 1,796 section 4 emergency admissions (for up to 72 hours). However, there were, in addition, 14,768 patients who had entered hospital on an informal (for those without capacity to consent) or voluntary basis (the latter with consent) who were sectioned once in hospital; thus 37 per cent of patients gain the status of section 2 or section 3 only after a negotiated admission to hospital. Bindman *et al* argue that this constitutes a lower working threshold for compulsory admission, since the use of compulsion via section 5(2) or section 5(4) only requires one professional opinion for the purposes of temporary detention;[53] and for the direct use of section 2 or section 3 in hospital, the authors assert that this can

---

[50] Høyer *et al* 2002.

[51] DoH/National Statistics 2002.

[52] The reasons for this increase are necessarily complex (see DoH/National Statistics 2002) but include the DoH drawing the disjunctive nature of 'health or safety' to the attention of practitioners, reinforced by *R v MHRT for the South West Thames Region ex parte Smith* (1998), and the pervasive influence of the 'climate of blame' in the 1990s. Over the 10 year period from 1990 there has been an increase in the use of compulsion by over 60%; notably, whilst the effect of the *Bournewood* judgment in the Court of Appeal contributed to the rise in 1998/9, it was followed by a drop in 1999/0 after the judgment was reversed by the House of Lords. This is perhaps one of the best illustrations of a direct influence between changes in the law and practitioner behaviour in mental health practice.

[53] Under the 1983 Act s 5(2) and s 5(4) are temporary holding powers. They permit respectively the patient's doctor to detain the patient for up to 72 hours, or a nurse, to detain for up to 6 hours, with a view to making a formal application for admission for assessment or treatment under the Act.

take place more readily where staff have acquired a sense of responsibility for patients and their risk management as a result of the patient's prior voluntary admission. Reflecting on Mr Draper's experience, it is entirely possible that many of those professionals who were planning to negotiate some kind of voluntary admission knew all too well that, after admission, executing a section would be unproblematic.

4.3 Predicting Violence

Many jurisdictions have admission and discharge criteria that incorporate some notion of 'dangerousness to others'. The 1983 Act is no exception, although its terminology of 'necessary for the health or safety of the patient or for the protection of others' is more broadly drawn than many other dangerousness criteria. Predicting and managing violence has thus become one of the key areas of study for those interested in the decision-making of mental health professionals. Here is not the place for a review of that literature;[54] however, one or two points are worth stressing. First, it is an enormously problematic area to research well. Second, as our knowledge of the largely tenuous, but occasionally robust nature of the relationship between mental disorder and violence has evolved, efforts have been made to design, assess and enhance the reliability of predictive tools to assist decision-makers in this field. The MacArthur Violence Risk Assessment Study has had this as one of its two core goals of over a decade of research. The work is methodologically highly impressive, and, whilst it relates only to acute civil in-patients in the US with a median length of hospital stay of 9 days, it is based on a sample of 1,139 admissions and uses a triangulated method (patient interviews, interviews with collaterals—persons named by the patients as being someone who would know what was going on in their lives—and official documents, namely arrest and hospital records). From this data set the authors have produced a complex iterative classification tree that derived from 106 risk factors; the authors were further able to identify a smaller number of major factors associated with either a high or low risk of violence. The patients could be allocated on the basis of the model to one of five risk categories.

Whilst this model seemingly surpasses a better statistical threshold than anything else that is currently available,[55] it still only produces a 76 per cent probability of predicting one event of violence over a 20 week period for those in its highest risk category (some 60 plus patients out of its original sample). To what extent this is useful where or if decision-making bodies have to apply a 'beyond reasonable doubt' standard to their decisions is debatable. The authors modestly assert that this predictive model should act as only one tool in the array of measures available to decision-makers; equally, they point to the

---

[54] Monahan *et al* 2001.
[55] See the review by Buchanan and Leese 2001.

predictive power of those in the lowest risk category (some 350 patients fell into the 1 per cent risk of a violent incident over a 20 week period) which should assist decision-makers in identifying those for whom coercive measures are no longer necessary.[56] Paradoxically, whilst the tool does live up to its aim of having been produced on the basis of the best 'science' on violence risk-assessment possible, and the authors are currently working on a computer based, clinician-user-friendly programme to apply the findings, it remains vulnerable in its application. Since patients will have to be allocated by clinicians, or other decision-makers, at each of the classification points to one of a choice of categories, it remains possible that its ultimate predictive power will be undermined where clinicians 'play cautious' and allocate those they believe to be more dangerous, to the categories that they believe will predict dangerousness.[57] And anyway, as with most prediction instruments, the tool fails to capture the contextual factors that even the authors acknowledge are critical for the manifestation of violence. Thus, even as sophisticated a tool as this one remains vulnerable to the ineffable human factors in decision-making.[58]

4.4 Community Treatment Orders (CTOs)

The Mental Health Act 1983 has been regarded as outmoded and deficient in not permitting compulsory treatment in the community. The government plans to remedy this in its proposals for new legislation (see chapter 5). Suffice it to say here that many other jurisdictions (most notably 39 US States, Australia, New Zealand and four European Union countries[59]) permit what is commonly known as outpatient commitment. But, such schemes remain controversial and assessing their effectiveness is highly problematic.[60] In proposing such new legislation the government is reflecting not only the reality of the location of the vast majority of modern mental health care, but it is also fulfilling what are the evident wishes of many (but not all) practitioners (both in real life and in the current study) for such an order to be added to the array of other forms of control practitioners currently enjoy.

However, do the practitioners' beliefs in the efficacy of such legal orders have any empirical basis? Again, designing a methodologically rigorous study of outpatient commitment orders has not proven easy, and even the two randomised controlled trials that are now available from North America have attracted criticism.[61] What the two studies seem to show would be of limited comfort to

---

[56] Steadman 2002.

[57] As noted by one of the Nordic authors, Høyer (personal communication).

[58] See, for a ground-breaking study, Hogarth 1971.

[59] See, for example Salize *et al* 2002:31 who note that of the 15 EU jurisdictions only Belgium, Luxembourg, Portugal and Sweden have compulsory out-patient treatment.

[60] Høyer and Ferris 2001.

[61] Appelbaum 2001; Dawson 2003; Dawson *et al* 2003.

those who adhere to a belief in the efficacy of legal orders.[62] The Steadman *et al* study concluded that 'the court order itself had no discernible added value in producing better outcomes' whilst the Swartz *et al* study found lower rates of criminal victimisation and arrest, and lower rates of violence, but only amongst those who were subject to extended out-patient commitment. More notably, both studies reported that improving the availability and quality of mental health services led to better outcomes. Equally, a recent study using matched controls in Western Australia demonstrated that the imposition of a compulsory order is no more effective than not enforcing community treatment.[63] As Monahan *et al* observe, out-patient commitment is only one of a growing array of legal tools used to mandate treatment adherence in the community (others would include advance directives, treatment involving the social welfare system where benefits or housing can be used as leverage, and the avoidance of jail) and it is therefore unlikely that the mere presence of a legal order would exert any significant additional effect on treatment compliance.[64] However, what is of interest is that the alleged power of such orders remains fixed in the thinking of some policy-makers and some clinicians, creating the basis for a future additional option for decision-makers. How popular it will prove in England and Wales once clinicians have direct experience of it (see below) remains an open question.

4.5 Other Types of Study

Other recent research, adopting a limited vignette approach, has used brief written descriptions of the salient facts and studied only individual decisions. For example, Morgan *et al* examined the differential application of the 1983 Act by a total sample of 67 GPs, psychiatrists and ASWs using a questionnaire containing 14 case vignettes.[65] Applying the Act individually, these professionals showed general agreement in situations involving 'danger to self' and 'danger to others', but the ASWs were less likely to detain than doctors on health grounds. Also, GPs tended to use the Act inappropriately, being too readily prepared to use it on health grounds where it was not for the assessment or treatment of mental disorder; one such example would be where it would assist surgeons to perform amputations.

Hassan *et al's* 1999 study, using telephone interviewing based on one brief case-history, questioned how conversant those doctors who work in accident and emergency departments (A&E) are with the law on capacity to consent to treatment. They found that '(a)n appreciable number of doctors at all levels of seniority would have contravened the existing legal rights of the patient in our

---

[62] Swartz *et al* 1999; Steadman *et al* 2001.
[63] Preston *et al* 2002.
[64] Monahan *et al* 2002.
[65] Morgan *et al* 1999.

scenario had they been dealing with a real patient'.[66] Indeed, over 40 per cent of these A&E doctors would have incorrectly detained at common law a patient deemed mentally competent; and nearly half of them would have then gone on unlawfully to treat the patient 'in her best interests'. Since, in practice, this could lead to charges of battery or to a civil action for negligence, it is vital that practitioners' perceptions and misperceptions of their legal roles are better understood by those responsible for law reform and for the promulgation of any new law.

Research on the critical role of the ASW in challenging a medical perspective has also been undertaken. For example, Walton found 18 per cent of patients for whom two doctors had already recommended compulsory admission being dealt with in an alternative way by the ASW in the case.[67] Further work supporting this finding has been published by the Social Services Inspectorate.[68] Their report, based on an inspection of ASW services in 10 local authorities, noted that only 65 per cent of patients assessed by ASWs (most of whom would have been referred by a doctor as needing compulsory admission) were subsequently detained under the Act, with informal admission or alternative care being arranged for a further 23 per cent of patients. The Social Service Inspectorate reported that ASWs can sometimes be criticised by other professionals as pedantic in their adherence to good practice (that is, good practice as set out in the Code of Practice published pursuant to the 1983 Act); in short ASWs had to resist expedient measures to protect the rights of individual users. Indeed, ASWs were found to challenge casual use of the Act, whereas clinicians perceived the Act as a bureaucratic burden and as a restriction on their clinical freedom. Even so, disagreements were reputedly rare, with negotiation rather than conflict being the norm.

The Mental Health Act Commission (the body responsible for monitoring the conditions under which detained patients are held and treated) also conducts research, with particular respect to the areas for which it has statutory responsibility. The most recent and most relevant study for the purposes of this book concerns its survey of ect facilities in England and Wales.[69] Some 230 hospitals in England and Wales administer ect; yet, in approximately 20 per cent of these hospitals there were substantial departures from best policy, practice or training guidelines. Whilst not a study of the use of law per se, the preliminary findings suggest a worrying lack of rigour about the way in which ect, perhaps the most controversial treatment given with any regularity to patients, is administered.

---

[66]   1999:109.
[67]   Walton 2000.
[68]   Social Services Inspectorate 2001.
[69]   For a report of the preliminary findings of this survey see MHAC 2002.

5. WHAT DOES THE CURRENT STUDY ADD?

Whilst eclectic in content, the research reviewed above provides some indication of the nature of research studies in decision-making in mental health law. Some of the studies are of the 'how often' or 'how many' variety. But most seek to answer 'what', 'how' and 'why' questions. It is evident that such research can most helpfully facilitate an understanding of the meaning of phenomena from the perspective of those being studied.[70]

The study which forms the basis of this book is an example of this latter approach, since it has focussed on non-legal heuristics in a specialist legal field; in short, it provided insights into professionals' reasoning processes in a quasi-legal decision-making setting. Since it is a study of how people make, explain and justify their decisions, both individually and in pairs, the specialist literature on human factors in decision-making, on common cognitive errors and on the behavioural aspects of decision-making, is relevant.[71] This literature has previously been applied both in the context of decision-making in mental health practice[72] and in legal contexts.[73] What the current study has done is to provide an understanding of its applicability in the context of duo-disciplinary decision-making in mental health law.

Whilst the findings detailed in this book are open to all the limitations of any *in vitro* study, some attempt was made in the research design to minimise these by employing real life subjects (that is, not the ubiquitous research subject, the impoverished student) and giving these mental health practitioners materials that were as ecologically valid as possible. By this stage it should be apparent that the methodology adopted attempted to mimic the actual process by which decisions are reached in 'real' assessments whilst at the same time permitting the decision-making of a substantial number of practitioners about identical 'patients' to be studied. Whilst the decisions made should not be regarded as in some way typical, they do illustrate the range of decision processes and reasoning styles that might be employed by professionals in real life.

The methodology adopted also permitted practitioners' decision-making to be subject to fine-grain examination, including detailed deconstruction of the decisions made in their immediate aftermath. In real life, such opportunities rarely present themselves where practitioners are necessarily caught-up in dealing with the situation, the parties involved and in following through their decisions. In contrast, the controlled environment provided by the study permitted an analysis of the interactions between the professionals, thereby giving some understanding of both their individual thought processes and the potential corruptions of relevant legislation and the more subtle sign-posting of these

---

[70] Buston *et al* 1998:197; Greenhalgh 1997.
[71] See for example, Baron 1994, Dawes 1988, Fitzmaurice and Pease 1986.
[72] Bartlett and Phillips 1999.
[73] See McEwan 2000 and Peay 1999.

intentions, which occur when participants are faced with problematic cases and/or necessarily complex decisions. Moreover, understanding the ways in which any identifiable decision-making styles can variously affect, or even distort the intended effects and the effectiveness of mental health law from that intended by policy-makers, is important to any purposeful reform of mental health legislation.

To illustrate, the *ALCESTE* analysis touched on in chapters one and two of the styles of discourse adopted by the ASWs and the psychiatrists shows how psychiatric discourse is more dominated by issues of risk. In the recent climate, where psychiatrists have found themselves most publicly criticised before, during and after Inquiries following homicides committed by psychiatric or former psychiatric patients, this is perhaps not surprising. However, it is unlikely to be a matter of direct experience for the clinicians involved in this study. Nonetheless, the psycho-legal research has illustrated a more pervasive influence, namely, the reliance people place, in the absence of other information, on what is known as the 'availability heuristic'. That is, the ease with which instances of the matter to be predicted come to mind, influences how probable it is thought to be likely to recur.[74] Another factor, the role of the 'simulation heuristic', namely, the notion that people try to match the attributes of a given scenario to those already experienced, may also be at work here. Together, these heuristics help to explain how fear can become a predominant factor in decision-making in mental health; both the media's coverage of untoward events and the examination of them through the inquiry process can distort the practitioner's perception of the frequency of such events.

However, some practitioners have other experiences on which to draw. Thus, those ASWs with 'out-of-hours' experience (and in this study there were a number of such practitioners who specialised in dealing with both forensic patients or with having to make decisions when team back-up was not so readily available) were able to accommodate the prospect of managing Mr Draper in the community. Others, who had little or no similar experience, were much more ready to employ a Mental Health Act section, possibly because the information on which they had to draw was of negative outcomes. Being able to envisage alternative outcomes was thus critical in making decisions that would facilitate, rather than pre-empt, such outcomes. Thus, real world relevant experience can be an advantage as an aid to avoiding casual or inappropriate use of the Act.

The study also provides evidence of the operation of a number of other common decision errors. Thus, the discussion in chapter three of the proposition that the use of ect was successful even with non-compliant patients was an example of the tendency of decision-makers to ignore the totality of their track record and give potentially spurious credence to their knowledge of their successes. Similarly, there was evidence of the common failure of people rarely to revise their views in the light of new information; in the study, some of the

[74] Kahneman *et al* 1982.

psychiatrists remarked that Mr Draper did not appear to be as ill in the video as they had expected him to be on the basis of the case history. However, they interpreted this as something deficient in the video or the assessment, rather than questioning whether their own initial assumptions were correct and integrating the new information accordingly. Their view as to what should happen next did not change.

6. WHAT RELEVANCE HAS THE RESEARCH TO LAW REFORM?

The relationship between the research findings and the proposals for law reform in the Draft Mental Health Bill 2002 are discussed at greater length in chapters five and six. One specific point is worth stressing here. The Draft Bill seemingly envisages not only a change in the personnel to be involved in the decision to put someone into the process of compulsory assessment (the proposal in the 2002 Bill is for two registered medical practitioners and one approved mental health professional, with the latter group going wider than ASWs to include, for example, appropriately qualified nurses) but also a change in the method of reaching the decision. For, under clause 13, it was proposed that each of the three professionals must record in writing their own determination and the reasons for it. If, at any point, any of the professionals reached the view that not all the relevant conditions were met for assessment, then none of the other examiners could carry-out an examination.[75] This reliance on individual decision-making and requiring justification for those individual decisions seems likely to have the impact of making compulsory assessment more difficult than under the current regime of joint assessment, where the ASW acts to initiate the application for a section having obtained two medical recommendations. Conversely, clause 10 of the Draft Bill required the examiners, if determining that it is not appropriate for the assessment to be carried-out in hospital (that is, that the assessment could as readily be done in the community) to

> specify the requirements to be imposed in respect of the patient to (a) secure that the assessment be carried out, or (b) protect his health or safety or other persons against the risk by reference to which the examiner determined whether the third of the relevant conditions is met in his case.

Since the relevant 'third' condition requires decision-makers to be satisfied of the necessity for medical treatment in the interests of the patient's health, or safety, or the protection of others, in essence this clause requires those asserting that assessment *can* be carried out in the community to establish *how* risk is to be managed. It would seemingly have propelled decision-makers with a safety-first bent to opt for hospital assessment.

The relationship between the commissioning of research and the impact that any of its findings might have on subsequent policy development or law reform

---

[75] See clause 11 of DoH 2002.

is a complex one. Kane's crucial work in this field is reviewed in the last chapter.[76] However, suffice it to say here that researchers wisely generally justify their activities not on the basis that their findings have a direct impact on policy, but rather on the grounds that the enhancement of reliable knowledge is a good thing in and of itself.

[76] Kane 2002.

5

Legal and Policy Context

I T WOULD NOT be uncommon for a chapter on the legal and policy context of mental health decision-making to commence with a historical synopsis of the developments and tensions in law. Whilst passing reference will be made to this historical context, it will be no more than passing reference. The task has already been done excellently elsewhere and it would be tedious and redundant to replicate this.[1] Nor does this chapter focus on the law per se; the most relevant sections of the current Act for this book are reproduced in Appendix 1 and an authoritative treatise on the law is also readily accessible.[2] In any event, to concentrate on the law, its development or the tensions inherent in it would be potentially misleading, for the focus of this book is not on how lawyers perceive these tensions or their historical genesis, but on how non-lawyers deal with them. Moreover, since the research suggests that non-lawyers do not give law the eminence or priority that lawyers do and that its application may fall far short of that expected by Parliament and the law's draftsmen, a more rounded approach to understanding the relevance of law is most apt. Thus, whilst this chapter will look at legal and policy developments, particularly since the 1983 Act, it will also strive to place them into their practical context, namely that of the other relevant matters ongoing in the professional lives of mental health practitioners. Even this task will necessarily be limited.

The primary focus here is on the process of reform since 1998, giving the chapter not so much a retrospective focus from the point at which the practitioners took part in the study, but a prospective one. The year 1998 is significant since it marks the point at which activity with respect to mental health law reform acquired a sense of urgency and momentum, even if the momentum was not unidirectional. It was also the year when the Expert Committee (the Richardson Committee) was set up to advise the Minister of State at the Department of Health on the scope of the necessary changes to mental health law. At this point it is important to reiterate the health warning provided in the Preface to this book; I was a member of the Richardson Committee and, despite the central tenets of its report being rejected in the subsequent process of law reform, I remain wedded to its focus on non-discrimination and autonomy as guiding principles for modern mental health legislation. Everything that appears here is therefore biased, for I cannot claim the moral superiority of a neutral academic observer.

---

[1] See, for example, Fennell 1996, Unsworth 1987, Jones K 1993.

[2] Jones R 2002. See also Bartlett and Sandland 2000, or Hoggett 1996 for a general commentary on the field.

That said, a number of milestones have been passed. These include the publication of the Richardson Report in November 1999[3] and the concurrent publication of the Government's response to it in the form of a Green Paper;[4] the further publication of a White Paper in December 2000;[5] the publication of a Draft Bill in June 2002;[6] the response to it by the Joint Committee of the House of Lords and House of Commons on Human Rights;[7] and finally, an assurance by the Secretary of State for Health that a Bill would be presented to Parliament in the then forthcoming session, despite there being no mention of such legislation in the Queen's Speech in November 2002.[8]

Whilst the path the government has pursued has been fairly consistent, with its emphasis on risk and public protection as abiding themes in law reform, it represents a profoundly different approach from that of the Richardson Report. This is discussed further below. However, one point is worth emphasising here since it has had a bearing on the working lives of all those involved in mental health care and policy. The compilation or publication of all of these documents has entailed associated periods of consultation with both the professions, interested parties and the public generally. Richardson engaged in two rounds of consultation prior to its final publication;[9] and formal consultation took place in respect of both the Green Paper and the Draft Bill. For the White Paper the consultation process was selective and informal. This welter of response elicitation has left the professions probably bewildered, and certainly feeling besieged. Indeed, the publication of a critical joint statement by the Royal College of Psychiatrists (RCP) and the Law Society on the day of the release of the Draft Bill in June 2002 was testament to the extent to which government policy and the views of practitioners had diverged, possibly irrevocably, during this process. However, there will be more of this later. The chapter starts, so as not to disappoint, with a (brief) potted history.

1. 1890 AND ALL THAT

Three core issues have dominated contemporary discussions of mental health law and mental health practice. First, the conflicting roles played by mental health care professionals and others in treating and caring for those with men-

---

[3] Richardson 1999.

[4] DoH 1999.

[5] DoH/Home Office 2000.

[6] DoH 2002.

[7] Joint Committee on Human Rights 2002.

[8] Curiously, whilst there was no mention of the Draft Mental Health Bill in the Queen's speech, on the next day Alan Milburn announced to Parliament that a Bill would be brought forward once the DoH had finished considering around 2,000 responses submitted during the consultation process on the Draft Bill; Hansard 14 November 2002.

[9] The DoH did not put the final Richardson Report out for consultation, but rather engaged in a limited consultation on its own Green Paper, which had confusingly incorporated some of Richardson's specific proposals, but without their underpinning framework.

tal disorder. Second, the relationship between mental health and risk, that is both the risk of serious harm that patients may pose to themselves or others and the 'clinical risk' that a therapeutically achievable maximum state of mental health might not be realised for the patient if compulsion is not used. And third, the notion of rights. This last core issue embraces the right not to be detained, the right to refuse treatment and, more controversially, to have treatment, and finally, the right to challenge decisions made by professionals about whether or not, and in what circumstances, treatment should be given. This third notion of rights is particularly problematic. Patients generally have no right to a particular form of treatment, but equally health care professionals have an ethical and legal duty to provide care of a particular standard. The relationship is perhaps best conceived as an axis of entitlement and duty. However, the situation is further complicated by the way in which mental health law sustains the anomalous position whereby patients with mental health problems who retain their capacity (but who are not subject to the Mental Health Act 1983) have an absolute right to refuse treatment, but those suffering with similar problems who are subject to the 1983 Act have no right to refuse treatment for their mental disorders, even if they retain all of the elements required to satisfy the notion of legal capacity. Yet those very same people will enjoy an absolute right to refuse treatment for their physical disorders. Since the boundaries between physical and mental disorder are not uncommonly blurred, this illogicality in the law creates potential role confusion for clinicians; in what contexts should they be negotiating consensual treatment with patients and when should they properly have resort to compulsion, with all of the consequences that may bring for the conventional doctor-patient relationship?

The triumvirate of roles, risks and rights, crudely set out above, pulls in conflicting directions and with varying forces. During the last 110 years each has held sway in mental health legislation. Kathleen Jones, for example, has characterised this as the movement of a pendulum between legalism and medicalism. It is only possible to give a flavour of her argument here, but in essence, legalism attempts to regulate the coercive aspects of psychiatric practice through the imposition of legal safeguards, and medicalism re-interprets the coercive aspects of psychiatric practice as treatment, and accordingly makes them subject to clinical judgement and not legal regulation.[10] Indeed, a rights-based approach can be portrayed as being anti-therapeutic. Adopting this analysis has led lawyers and historians to portray the *Lunacy Act 1890,* which required judicial certification for virtually all admissions,[11] as the highpoint of legalism.[12] In contrast, the *Mental Treatment Act 1930,* by introducing voluntary admission by written

---

[10] Jones K 1993.

[11] As Fennell 1996:9 notes even patients with voluntary boarder status could be treated without their consent.

[12] Before that time, dealings with those suffering from mental disorder had gone through a number of different phases; see Glover-Thomas 2002 for a brief history and Scull 1993, Parry-Jones 1972 or Jones 1972 for more detailed analysis.

application and temporary admission for non-volitional patients, began a move towards early treatment without unnecessary legal impediments. The *Mental Health Act 1959* built on this; judicial certification was replaced with multi-disciplinary professional discretion as the basis for the determination of the use of compulsion. By the time the *Mental Health Act 1959* was enacted, the pendulum is portrayed as having swung to the opposite extreme to the 1890 Act, so that the 1959 Act represents the highpoint of medical discretion. Indeed, as Fennell notes, in recent times it was only during the currency of the 1959 Act that there was no central authority (like, for example, the Mental Health Act Commission) to exercise supervision over the conditions and treatment of detained patients.[13]

The latter part of the 20th century saw legislation with (once again) a somewhat greater emphasis on rights. The *Mental Health Act 1983* was a swing back in the direction of legalism, or rather of a new legalism since it embodied not only notions of due process, but also Gostin's promotion of the idea that patients should have a right to care in the least restrictive setting.[14] Thereafter, the focus of new legislation shifted much more clearly towards risk management, with the *Mental Health (Patients in the Community) Act 1995* incorporating a new power into the 1983 Act to 'take and convey' patients who were non-compliant with treatment in the community back to hospital. Finally, with the passage of the *Human Rights Act 1998,* which incorporated the European Convention on Human Rights into domestic law, the era of rights-based thinking heralded by the 1983 Act arguably came properly into being. Yet, its delivery does remain arguable, for the ECHR's 1950s thinking sets, by current standards, a remarkably low threshold for the satisfaction of rights. Thus, for example, Article 5(1)(e) refers to 'the lawful detention of persons for the prevention of the spreading of infectious diseases, of persons of unsound mind, alcoholics or drug addicts or vagrants', thereby consigning those with mental health problems alongside the 'dangerous and undesirable'. To date, human rights challenges to mental health law have produced perhaps less than their proponents might have wished, but arguably more than pessimists might have expected.

Of course, not all of those who have analysed these historical trends agree with Jones' pendulum portrayal. Most notable, and most relevant for this study, is Fennell's argument that it is more helpful to look at the changes in mental health law in terms of the 'promotion, development and legal recognition of clinical authority'.[15] Placing the emphasis as he does more on the conditions

---

[13] Fennell 1996:6.

[14] Further analysis of the ideology of entitlement is provided in Gostin 1983. Under s 26 of the 1959 Mental Health Act (the equivalent of s 3 under the 1983 Act) it was only necessary to state why no other method of dealing with the patient was appropriate, see s 26(3)(b). Under s 3(2)(c) of the 1983 Act this was strengthened to a requirement that treatment 'cannot be provided unless he is detained under this section'. See also DHSS 1976.

[15] Fennell 1996:13.

under which psychiatry has treated patients with mental disorder without their consent, flavours the analysis with notions of fundamental human and civil rights; but it also makes the focus, at least in part, one that entails ensuring that these decisions are made only following a proper evaluation of risks and benefits by the professionals involved.

2. SETTING THE CONTEXT OF REFORM

Of the 106 practitioners who took part in the research few had had experience of working with anything other than the 1983 Act; and a number demonstrated less than full familiarity even with that Act. As such, it makes little sense to attempt any practical contextualisation of the law prior to 1983; indeed, this Act anyway represented a sea-change in respect of certain aspects of the law, particularly with regard to enhanced safeguards for patients.[16] These enhanced safeguards were themselves subject to criticism relatively early after the passage of the 1983 Act. Thus, MHRTs came under critical review both in respect of their decision-making[17] and in the 1990s, in respect of the extent to which their structure and procedures breached the rules of natural justice.[18] However, these research studies had little real impact on the working lives of practitioners; much more fundamental were the consequences that stemmed from attempts to treat and care for progressively greater numbers of patients in what were regarded as more appropriate non-hospital based locations. Thus, the shift to community care, which had been ongoing throughout the 1960s and 1970s, and the reduction of psychiatric in-patient facilities for the mentally ill and impaired, which had acquired impetus from the 1961 Hospital Plan,[19] changed the nature of the responsibilities of both psychiatrists and ASWs (and their predecessors). In addition to this, in the 1990s the growth of diversion for mentally disordered offenders from the penal system involved psychiatrists in aspects of the court structure extending beyond their traditional role of preparing reports for the court at the point of sentence.[20] Paradoxically, at more or less the same time that the psychiatric profession was becoming more guarded about its ability successfully to treat certain categories of patient and there was another wave of disenchantment with the effectiveness of the latest psychiatric drugs,[21] the profession's responsibilities were being extended into fora where it was progressively difficult to ensure effective treatment.

[16] For example, the introduction of Part IV of the Act relating to consent to treatment, the establishment of the Mental Health Act Commission, the role of SOADs and the extension of the power to discharge restricted patients by MHRTs following *X v the UK* (1981).

[17] Peay 1989.

[18] Richardson and Machin 1999, 2000.

[19] See Glover-Thomas 2002:66.

[20] On diversion specifically see Cavadino 1999, James 1999 and Burney and Pearson 1995. On policy generally relating to mentally disordered offenders see Fennell and Yeates 2002, and Peay 2002.

[21] See Cohen 2002, Koerner 2002 and Richardson 2001.

It was perhaps inevitable that the locus of the scandals of the 1950s, which had been institution-based, would relocate to the community.[22] In 1992, three events seared themselves into professional memories and, more arguably, into the public's mind; the killing of Jonathan Zito by Christopher Clunis, Ben Silcock climbing into the lion's den at London Zoo and the killing of Katy Sullivan, a student worker at a MIND hostel.[23] In 1993 the then Secretary of State for Health, Virginia Bottomley, produced a 'Ten Point Plan' as a response to what was perceived as rising public concern about care in the community. The 10 point plan led to a number of initiatives which would impact negatively on professionals, for example the introduction of Supervision Registers[24] and the requirement for mandatory inquiries following any homicide by any user or former user who had had contact with the mental health services in the previous 12 months.[25] In contrast, the introduction of 'after-care under supervision'[26] was initially limited in its impact on professionals, since it was little used in its early days. Perhaps of more immediate benefit was the issuing of guidance on risk assessment and discharge, which was designed to assist professionals in the task of risk management.[27] But, all of these developments notably had risk at their heart; professionals were being left in no doubt about their responsibilities and the censure they would attract if things went wrong.[28]

By the turn of the millennium the deluge of Inquiry Reports, whilst fascinating in their detailed analysis of who had said and done what to whom, and who had concurrently failed so to do, had begun to tell a familiar tale. The Inquiries were peppered with examples of inadequate communication, a failure to document or synthesise information, services and people under pressure and of professionals developing strategies to manage or avoid the unmanageable.[29] Meanwhile an alternative approach, of systematic audit, emerged with the establishment of the Confidential Inquiry into Suicide and Homicide. This painted a somewhat different picture and, although *ad idem* with the Inquiry Reports' findings that few of the Homicides could have been predicted (indeed Community Treatment Orders, for example, were estimated as likely to prevent only 2 homicides a year of the 50 or so committed by people who had had prior contact with the mental health services[30]) the Confidential Inquiry indicated that a better strategy on suicide prevention could save a significant number of the 1,000 people per year who took their own lives. Around the same time as this

[22] Rose 1986.

[23] See specifically Crichton and Sheppard 1996:66.

[24] Now abandoned, but see Baker 1997, and Fennell and Yeates 2002.

[25] See generally Peay (ed) 1996.

[26] See the 1995 Act above. See also Hadfield *et al* 2001, and Pinfold *et al* 2002.

[27] As Buchanan 2002:252 demonstrates, in the 10 years since 1990 there were 19 separate publications of 'central guidance on mentally disordered offenders'.

[28] Ben Elton's satirical novel Popcorn, published in 1996, captures, in its closing pages, the diffusion of responsibility in the aftermath of tragedy, and hence the multiplicity of problems faced by the Inquiries.

[29] Peay (ed) 1996, Sheppard 1996; Rumgay and Munroe 2001.

[30] Appleby 1999:73; see also Appleby *et al* 2001.

knowledge about relative risk was most likely to be permeating into the public's consciousness,[31] the focus of policy also began to shift. Whilst almost imperceptible, the shift was in an appropriate direction, namely from risk to others, to risk to the patients themselves.

Thus, shortly before the establishment of the Richardson Committee, Professor Graham Thornicroft was asked by the Department of Health to chair a committee to recommend a series of national standards for care. His committee, which involved professionals, users and carers, led to the publication of the National Standards Framework (NSF) in 1999.[32] This was designed to assist in developing the kind of services that would encourage potential users to seek help earlier. Strikingly, Standard One included the need for Health and Social Services to 'combat discrimination against individuals and groups with mental health problems and promote their social inclusion'. The year 1999 also saw an attempt to modernise the care programme approach (CPA), streamlining patients into either standard or enhanced care programmes.[33] First introduced in 1990, the CPA had required a written care plan based on an assessment of a patient's needs, and a key worker to ensure that services were delivered; it applied to all patients who had been in contact with specialist psychiatric services. In keeping with the much earlier shift to community care, its emphasis was on patients in the community; and, with the introduction of the NSF, those on CPA were to have 24 hour access to services.

Of course, all of the negative publicity emerging from the 'Inquiries after Homicide', had helped fuel concern about discrimination against those with mental health problems. In 1998 the Royal College of Psychiatrists also commenced a five-year anti-stigma campaign[34] entitled 'Changing Minds' which was designed to increase public and professional understanding of different mental health problems and to reduce the stigma and discrimination against sufferers. Related to this campaign in 2001 *Every family in the land: understanding prejudice and discrimination against people with mental illness* was published by the Royal Society of Medicine.[35] This presaged what was to become the 'one in four' slogan promoted by the RCP, but originating with the WHO, to draw attention to the statistical fact that a quarter of the population would encounter mental health problems at some point in their lifetimes.

3. RICHARDSON AND AFTER

The triumvirate of role conflict, risks and rights outlined above was joined in the 1990s by a fourth core issue; this was the role, if any, to be played by capacity in

[31] Gigerenzer 2002.
[32] DoH 1999b.
[33] Department of Health 1999a.
[34] See www.rcpsych.ac.uk/campaigns.
[35] Crisp (ed) 2001; this CD rom contains a synthesis of practitioner and academic writings on mental health and discrimination.

the scope of law reform. The Law Commission had already spent some six years exploring reform of the law relating to mentally incapacitated (and capacitated) adults. This process, together with their recommendations for reform, had undoubtedly done much of the ground-work in raising legal and professional awareness of the importance of the concept of capacity.[36] Whilst the Richardson Committee was amongst the first formally to endorse and apply this capacity-based approach in respect of mental health law reform,[37] it was apparent that capacity-respecting legislation already had widespread if cautious support. This was revealed both in the processes of consultation conducted by Richardson and then by the government, but also support was evident in research conducted for the Department of Health.[38] Curiously, the notion of impaired decision-making ability, with its clear undertones of a capacity-based approach, was favoured in the recommendations for revisions to Scottish mental health legislation.[39] However, as will emerge below, the currency of capacity in the reform process in England and Wales was seemingly short-lived, as the government rejected it in favour of an approach based on risk. If capacity were to have had an important role south of the border, how might that have impacted on practitioners who were already ethically torn between the competing demands of rights, risks and their roles in health promotion? Indeed, could adoption of a capacity test have even eased any ethical dilemmas they might experience?

Since it would be impossible to focus on all of the permutations and perambulations of the various official proposals for reform of legislation, the discussion below will deal primarily with the ambit and nature of the criteria for admission into compulsion. These are critical. Not only will they ultimately act as the filter to compulsion, but they will also crystallise the various normative approaches adopted; that is, how ought the law to be applied?

3.1 The Richardson Approach

In October 1998 the Department of Health established an independent Expert Committee, with a multi-disciplinary membership of 12 practitioners and academics chaired by Professor Genevra Richardson, to advise the Minister on the necessary scope of reform to mental health legislation. The Richardson Committee's brief was daunting. Daunting not only because they were encouraged to think in terms of 'root and branch' reform which, given the complexity

---

[36] Law Commission 1995.

[37] Whilst the two areas of law reform do overlap, mental health law has been primarily concerned with people suffering from mental (psychiatric) disorders and incapacity legislation primarily with people who lack the capacity to make specific decisions but largely not by reason of mental disorder. In many cases, this is a false dichotomy, and adopting a capacity-based approach to both areas of law reform could have achieved greater coherence in the law.

[38] See DoH Consultation; Roberts *et al* 2002.

[39] See Millan 2001 and Scottish Executive 2001. Scotland has already legislated on incapacity, see *Adults with Incapacity (Scotland) Act 2000*.

of the issues, was manifestly challenging, but also because of the imperative to 'get it right'. The opportunity for such reform comes rarely. At that time, mental health legislation had last been subject to fundamental reform in 1959, so this initiative at the turn of the millennium was likely to set in stone for many years the tone and tenor of the framework for compulsory care of those with mental health problems.[40]

The Committee's deliberations were confined by an unusually short time-frame. However, between October 1998 and July 1999 they commissioned expert reports, benefited from two rounds of public written consultation and received submissions from users and carers, public and professional bodies and from individual practitioners and academics. They also held public and private seminars with experts from other European and English speaking jurisdictions and visited various facilities in England and Wales.[41] As already adverted to above, at the end of this extensive consultation process the Richardson Committee concluded that non-discrimination on grounds of mental ill health should be a core principle of any legislation underpinning the delivery of mental health services. In advocating that approach they were at one with the recommendations of, for example, the World Health Organisation, the US Surgeon General and, more parochially, the Department of Health's own National Standards Framework.[42] In principle, therefore, non-discrimination appeared non-controversial.

Whilst the principled basis for adopting non-discrimination was compelling, its practical consequences were potentially problematic.[43] Problematic since practitioners claimed that capacity was an issue with which they were not familiar when making decisions about the use of compulsion. Whilst this was self-evidently true, since change in the legislation was being proposed, capacity was not an unfamiliar concept to practitioners. Indeed, it guided their practice in all other fields where compulsion was not used. And herein lay the attractions of a capacity-based model, for it would resolve one problem in the existing legislation that was logically and legally indefensible; namely, that detained patients with capacity had their decisions to refuse treatment for their physical disorders respected, but that their decisions concerning treatment for mental disorder could be overridden. One of the Committee's key principles was that 'wherever possible the principles governing mental health care should be the same as those which govern physical health'.[44] Thus, in so far as was possible, people with mental disorder who retained the capacity to refuse treatment should have that decision respected, as they would have their decisions respected about treatment for their physical illnesses. Given this, it was curious that capacity should have been seen as an alien concept, since it was already integral to the legal basis on

---

[40] For a context to Richardson see Eastman and Peay (eds) 1999.
[41] Richardson 1999:129–39.
[42] World Health Organisation 1996; Surgeon General 1999; Department of Health 1999b.
[43] Richardson 1999, Richardson and Peay 2000.
[44] Richardson 1999:21.

which practitioners made decisions about the treatment of patients with physical disorders, or of patients with either mental or physical disorders who were not subject to compulsion, and in respect of patients who were subject to compulsion for their mental disorders, but who also had somatic disorders. In respect of treatment decisions about the latter, a test of capacity already applied.

In adopting this essentially non-discriminatory approach the Committee had attributed primacy to the concept of autonomy as a good in itself. This was by no means novel,[45] for it was consistent with the approach adopted by the courts in England and Wales for adult individuals with capacity.

> An adult patient . . . has an absolute right to choose whether to consent to medical treatment, to refuse it or to choose one rather than another of the treatments being offered . . . This right of choice is not limited to decisions which others might regard as sensible. It exists, notwithstanding that the reasons for making the choice are rational, irrational, unknown or even non-existent.[46]

In the case of Ms B,[47] a woman who wished to be taken-off a ventilator, a course of action that would lead quickly and inevitably to her death, the court noted:

> it is a question of values . . . we have to try inadequately to put ourselves into the position of the gravely disabled person and respect the subjective character of experience. Unless the gravity of the illness has affected the person's capacity, a seriously disabled patient has the same rights as the fit person to respect for personal autonomy. There is a serious danger, exemplified in this case, of a benevolent paternalism which does not embrace recognition of the personal autonomy of the severely disabled patient.

Whilst this makes clear that even imprudent and life-threatening decisions must be respected, the principle *has* been limited for those where the fulfilment of their autonomous and capacitous choices may do harm to others, or harm to themselves if made incapacitously. JS Mill[48] expressed it thus:

> The only freedom which deserves the name, is that of pursuing our own good in our own way, so long as we do not attempt to deprive others of theirs, or impede their efforts to obtain it. Each is the proper guardian of his own health, whether bodily, or mental and spiritual. Mankind are greater gainers by suffering each other to live as seems good to themselves, than by compelling each other to live as seems good to the rest.

Or, in the more frequently cited passage:

> . . . the only purpose for which power can be rightfully exercised over any member of a civilised community, against his will, is to prevent harm to others. His own good, either physical or moral, is not a sufficient warrant.

---

[45] Ashworth 1999:27–28; Gunn 2000.
[46] *Re T (Consent to Medical Treatment) (Adult Patient)* [1993] at 113.
[47] *B v An NHS Hospital Trust* [2002] at para 94.
[48] Mill [1859]1991:17.

However, this doctrine was meant to apply only

> to human beings in the maturity of their faculties. We are not speaking of children, or
> of young persons below the age which the law may fix as that of manhood or wom-
> anhood. Those who are still in a state to require being taken care of by others, must
> be protected against their own actions as well as against external injury[49]

The perimeters and parameters of the debate were thus long-standing. After two
rounds of extensive consultation the Richardson Committee recommended that
some criteria should be common to all compulsory orders; namely, the presence
of mental disorder of such seriousness that the patient requires care and treatment under the supervision of specialist mental health services; and that the care
and treatment proposed for and consequent upon, the mental disorder is the
least restrictive and invasive consistent with safe and effective care; and that the
proposed care and treatment is in the patient's best interests.[50] Thereafter, a
capacity test would apply. For those who *lacked* capacity the compulsory order
would have had to have been 'necessary for the health or safety of the patient or
for the protection of others from serious harm or for the protection of the
patient from serious exploitation that s/he be subject to such care and treatment,
and that such care and treatment cannot be implemented unless s/he is com-
pelled under this section'.[51] For those who *retained* the capacity to consent
Richardson proposed two alternative approaches, which are described respectively as the consistent and the pragmatic approach to autonomy. Both
approaches would have permitted compulsion where people other than the
patient were at risk. The dividing line concerned the protection of the patient
from him or herself. Thus, for the consistent approach there would have needed
to have been 'a substantial risk of serious harm to the safety of other persons if
s/he remains untreated'. For the pragmatic approach the criteria would have
been wider with 'a substantial risk of serious harm to the health or safety *of the
patient* or to the safety of other persons' etc (emphasis added). In setting out
these two approaches the Richardson Committee was, in essence, marking out
the terrain covered by a longstanding debate between the attractions of an
autonomy-based approach and those grounded in paternalism. The point at
which the Committee divided concerned whether patients with mental disorder
should 'enjoy' the same right to harm themselves as those suffering from physical disorder, or whether those patients who retained capacity in the context of
a mental disorder should nonetheless be protected from themselves. Whilst the
logic of the latter paternalistic approach may be harder to grasp, it is not hard
to appreciate why the view might be taken that capacity in the context of mental disorder cannot be wholly equated with capacity in the context of physical
disorder, so that allowing those with mental disorders to harm themselves feels
unconscionable to those with a paternalistic bent. The Committee laid bare the

---

[49] 1991:14.
[50] Richardson 1999: 70.
[51] Richardson 1999: 70.

difficulty of the task that needed to be addressed, but argued that the choice between principled autonomy and pragmatic paternalism was essentially a moral one, and one for politicians and not the Committee to take.[52]

In respect of capacity per se the Committee believed that unlike 'appropriateness' (see chapter one) it did have an independent value and meaning 'the core of which is accepted by all those involved in the operation of mental health legislation: mental health professionals, users, carers and lawyers'. The Committee continued thus 'In our opinion the introduction and development of the concept of capacity will lead to a more precise and objectively justifiable use of compulsory powers'.[53] Notably, the Committee had already accepted that the concept, as an element in the criteria for admission, would require extensive training and refinement as experience of applying it grew. Finally, the Richardson Committee proposed that there should be a health intervention of likely efficacy available (that is, one going beyond the treatability criterion in the 1983 Act) for all patients who retained capacity; namely, that there should be 'positive clinical measures included within the proposed care and treatment which are likely to prevent deterioration or secure an improvement in the patient's mental condition'.[54] In recommending 'positive clinical measures' the Committee was endeavouring to find a form of words that would both prevent mere containment in a therapeutic environment and avoid clinicians excluding those who were harder to treat solely with medication under a traditional psychiatric model. However, whatever form of words were ultimately to be adopted, the Committee was clear that a health benefit criterion was vital. The absence of one, the Committee observed with some prescience, would be to require health professionals to 'engage in activities which they would regard as inappropriate and possibly unethical'.[55]

3.2 The Green Paper

The concurrently published[56] Green Paper formed a stark contrast with the Richardson Report. The former has been described as taking parts of the skeleton of Richardson, but abandoning its ethical heart and its principled musculature.[57] Where Richardson was urged to be radical, the Green Paper's conception of modernising mental health services entailed a controlling and cautionary emphasis; its vision was retrograde. Crudely, risk was the pervasive theme, with

---

[52] Richardson 1999: 20.
[53] Richardson 1999: 92.
[54] Richardson 1999: 70–71.
[55] Richardson 1999: 71.
[56] Whilst the Richardson Report was delivered to the Minister in July 1999, its publication was delayed by the DoH until it was possible for them to publish their own Green Paper, which was a partial rebuttal of Richardson and a rejection of the capacity-based approach.
[57] See generally Peay 2000.

notions of rights and the problems arising out of role conflict playing a sub-sidiary role and capacity being relegated as 'largely irrelevant'.[58]

The tone of the two documents was markedly different, with Richardson's emphasis on non-discrimination, patient autonomy and capacity and the Green Paper focusing on risk as being a, if not the, key factor on which compulsion should turn. Moreover, whilst Richardson provided a reasoned justification for its approach, the Green Paper assumed risk to be an aproblematic notion and one that required no justification beyond recitation of the Government's desire for services that were 'genuinely safe, sound and supportive'. Finally, whilst the Green Paper urged that the provisions of a new Act should be 'fairly and con-sistently implemented',[59] 'clear',[60] and that people with mental illnesses 'should be treated in the same way as people with any other illnesses'[61]—all laudable intentions—it then advocated criteria for compulsion that were so broadly drawn that it was almost impossible to conceive of an individual who was suf-fering, or had suffered, from mental disorder who would *not* fall within the pro-posed criteria.[62] Thus, the Green Paper's criteria had the *potential* to make compulsion the rule for the treatment of mental disorder. Since the criteria clearly could be discriminatory against those with mental disorder, it is perhaps understandable that this Green Paper also abandoned Richardson's recommen-dation that the principle of non-discrimination should be a central tenet of any new Act.

Consistent with this shift away from patient-oriented principles, the Green Paper generally focussed on the views and interests of others rather than on the service user, so that Richardson's preference for a patient based 'best interests' test became in the Green Paper 'best interests should be determined by members of the multi-disciplinary care team, and based on their professional opinion';[63] similarly, whilst Richardson wanted treatment to take account of the safety of 'other patients, carers and staff' the Green Paper put the emphasis on the patient's 'safety *and the safety of the public*'. Richardson also stressed the need for evidence-based practice to take account not only of research evidence, but also of the views of service users; the Green Paper dismissed evidence-based practice as already being part of clinical governance. Finally, while Richardson stressed the need for advance agreements about care to be considered routinely,[64] the Green Paper did not endorse this view. Thus, Richardson's approach had a primary focus on the patient and attempted to facilitate and encourage patients into treatment; the Green Paper had a much greater emphasis on the interests of the public, consistent with its overarching theme of

[58] DoH 1999: 32.
[59] DoH 1999:10.
[60] DoH 1999:11.
[61] DoH 1999:9.
[62] DoH 1999:32–33.
[63] DoH 1999:34.
[64] Richardson 1999:106.

managing risk, and thus emphasised the need for widely drawn powers of compulsion.

In rejecting Richardson's capacity-based entry criteria, the Green Paper commented:

> The principal concern about this approach is that it introduces a notion of capacity, which, in practice, may not be relevant to the final decision on whether a patient should be made subject to a compulsory order. It is the degree of risk that patients with mental disorder pose, to themselves or others, that is crucial to this decision[65]

Moreover, the Green Paper wholly failed to address the ethical problem laid bare by Richardson as to whether a consistent or a pragmatic approach to autonomy ought to be adopted; in essence it merely elided the two and then effectively dismissed the moral dilemma they posed by proposing a model without a capacity test.[66]

3.3 The White Paper

The Green Paper was not received well.[67] It was followed in December 2000 by a White Paper that revised the entry criteria proposed in the Green Paper. Whilst the introduction to the White Paper put great stress on the level of financial investment there was to be in mental health, and on other government initiatives to regulate standards of care (for example, on NICE, CHI and the NSF), legal reform was evidently still to be driven by risk; and the second part of the White Paper buttressed this approach by incorporating proposals for the new category of Dangerous People with Severe Personality Disorder (DSPD).[68]

The White Paper was also quickly subjected to critical analysis.[69] As Genevra Richardson, writing in a personal capacity, pointed out, rejecting capacity as an entry criterion was not sufficient, something had to be put in its place since not everyone suffering from a mental disorder should be vulnerable to the application of compulsory powers.[70] Risk and medical paternalism, the Green Paper's approach, were too broad. The White Paper did differentiate between those who were a risk to others, and those who needed compulsion in their own interests. However, for the second group it went on confusingly to place reliance on the notion of a patient's mental disorder warranting specialist care and treatment *'in their own best interests'*. This was confusing since best interests is the basis on which treatment is administered under Common Law[71] to those without the capacity to consent to it, and yet the White Paper proposed to use it for

---

[65] DoH 1999:32.
[66] DoH 1999:31.
[67] Bowen 2000, Peay 2000, Zigmond and Holland 2000.
[68] Prins 2001, 2002, Fennell 2001.
[69] Richardson 2001.
[70] Richardson 2001:425. This point was also made by the Percy Commission 1957.
[71] *F v West Berkshire Health Authority* [1990]; *Airedale NHS Trust v Bland* [1993].

patients with capacity. In contrast, in *Ms B v An NHS Hospital Trust*, the case concerning the woman who wished to be taken off a ventilator, the court noted how straightforward and robust the law was on this issue:

> If mental capacity is not in issue and the patient, having been given the relevant information and offered the available options, chooses to refuse the treatment, that decision has to be respected by the doctors. Considerations that the best interests of the patient would indicate that the decision should be to consent to treatment are irrelevant.[72]

Moreover, the Law Commission had also dealt with best interests in its Report on Mental Incapacity.[73] Yet the White Paper wanted the concept to perform a crucial gate-keeping role. As Richardson observed, 'Best interests, undefined, is too slippery a concept to provide the basis for a major deprivation of individual rights'.[74]

For the first group of patients, those who posed a risk to others, the White Paper introduced another controversial notion, namely that if the care and treatment plan did not treat the underlying mental disorder (that is, it did not have a health benefit to the patient) it must 'manage behaviours arising from the disorder'. This smacked of preventive detention ousting health benefit, alleviated only by the impression given that innovative treatment techniques would be developed to address the needs of this problematic group of treatment resistant patients. However, the government clearly did not have enough faith in the professionals' ability to *deliver* such programmes for health benefit to be made a requirement in potential legislation.

Either way, in the 17 months after the publication of the White Paper and before the release of the Draft Bill, further informal consultations on these criteria were held. More permutations were discussed, none of which seemed to satisfy. When the Bill was finally published, it appeared as if the government were planning to place reliance on a set of criteria that looked remarkably similar to those embodied in the 1983 Act, but broadened by the adoption of a very wide definition of mental disorder without exclusions and unrestrained by a workable treatability test. Thus, it looked as if the government were prepared to promote criteria that would be wide enough to permit compulsion for all, where the entry examiners felt this was necessary and where the new Mental Health Tribunal, applying the same broad criteria, did not object.

4. DRAFT MENTAL HEALTH BILL 2002

With the publication of the Draft Mental Health Bill 2002 this saga entered its endgame. 'Entered' is the pertinent word, since the government announced a

---

[72] *B v An NHS Hospital Trust* [2002] at para 100ii.
[73] Law Commission 1995.
[74] Richardson 2001:429.

further period of consultation on its Bill. The preliminary response to the Bill was hostile and the key professions and other groups involved formed an alliance in opposition to it.[75]

Whilst much might be said about the presentation of the need for new legislation, with the government asserting that the Draft Bill would improve public safety and increase consistency in application of compulsory powers, there were, in reality, four driving factors behind the reforms; the need to make legislation Human Rights compliant (and thereby avoid what was becoming a torrent of judicial reviews—albeit mostly unsuccessful—on vulnerable areas under the 1983 Act);[76] a perceived need to extend the locus of compulsory treatment from hospital into the community; a desire to ensure that 'dangerous people with severe personality disorder' (as they had become known in the late 1990s)[77] would be brought within the ambit of the Act, even if deemed untreatable by psychiatrists, and subject to restraint and management; and finally, to fill the '*Bournewood* gap' by extending some safeguards to compliant but incapacitous patients.[78] Since the government had given an assurance in the House of Lords in the case of *Bournewood* that action would be taken to protect this vulnerable group, these primarily informal patients became to be perceived as an urgent legal problem.[79] Yet, the most obvious solution, that of implementing the Law Commissions's recommendations on mental incapacity, seemed, until late in the process of mental health law reform, to have been side-lined.[80]

4.1 Community Treatment Orders and the DSPD Initiative

The two areas above where the government had made its intentions very plain throughout the process of review and reform concerned community treatment orders and untreatable psychopaths (the DSPD initiative). For the former, there was already a long and inauspicious history of attempts to invent and implement a satisfactory CTO[81] dating back to the decision in the cases of *Hallstrom*

---

[75] See 'Rights not Compulsion', the Mental Health Alliance's campaign in respect of the Draft Bill and the Press Statement 'Unique and United'—on the Alliance, RCP and Law Society web pages, 6 August 2002.

[76] See, for example, *Johnson v United Kingdom* (1997); *R (on the application of H) v Mental Health Review Tribunal for North and East London Region* [2001]; *Benjamin and another v United Kingdom* (2002); *R (on the applications of KB, MK, JR, GM, LB, PD, and TB) v MHRT and the Secretary of State for Health* [2002]; *R (on the application of B) v Mental Health Review Tribunal* (2002); *R (on the application of IH) v Secretary of State for the Home Department and the Secretary of State for Health* [2002].

[77] Home Office/DoH 1999, Home Affairs Select Committee 2000.

[78] *R v Bournewood Community Mental Healthcare NHS Trust ex parte L (Secretary of State for Health and Others Intervening)* [1998]. See also, Eastman and Peay 1998, Glover 1999.

[79] The relationship between the need for an Incapacity Act and a new Mental Health Act is discussed in Richardson 2002.

[80] See Law Commission 1995. On 16 December 2002, the Lord Chancellor's Department announced that it would be taking forward Incapacity legislation, when time permits.

[81] For a review see Exworthy 1995.

and *Gardner*.[82] This judgment made plain that psychiatrists could not use a strategy that had developed of renewing sections on patients who were on leave in the community, then granting them further leave under the section (invidiously known as the long-leash approach). Thereafter, a number of formal alternatives were proposed and rejected, culminating in what became section 25A 'aftercare under supervision'. But, the section was not greatly used, partly because it was seen more as imposing bureaucratic requirements on psychiatrists than on restraining patients and partly because it still required patients who refused medication to be brought back to the hospital for the administration of medication, via re-sectioning if the patient refused.[83] Or as Baroness Jay put it, this was a 'classic case of taking a horse to water but not being able to make it drink'.[84] For this was a power only to 'take and convey'. Finally, the decision in *ex parte Barker*[85] in effect gave back to psychiatrists the power they thought they had had before *Hallstrom*.[86]

This saga of ineffective legislative and policy initiatives had rebounded on the Richardson Committee. As intimated above, whilst the Committee had been asked to undertake a 'root and branch review' and to adopt 'a fresh approach and find innovative solutions',[87] one policy objective was stated with remarkable clarity. Indeed, it was presented as critical to the whole programme of reform. That objective was the need for the Committee to address the issue of compulsory treatment in the community. As Paul Boateng put it:

> ... if there is a responsibility on statutory authorities to ensure the delivery of quality services to patients through the application of agreed individual care plans, so there is also, increasingly, a responsibility on individual patients to comply with their programmes of care. Non compliance can no longer be an option when appropriate care in appropriate settings is in place. I have made it clear to the field that this is not negotiable.[88]

Thus, 'non compliance is not an option' was to apply both to patients and to clinicians.

When the Green Paper was published, setting out its objectives in its foreword 'to modernise the legal framework within which mental health care is delivered' it was clear that CTOs were also to be central to its programme of modernising mental health services. And, whilst it is possible to construct arguments favouring

---

[82] *R v Hallstrom, ex parte W (no 2); R v Gardner ex parte L* [1986].

[83] See Bindman 2002. Aftercare under supervision is thought primarily to be useful for the small group of patients who are prepared to respect the legal framework.

[84] Hansard HL Vol 563 col 152.

[85] *B v Barking Havering and Brentwood Community Healthcare NHS Trust, ex parte Barker* [1999]. For commentary see Lewis 2000, and see also *R (on the application of DR) v Mersey Care NHS Trust* (2002).

[86] Peay 1986.

[87] Speech by Paul Boateng MP, then Parliamentary Under Secretary of State for Health, delivered at the first plenary meeting of the Richardson Committee. Reproduced in Richardson 1999:140–45.

[88] Richardson 1999:142.

compulsory treatment in the community,[89] the emphasis in the Green Paper was a controlling and cautionary one. This was explicit in its discussion of the need for compulsory care and treatment in the community.

> ... too often, patients treated in hospital—both formally and informally—fail to fol-
> low their treatment plans on discharge and need to be re-admitted to hospital because
> their condition deteriorates following loss of contact with care services. It is totally
> unacceptable that a group of patients who are known to pose a risk either to them-
> selves or to others when they fail to comply with treatment, should so easily drop out
> of care in this way—sometimes with tragic results.[90]

Given this overriding policy imperative, it came as no surprise that the seamless use of a compulsory care plan bridging both hospital and community settings was also a central plank of the Draft Bill's framework.

The other area where legislation looked inevitable related to the government's well-documented intentions with respect to DSPD. Although the Draft Bill formally made no mention of DSPD, it created the legislative possibility for the care and detention of this 'group' since it would permit compulsion where there was a 'substantial risk of causing serious harm to other persons'.[91] Curiously, there had been a shift from the White Paper's preference for the use of the term 'significant risk'.[92] Yet, under the Draft Bill proposals, for this group it would be sufficient that medical treatment be provided to the patient for the protection of those other persons (that is, there need be no health benefit for the patient) and that compulsion need not be the only way of providing treatment (that is, even those volunteering for treatment could be dealt with on a compulsory basis).[93] With its broadly drawn definition of both medical treatment and mental disorder and the proposed abolition of the treatability test, the Draft Bill would permit a form of humane containment under medical supervision for the DSPD category (and all others who posed a substantial risk of serious harm).

The government presented the initiatives on CTOs and DSPD (neither of these terms appear in the Bill) as modernising the Act. Thus, the existing leg-

---

[89] See generally Richardson 1999. For example, using compulsion in the community can, where the criteria are tightly drawn (as with Richardson's capacity-based model), constitute a lesser net loss of a patient's civil liberties since compulsory treatment will not inevitably also entail loss of liberty. Moreover, it is also argued that whatever benefits compulsory treatment may bring, can also be enhanced by the patient being at liberty.

[90] DoH 1999:37.

[91] See clause 6(4)(a) of the Draft Mental Health Bill DoH 2002.

[92] DoH/Home Office Part II 2000:14.

[93] The decisions in *Reid v Secretary of State for Scotland* [1999] and *Anderson, Reid and Doherty v The Scottish Ministers and the Advocate General for Scotland* (2001) had seemingly confirmed that untreatable restricted patients could be held on grounds of public safety without breaching Art 5(1)(e) of the ECHR. Curiously, this view has been challenged by the Joint Committee on Human Rights, who asserted that *Anderson* cannot be regarded as supporting the compatibility of the Draft Bill with the ECHR since *Anderson* applied to restricted patients who had committed very serious criminal offences and who were being treated for mental disorder, and the Draft Bill would permit non-therapeutic detention of persons who had no conviction for an offence of violence on the basis of 'speculation about possible future behaviour and resulting risk to unidentified persons', 2002:para 46.

islative framework was deemed out-of-step with current practice, with new drug treatments and with different patterns of care. Moreover the existing legislation was characterised as excluding people at risk to themselves or others with personality disorders, since the 1983 Act's treatability clause for those with psychopathic disorder effectively excluded from compulsory care those with personality disorder who were regarded as untreatable by the professions. Indeed, the government presented the existing legislation with its treatability clause as creating a basis for psychiatrists to reject from services those for whom the government thought there ought to be greater therapeutic endeavour. The government also placed great stress on strengthening the protections to patients, with the new role of the Mental Health Tribunal, the new specialist advocacy services, the proposal to allow patients to choose their own representatives and the introduction of individual care and treatment plans being designed to produce a greater focus on individual health needs. All of this could have been very reassuring but for the fact that the sections on taking account of the patient's interests were to be effectively downgraded by being located in a Code of Practice.[94] Yet, the current Code has no statutory force, as the courts have recently re-asserted in a case concerning the use of seclusion.[95] The Code is thus no more than guidance and practitioners are not required to do any more than have regard to it.

4.2 Outstanding Questions

The Draft Bill was not without merit. Commentators pointed to the new tribunal system which would be responsible for authorising longer-term care and treatment plans, the new right to advocacy and the new role of the nominated person as features that should be welcomed. However, even those aspects of the government's proposals had their critics; in this context the government persisted with its assertion that it was keen to 'get the legislation right'. Yet, as the Draft Bill received almost universal condemnation from user and carer groups, practitioners and academics it is perhaps more pertinent to ask in what way did the government get it so badly wrong?

First, the conditions for the use of compulsion were extremely wide, creating a fear that almost anybody could be brought within them on, in the first instance, the say of practitioners; whilst practitioners were anxious that they would be held responsible for not using compulsion in cases where patients fell within the conditions. In essence, the entry conditions would have returned the law to a position back before the 1960s. Second, the Bill was conceived as moving in the wrong direction. Even the Macmillan Report,[96] which preceded the

---

[94] In contrast, the need to consult carers about medical treatment was in the Draft Bill (clause 26(4)(b)).

[95] *R (on the application of M) v Secretary of State for Health* (2002).

[96] Report of the Royal Commission on Lunacy and Mental Disorder 1924–26 Cm 2700.

Mental Treatment Act 1930, argued that a clear demarcation between mental and physical illness could not be established,[97] so that it was a retrograde step to promote a Bill which made the distinctions even greater, rather than moving in the direction of trying to ensure that people with mental health problems were treated on a non-discriminatory basis (that is, on the same basis as they would be treated in respect of physical problems). Third, the Bill was at odds with a number of positive service and policy developments that the same government had initiated. Any Act based on the Draft Bill 2002 would thus have created conflict between practitioners' legal duties and the direction of their day-to-day working lives. At worst, any Act would be premature, since it would have come before these laudable service developments (for example, the NSF and the injection of considerable financial resources as a result of making mental health a priority area for health care alongside cancer and coronary care[98]) had had an opportunity to impact on practice.

However, this saga took another twist. Two days before the Queen's Speech in November 2002, the Joint Committee on Human Rights published its Report on the Draft Mental Health Bill.[99] Whilst the Committee acknowledged that the Bill would make major improvements to the human rights safeguards of those involved in the mental health care system, 13 areas were identified as giving the Committee cause for concern on human rights grounds. These included the definition of mental disorder, the absence of a treatability requirement with its implications for preventive detention, the need for provisions concerning advance directives and the uncertain legal status of the Code of Practice. In short, the Report eviscerated the central tenets of the Draft Bill, and did so on the basis of potential human rights incompatibilities with the ECHR. To widespread surprise the Bill was not included in the Queen's Speech. And, more curiously still, on the following day the Secretary of State for Health announced in Parliament that the government would be bringing forward a Mental Health Bill during that session once the Department of Health had had an opportunity to consider the 2,000 plus responses it had received in the consultation exercise for the Draft Bill.[100] With a full legislative programme and no clear sense of how the government might amend its Draft Bill, the provenance of any new legislation must be doubtful. The resulting interregnum may prove beneficial in the long-run, but in the short-term the deficiencies and uncertainties of the current legislation will serve neither the interests of patients nor practitioners.

Two questions remain hanging. Are the law and good clinical care inevitably going to be in opposition to one another? In the most contentious area, that of patients' rights, the answer is no. In the field of physical health care a divisive approach is not at all evident; patients have the ultimate right to refuse treat-

---

[97] See also Matthews 1999.
[98] NHS National Plan 2000; but see also Brindle 2002, who documents DoH concerns that much of the new earmarked money for service improvements has been diverted into other health budgets.
[99] Joint Committee on Human Rights 2002.
[100] Hansard 14 November 2002.

ment, but they cannot force doctors to give particular forms of treatment; a compromise exists which works happily enough in practice. And secondly, are the oppositions painted by the academic commentators necessarily reflected in practice? Again, no, for as Glover-Thomas notes, even the 1890 Act (with its requirement that decisions to detain an individual in an asylum had to be made by a justice of the peace) may not in practice have embodied an effective legal safeguard since the justices felt ill-equipped to make judgments about a medical issue and preferred to defer to the medical opinions, effectively rubber-stamping applications.[101] The moral appears to be that unfamiliarity breeds caution.

5. CONCLUSIONS

The three core tensions of rights, risks and role conflict, together with developing concern about the role of capacity in mental health care, are manifest in this review of legal and policy development. Whilst the recent debate around law reform has been dominated by the pervasive issue of risk and the seemingly unpersuasive role of capacity, the thinking and practices of mental health professionals have perhaps been more focussed on issues of role conflict. However, are practitioners necessarily *ad idem* with the debates and developments in law reform? Chapters one to three would suggest a clear gulf in some areas. In others, for example, practitioners' desire to have more control over their patients in the community, it is hard to ascertain which comes first, the desire for more control or the desire to avoid something going wrong and being publicly pilloried for it. Equally, it is not clear whether what practitioners really want is the power to exercise more legal control, or rather more resources for patients in the community, or both.

There certainly is a gap between notions of how professionals ought to behave and how, in reality, their work is only marginally informed by laws designed to achieve the dominant policy objectives of the current era. This is the familiar gap between rhetoric and reality; but in the field of mental health the gap is widened by the premium on self-regulation; thus, the way in which non-lawyers understand and apply law is of critical importance.

Whether non-lawyers, even those with a passionate interest in law, will have got to grips with the four sets of criteria published over the previous four years is another question. The possibility remains that the legal ferment is confined to a few *cognoscente* whilst most practitioners struggle with the realities of daily care.[102] ASWs, for example, have been as perturbed by the possible loss of their independent role (to be replaced by an approved mental health professional,

---

[101] Glover-Thomas 2002:19–20.
[102] For an analysis of the latter by one of the former see Zigmond 2002, and a response by Chris Burford on the subsequent pages of the mental health law web based discussion group.

who might be an appropriately experienced nurse) as by the minutiae of the grounds and procedures by which they might, or might not, seek to exercise compulsion.[103] Meanwhile psychologists, who are likely to gain a role under the Draft Bill, have expressed opposition to the concept of DSPD but a willingness to act as clinical supervisors.[104] Accordingly, role conflict looks as likely for them as it is currently experienced by psychiatrists.

Assuming that the detail of the various legislative proposals are not uppermost in the minds of practitioners, it is also hard to judge which of the rhetoric impacts most on professionals. For the rhetoric is not 'joined–up'. On the one hand we have repeated assertions of the need to ensure public safety and the government's preparedness to act (although Ministers are equally aware of the impossibility of securing public safety) and, on the other, we have assurances about respecting the rights of those with disabilities;[105] for example, Andrew Smith, the then Secretary of State for Work and Pensions stated:

> The government is totally committed to delivering enforceable civil rights for disabled people. We are leading the way in Europe, with the most comprehensive and far-reaching package of rights.[106]

Yet the Department of Health seems either to be prepared to pursue a discriminatory approach despite this or not to be alive to the notion that disability includes mental disability.

Of course, the rhetoric sets the tone for what it is possible for professionals to do. And the current climate is undoubtedly one of uncertainty. Dr Mike Shooter, the then incoming President of the RCP, remarked in an interview given just prior to his appointment, that psychiatrists' natural constituency were patients and carers, and that recently the College had spent too long looking in the direction of the Department of Health. These comments spoke volumes not only of the sheer exhaustion that the process of consultation must have had on key professionals and professional groups, but also of an alliance that is much more in keeping with the relationship between doctors and patients in 'physical' medicine.[107] These groups should have similar objectives; and, where patients have the capacity to make decisions, as is normally the situation, doctors will respect patients' judgements. They may not agree with them, but they are prepared to adhere to them. Not so, the law will say, in the practice of mental health. But, given the findings of this study presented in chapters one to three, to what extent doctors will follow the law, rather than their own ethics and instincts, remains to be seen.

---

[103] Although see ch 6 where it is noted that BASW are extremely concerned about the relationship between the new criteria and impossibility of ASWs maintaining an independent role.
[104] Cooke *et al* 2002.
[105] Severe mental illness comes within the terms of the *Disability Discrimination Act 1995*.
[106] Letter to the Guardian 19 July 2002.
[107] 'All in the Mind' BBC Radio 4, 10 June 2002.

6

Conclusions

T HE QUOTATION AT the beginning of this book merits re-reading. For it is not hard to discern in this psychiatrist's words a sense of desperation, nor to avoid what is a call for clarity in legislation and defined limits on the responsibilities of practitioners. Whether these goals are attainable forms one of the themes central to this chapter.

However, before turning to these issues it is worth recapping the main findings from the empirical research. Clearly, there was considerable variation in decision outcomes, both between and within the professional groups; in short, no single case did appear the same to any two practitioners. There was also evidence that joint decision-making did reduce this variability, but only at the expense of favouring either one professional group, where the law gave that group formal authority to make the decision, or the views of particularly forceful individuals. A third evident factor was the role played by a cautionary approach, whether that was induced by clinical risk or a perception of the risk of harm to others; in each case this could impel a decision to do something, rather than to let a situation develop without the use of compulsion. Fourth, the practitioners commonly expressed and experienced confusion and anxiety about the law, tempered by an avoidance of its detail when they felt morally or professionally bound to take another course. Of course, all of these findings may pan out somewhat differently in the real world where the nature of a professional's practice,[1] their caseload, their access to good facilities and whether or not they have had prior dealings with a patient, may all impact on any given decision. In addition, the relatively unstructured nature of real-life joint decision-making, where parties are not required formally to commit themselves to a prior position, may further water-down whatever restraining or directional impact the law might otherwise have; fluidity favours consensus; consensus favours a best interests based approach; best interests favours a professional view, and not one naturally favouring patient autonomy. Accordingly, the decision outcomes in this study should be treated with some caution. However, as was stressed in the Preface, the research findings should not be judged merely by the nature of the decisions made, but as, if not more, importantly by the reasons the practitioners gave for those decisions. And these reasons varied as much as did the outcomes. Thus, the very malleability of 'facts' will confound any aspirations the law may have towards clarity and consistency.

---

[1] In December 2002, shortly before the submission of this manuscript, I tried out the case of Mr Draper with some 20 forensic psychiatrists at the Institute of Psychiatry in London. Curiously, not

As to the body of this chapter, the first section discusses the internal conflicts within law where it strives to achieve these goals of clarity and consistency, and examines the external problems of applying law, where it is argued that multi-disciplinary settings can undermine the law's internal logic in unanticipated ways. The second section looks briefly at the difficulties of working in chaotic and complex situations. Curiously, the elaborate machinery the law employs for making binary decisions in a litigation context seems not to be mirrored in those fields, including mental health law, where the decisions are much more complex. Here the machinery is of a more rough and ready nature.[2] The chapter then questions the extent to which law reform in this field is, or can be, influenced by research, based on the premise that research-informed law may at least have a greater relevance to the real world and thereby to the attainment of consistency, than is likely for law designed around ideology or policy. Finally, the chapter makes some waspish comments about the effectiveness and acceptability of the likely reforms proposed, in so far as it is possible to ascertain their ambit and given their seeming failure to adopt principles grounded in working practices.

When reading this review it would be wise to bear in mind that the law is applied, and intended to be continued to be applied, at least in the first instance, by non-lawyers. Throughout this study it has been clear that non-legal practitioners operate from a value base that is not necessarily shared by the law. In this context, it has been tempting to set-up the decision-making of non-lawyers as somehow straying from an ideal that would be attainable were lawyers charged with the decisions. This is not necessarily the case. Indeed, even the most eminent of lawyers has acknowledged both the partial nature of a judge's knowledge of the law and the pull of desirable outcomes:

> the judge's vision of the law tends to be fragmented; so far as it extends, his vision is intense; and it is likely to be strongly influenced by the facts of the particular case . . . If I were asked what is the most potent influence upon a court in formulating a statement of legal principle, I would answer that in the generality of instances it is the desired result in the particular case before the court.[3]

And, whilst it might be asserted that judges are generalists and inevitably have only a fragmented view, other research has demonstrated that specialist lawyers in the mental health field, for example legal members of the MHRT, are prone to instrumental reasoning and torn by similar dilemmas when dealing with particular cases.[4] Accordingly, I have striven to avoid my more natural tone, of being hectoring and judgemental, and inclined towards one that is cautious and questioning.

---

one of them favoured using compulsion. As they observed, given their predominantly forensic caseload, this looked to them like a 'soft' case.

  [2] I am grateful to Brenda Hale for this insightful point.
  [3] Lord Goff 1988 at 30–1.
  [4] See Peay 1989, chs 5 and 9.

1. CLARITY AND CONSISTENCY

It might be apposite to start with the observation that whilst clarity and consistency are valued by the law, neither are necessarily its hallmark in the mental health field. In respect of consistency, this may be partly attributable to the phenomenon of the pull of desirable outcomes, since in this interdisciplinary field there is considerable disagreement about what should constitute a desirable outcome. However, consistency is also peculiarly vulnerable to the shifting influences of the passage of time, the context against which a decision is made and the influence of the particular decision-maker or makers involved. The recent history, discussed in chapter five, of the courts' approach to the proper use of renewal of detention by the RMO under section 20 of the 1983 Act and the subsequent granting of leave under section 17 provides an object lesson. The imaginative use of leave combined with the renewal of the section 3 had effectively enabled clinicians to give themselves the equivalent of a community treatment order. Yet, in 1985, when this strategy was first challenged—a strategy that was notably thought to be in accordance with good modern psychiatric practice and in the best interests of patients—Mr Justice McCullough observed:

> There is, however, no canon of construction which presumes that Parliament intended that people should, against their will, be subjected to treatment which others, however professionally competent, perceive, however sincerely and however correctly, to be in their best interests. What there is is a canon of construction that Parliament is presumed not to enact legislation which interferes with the liberty of the subject without making it clear that this was its intention.[5]

He went on to find that a patient's detention could *not* lawfully be renewed whilst the patient was on leave of absence from the hospital, thereby denying clinicians the opportunity to compel patients to accept their medication in the community. Fourteen years on, the Court of Appeal overruled this finding,[6] and in a subsequent case the ambit of the judgment was extended.[7] Indeed, the conditions for renewal became so generous that a patient on leave who was receiving occupational therapy and who attended the weekly ward-round was nonetheless held to be a patient whose detention could be renewed under section 20. Thus, the distinction between receiving treatment as *an in-patient* and receiving treatment *at a hospital* was found to be 'too subtle'. Moreover, treatment was now to embrace providing the opportunities for attempted dialogue between doctor and patient. In so deciding, the court effectively provided for clinicians the basis of a community treatment order, a provision which policy-makers seemingly had had too much difficulty in designing for the legislature to enact in the previous decade and a half. Whether it is desirable that the courts

---

[5] *R v Hallstrom, ex parte W (no 2); R v Gardner, ex parte L* [1986] at pp 1104.
[6] *B v Barking Havering and Brentwood Community Healthcare NHS Trust* [1999].
[7] *R (on the application of DR) v Mersey Care NHS Trust* (2002).

should step-in to fill perceived legislative gaps in this way is debatable, but what is crucial about the judgment is that it marks a shift in tone. Previously, the courts had stood firm against endorsing clinical strategies just because they were thought to be in a patient's best interests; yet, these decisions show the courts positively encouraging practices deemed to have therapeutic value, even if that required a fundamental re-evaluation of the ambit of legislation. Thus, even amongst lawyers consistency can be a contingent value.

On the other hand, clarity in legislation is a prerequisite for attaining legal certainty; and legal certainty is critically important where deprivation of liberty is concerned. As the European Court of Human Rights (ECtHR) asserted in the case of *Kawka v Poland*:[8]

> where deprivation of liberty is concerned, it is particularly important that the general principle of legal certainty is satisfied. It is therefore essential that the conditions for deprivation of liberty under domestic law should be clearly defined, and that the law itself be foreseeable in its application, so that it meets the standard of 'lawfulness' set by the Convention, a standard which requires that all law should be sufficiently precise to allow the person—if needed, to obtain the appropriate advice—to foresee, to a degree that is reasonable in the circumstances, the consequences which a given action may entail . . .

The extent to which the ECtHR permits member states to enjoy some latitude in respect of the application and interpretation of the articles and underlying principles of the European Convention on Human Rights (ECHR) varies.[9] This latitude is know as a 'margin of appreciation', and it describes the measure of discretion that the ECtHR allows to member states when the ECtHR decides whether the action taken by member states is necessary to comply with key terms in the ECHR. This thereby enables the ECtHR to take account of differing cultures and traditions between member states. For example, what qualifies as 'unsoundness of mind'—the term used in respect of mental disorder—has been left to member states to determine individually on the basis of medical expertise.[10] Thus, precisely which mental disabilities should be included in, and which excluded from, mental health legislation will vary by jurisdiction.

But, do member states enjoy an equal discretion in respect of the circumstances under which those who have this qualifying form of mental disorder may be deprived of their liberty? Article 5 of the Convention, which concerns the circumstances in which people may be deprived of their liberty, established a series of procedural requirements that have to be met.[11] These have been strictly interpreted; for example, a delay of eight weeks between the deprivation of liberty and a first review of that deprivation by a competent court will

---

[8] Application no 25874/94—Judgment 9 January 2001 at para 49.

[9] See Ashworth 2002: 75–77; Wadham and Mountfield 2000: 21–24.

[10] *Winterwerp v The Netherlands* (1979).

[11] Similarly, a focus on procedural fairness, now underpinned by the Human Rights Act 1998, has clarified the need for SOADs to provide reasoned decisions when authorising treatment for a non-consenting competent patient; *R (on the application of Wooder) v Feggetter* [2002].

constitute breach of the ECHR,[12] and thus invoke a right to financial compensation under Article 5(5).[13] Yet, the ECtHR has been much less clear-cut on issues of substance. Lewis, for example, has argued that it is 'surprising' that the Court has not yet laid down any such guidelines other than 'kind or degree' specifically concerning how severe or dangerous a person's mental disability needs to be to trigger compulsory detention.[14] If experience in the United States is a precursor of practice here, it is to be expected that such guidance will emerge in due course, if not shortly.[15]

On the basis of this study it is evident that the criteria as they currently exist hardly supply 'legal certainty'; it is accordingly unlikely that those proposed in the Draft Mental Health Bill 2002, which are even wider, would either. Legal certainty is a pre-requisite to attaining consistency; and consistency is valued, not at the expense of injustice, but because it promotes fairness in the treatment of individuals. Indeed, it is perhaps important to stress that legal certainty does not imply guaranteed outcomes, but rather that there should be some predictability in the way the law is applied and that its tenets should be reasonably accessible to those to whom it will be applied. Thus, people should both have an opportunity to moderate their behaviour so that they may stay within the law, and have some confidence that where it is necessary to have resort to the law that its application will not depend solely on factors such as the day of the week, the place of application or the individual or individuals who decide whatever may be at issue.

But would mere clarity in legislation suffice to promote these objectives? First, there is something to be said for everybody pointing in the same direction. Where there is a lack of agreement on the underlying principles to be applied or the desired objectives, anarchy in decision-making can result. It would be like trying to play Monopoly with some players going clockwise but others jumping across the middle of the board in order to enhance their own prospects of landing on advantageous squares. In contrast, having the overriding principle in section 1(1) of the *Children Act 1989* that 'the child's welfare shall be the court's paramount consideration' helps all involved at least to be working towards the same objective. Thus, legislation embodying principles, as the Richardson Committee favoured, has the advantage that a clear tenor and tone is set, making it more difficult for practitioners, and in particular non-legal practitioners,

---

[12] *E v Norway* (1990). The acceptable period more than 10 years on from this judgment is likely to be shorter, placing both the periods under the 1983 Act and the Draft Mental Health Bill in jeopardy.

[13] *Wassink v The Netherlands* (1990).

[14] Lewis 2002.

[15] For example, in 1972 the US Supreme Court in *Lessard v Schmidt* ruled that when doctors decide that a person is of sufficient 'dangerousness' to warrant compulsory confinement, that opinion must be 'based upon a finding of a recent overt act, attempt or threat to do substantial harm to oneself or another.' Lessard, 349 F Supp at 1082. In this country, cases have recently begun to invoke US jurisprudence in the context of Human Rights Act submissions; see, for example, *R(on the application of the Kurdistan Workers Party and others) v Secretary of State for the Home Department* [2002] and *A and others v Secretary of State for the Home Department* (2002).

to fail to appreciate the purpose or purposes of the legislation; moreover, principles can act as a guide to interpretation when the detail eludes or defeats those who are required to apply the law.

Although having clarity in law is inherently attractive, it will not necessarily ensure consistent outcomes. Aiming for consistent outcomes is, of course, only laudable when those outcomes are regarded as desirable and right. The study conducted here has largely not reached a judgement about what were the right outcomes (other than to identify those that were clearly legally 'wrong'). However, on the basis of this study one might conclude that the degree of variation in outcome creates grounds for arguing that there is some arbitrariness in decision-making. And, whilst decisions to deprive someone of their liberty or to give treatment against a patient's express choices may, in certain circumstances, be preferable to leaving patients at liberty or untreated, the risks and consequences associated with wrong choices in either case are not necessarily directly comparable. Thus, it has to be incumbent on decision-makers to strive after lawfully appropriate decisions.

Drawing firm conclusions on the basis of this study would also be unfair since the participants only had resort to less than wholly clear legislation; although there remains no complete agreement amongst those who would wish to see the 1983 Act reformed as to how it should be reformed, most are agreed that the Act is deficient and requires some reform. However, two factors were evident from the study. First, practitioners did not concern themselves with the detail of legislation but seemed to operate at a conceptual level in terms of what they thought the law did or ought to permit them to do.[16] Thus, clarity in these circumstances may be irrelevant. Secondly, a common phenomenon emerged; given the same factual situation participants placed on it their own interpretation and thus, their own unique solution. There is perhaps nothing surprising in this, since the situation may readily be compared to going to a film with a friend, or reading a book alongside a group of others. The disagreements that can arise after such an experience form the stuff of exchange. Hence, not only is the application of the law an interpretative exercise, but the construction of the facts to which the law might be applied is an equally fluid exercise. What this suggests is that law cannot make people see the world in the same way; all it can do is to place some restraint on how those individual views are imposed on others. And in some circumstances it may not even do that.

One strategy the law has adopted to try and achieve better decision-making outcomes is that of multi-disciplinary or multi-party decision-making. However, the research has also shown that although duo-disciplinary decision-making has the appearance of shared decision-making, and may make practitioners feel that they are not alone in carrying the responsibility for the decision made, it is evident that in practice, one practitioner or one party is likely to have more influence than the other or others. In the mental health context, for

[16] See also Halliday 2000.

specific decisions one party clearly does bear the burden as the primary decision-maker; which party that is depends partly upon the particular type of decision to be made. Thus, in respect of admission, the ASW has to initiate the process and can prevent the use of compulsion by refusing to sign the pink forms (although psychiatrists, in an attempt to gain leverage or cover themselves, may provide an opinion on a form that is given to the ASW but not subsequently used by them). Similarly, renewal requires action by the RMO; however strongly an ASW feels, their role, if consulted at all, is advisory in the process of discharge.

Thus, a clear legal framework can make practitioners stop and think about particular issues; it can also make them point in a particular direction; it can even, through the medium of duo-disciplinary (or multi-disciplinary) decision-making, make one practitioner take account of the views of another. All of this may help to achieve greater legal certainty. However, whatever legal framework is adopted and whatever procedures are required to facilitate decision-making, they cannot guarantee wholly consistent outcomes. This arises partly because of the individual influence that any decision-maker may exert beyond that attracting naturally to their statutory role. It will also be partly attributable to a series of interactive effects between the parties and the particular factual situation that are almost impossible to predict. Thus, the law cannot even guarantee that multi-disciplinary decision-making means consensus decision-making. Whilst clarity in legislation may promote legal certainty, it needs to be valued for reasons other than achieving it.

There is, therefore, considerable merit in recognising that there are limits in terms of what the law can do. And considerable merit in sharing decision-making with patients, or even giving their views primacy, as is the case in the treatment of somatic disorders where the patient has capacity. Making decisions for other people is frequently fraught; choosing a restaurant, a wine or a holiday destination can be highly problematic. More tellingly, in respect of giving presents, where the abiding adage is 'it's the thought that counts', we recognise that we often get it wrong about others' desires and needs. Accordingly, it should be less surprising that many mental health practitioners have come to welcome a capacity-based test or, if not one using that precise term, then one with a similar import, namely, the more politically acceptable test based on 'impaired judgement'. Either way, there is seemingly a grudging and growing acceptance that a test based on the patient's decision-making abilities may be in both the interests of patients and practitioners. Evidence of this can be found in the decision by the Royal College of Psychiatrists to join the Mental Health Alliance and its call for 'rights not compulsion' together with the Alliance's assertion that a law is needed that 'takes account of people's capacity to make their own treatment decisions'.[17] From the public's perspective, it is evident that

---

[17] See 'Rights not Compulsion' the Mental Health Alliance's campaign in respect of the Draft Bill and the Press Statement 'Unique and United', available on the Alliance, RCP and Law Society web sites, 6 August 2002.

we expect far too much from professionals, and expect things they cannot possibly deliver. Adopting an approach that gives greater weight to what patients want might help to ameliorate the public's expectations of the professionals. And, from the patient's perspective, it has not only been the law underwriting the paternalism of the professionals, but relatives and carers too who have colluded in denying patients (perhaps for the most laudable of motives) access to the very information that might assist them to make informed decisions. Thus, Mr Wright's hypothetical sister had never told him that he could not come and live with her; this simply was not an option, and he did not know this, basing all his plans around a fundamental misunderstanding. Whilst it is easy to understand why relatives and carers might similarly do this in real-life, preserving a short-term relationship with a patient over a longer-term and more amorphous one, such laudable motives are potentially self-interested. Yet relatives too need support, which is not always forthcoming, to enable patients to hear unwelcome but arguably necessary news.

The focus so far has been on the use and impact of written words. However, implicit in the discussion is an acceptance of the relative impotence of words in comparison with deeds. And, whilst the implications of the research may be familiar and uncontentious to psychologists, they are perhaps admitted less readily by lawyers who have always put tremendous stress on the power and significance of particular words. But it is evident here that non-verbal communication is also critical. Words play a part, but not necessarily the part or the most important part of what determines the actions that people take. Whilst the analysis presented here has been on the words used, partly because they have been the easiest factor to capture, much of their power has derived from who is using them, in what context and the other preconceptions, predilections and personal baggage that the participants brought. Who was ethically aware and in what way? Who was dominant? What anxieties were present in the context of the decision made, anxieties not only about what might happen to the patients and the uncertainty associated with potentially being blamed for making the wrong decision, but also anxieties about professional roles and professional turf? Describing what went on between the pairs, as opposed to what they said to one another and what decisions were made, has not been a preoccupation of this book. Yet, sitting watching these interactions it was clear that much else besides did go on. Indeed, their very variability makes it impossible succinctly to capture their essence. From pair-to-pair the exchanges could have a very different emotional tone. But, from my stance as observer, some of the discussions felt like being privy to a private courtship, others to a battle of wills and yet others to an exchange peppered with a world-weariness shared between the parties; sometimes, mutual professional respect was evident, sometimes not; and, occasionally, black humour pervaded the proceedings.

Given this, it is not surprising that there was as much diversity within the professional groups as there was between them. And given this diversity, it is equally unsurprising that the professional pairs also produced diverse decisions.

Joint decision-making in this format in these exercises did not produce consistent decision-making. The decisions were messy, but in so being, they reflected the complexity of the real world. And if joint decision-making does produce consistency in the real world (and other research evidence suggests that it does not) then what is likely to be occurring is not necessarily a restraint of the law, but the acquiescence of one party to another. It is superficial consistency. Ultimately, it is unlikely to be any other way. There is just too much going on; too many factors to take into consideration and too little control over how it is done. That these decisions are currently not subject to an open court-based review cannot assist this process; and, in this context, the recommendation in the Draft Bill 2002 that there should be a Mental Health Tribunal to approve the care and treatment plan and the use of compulsion is to be recommended.[18] However, given the broad criteria it is intended to apply, criteria which reflect broadly-based admission criteria, the restraint such a Tribunal is likely to be able to achieve must be regarded with some scepticism. Equally, whilst the Mental Health Act 1983 can be criticised for lacking any clear underpinning principles, the Draft Bill 2002 does not look likely to improve matters. Not only is there an absence of meaningful principles, but, by extending the use of compulsion into the community without any prior restraint deriving from a fixed number of hospital beds, the proposed legislation is likely to capture within its net people currently excluded from compulsion. Practitioners are likely to gain little solace from being left greater not less discretion, where that discretionary manoeuvrability brings with it more responsibility, but no clarity as to its use.

2. WORKING WITH CHAOTIC AND COMPLEX SITUATIONS

Even if I were competent to do it, which I am not, here would not be the place for a review of the relevance of chaos and complexity theory.[19] That said, this may be an approach which would provide some insight, particularly at the level of re-iterating common-sense truths. For example, it has been observed that three people making decisions is fundamentally different from two-party decision-making. Whilst this intuitively makes sense, in the scheme of Mental Health Act decision-making, where different parties bring greater or less authority to the decision-making forum, its precise impact is less clear-cut. Indeed, adding an extra decision-maker with limited authority may make little difference in practice to the likely outcome. One illustration would be where General Practitioners form the third party in the admission process; their role

---

[18] Resistance to the notion of the MHT approving care and treatment plans, more traditionally the preserve of clinicians, has been muted. Perhaps psychiatrists have accepted, as did the police with respect to the balance of power between themselves and the Crown Prosecution Service after the establishment of the independent CPS, that a narrower area of defined responsibility has its advantages.

[19] See Kiel and Elliott (eds) 1996.

here is justified partly on the basis that they are assumed to have unique longitudinal knowledge of the patient. However, it was evident from the discussions in the case of Mr Draper that this role, of third decision-maker, was really a formality. Whilst in this case it may be because the GP had sought a Mental Health Act assessment and was therefore likely to concur with the other professionals, it might also be questioned to what extent GPs do now have unique longitudinal knowledge. In too many cases, the GP is no longer the 'family practitioner' but another kind of GP, namely a group practitioner, perhaps with only cursory knowledge of the patient.[20] In these circumstances, their role is unlikely to be one of questioning the other two professionals since their claim to an area of family expertise may be less compelling now than it was when the Mental Health Act 1959 was first conceived.

Second, chaos and complexity theory remind us that there is always an interaction with the environment; what people do on a Friday evening will not necessarily be the same, given an identical factual situation, as they would do on a Monday morning. Equally, people learn from their experiences creating a further chronological factor. Thus, the interaction between the pairs of decision-makers in the case of Mr Wright had, as its context, their prior actions or inaction in the case of Mr Draper. In some cases it was evident that behavioural patterns had been set; in others, that one party or the other approached the second exercise in a more robust or combative manner.

Third, in a fascinating study of the moral dilemmas faced by health professionals and patients, Gorovitz observes a common experience; namely, that people often assert that they wish that they could do something, and then don't do it, when the preferred course of action is perfectly feasible, it just has not been given a sufficiently high priority to be selected.[21] In so doing, he cites Sartre's observation that we can choose over a much wider range of options than we commonly realise. This phenomenon is well-evidenced in the current study. Many of the participants felt that they had no choice but to do what they did; yet many did different things and felt equally constrained in so doing. One way of thinking about this is that practitioners were trying to simplify a complex world in an attempt to help them to reach decisions by foreclosing on certain options. However, if that foreclosure is inconsistent or unpredictable, then the outcome will be determined as much by chance (who comes to the decision) as by the application of law to a unique set of facts. Would merely informing practitioners that others had reached entirely different decisions with the same degree of confidence encourage them to think more fluidly? Or do practitioners need directly to experience such alternative decision-making, and to have it work successfully for them, to enable them to use it?

---

[20] Research would also suggest that GPs' relative lack of knowledge of mental health law is likely to place them at a fundamental disadvantage in respect of the other two parties involved in the decision-process; Peay *et al* 2001.

[21] Gorovitz 1982:68.

Whilst some options are treated inappropriately as unacceptable or impossible, others are discounted for reasons probably not anticipated by the original framers of the law. Take the case of after-care under supervision under section 25A. It is paradoxical that this provision was perceived to be an option in the case of Mr Wright (when arguably, the legal criteria were not readily fulfilled) and it was a popular decision choice, yet some practitioners ultimately shied away from it in the ensuing discussion. Whether this was because the section 25A was seen primarily as a section on psychiatrists (by making bureaucratic demands on them), or because a more attractive 'alternative' was available (for example, renewal followed by section 17 leave), is not clear. Any reluctance was unlikely to be based on experience of the provision since, at the time the research was conducted, little usage of the section 25A had occurred. Equally, most participants were probably unaware of either the description of the provision as 'a section on psychiatrists', or, for example, of the research based view that the provision has very little use for the determinedly non-compliant patient.[22] However, the preparedness of the practitioners to renew a section 3 and then use section 17 leave was, in practice, a creative way of achieving a community treatment order equivalent. Yet, pre *Barker,* making the decision to renew necessitated practitioners stretching the law.[23] And the use of the section 25A required them either to undermine the effectiveness of it by being fully honest with patients about their remit, or to engage in a strategy of providing less than full information. Were a ready-made CTO available, which permitted the use of compulsion in the community without the perception of bureaucratic legal restraints attached, its use is accordingly likely to be highly attractive as a preventive strategy.

Mental health law is not unique in its engagement with difficult issues. Indeed, many of the decisions to be made in the health and social spheres involve complex and conflicting imperatives. However, it is curious, as Brenda Hale has observed,[24] that the machinery for resolving these issues appears much less developed than that we apply to the comparatively straightforward binary decisions entailed in other areas of legal decision-making.

3. IS LAW INFORMED BY RESEARCH?

One of the questions posed in the Preface concerned whether the gulf between policy and practice can be crossed where each side pursues an agenda so little informed by the concerns of the other. The answer is perhaps self-evident. However, might policy development be better informed by evidence concerning practice via the medium of research? At one level, an attempt to facilitate this

[22] Pinfold *et al* 2002; Hatfield *et al* 2001.
[23] *B v Barking Havering and Brentwood Community Healthcare NHS Trust* , *ex parte* Barker [1999] and *R (on the application of DR) v Mersey Care NHS Trust* (2002).
[24] Personal communication.

was undertaken by government in the early stages of its process of mental health law reform. Not only was work undertaken to produce a systematic review of research relating to the 1983 Act,[25] but further work was commissioned on aspects of practice,[26] and a programme of research set-up to examine some of the areas where government ought to know more, but did not have the requisite research then available.[27]

Yet, as Kane observes, 'The relationship between research and policy-making is often uncomfortable'.[28] And it could be argued that a number of the researchers who contributed to the initiative would want to question the impact that their work had on the direction of reform. For it might appear to those outside of the policy-making inner sanctum that law reform was not much influenced by the research findings; indeed, the two appeared to run on parallel tracks, being within speaking distance but with little being heard.[29] On this, Kane most tellingly asserts that trust between researchers and policy-makers is crucial.

> To disregard or rubbish well presented, robust evidence, or to fail to collect informa-
> tion about the complexity of choices a policy-maker is facing, is to weaken the current
> and future influence of policy makers and researchers and the trust that their respec-
> tive constituencies invest in them.[30]

Kane has argued powerfully that whilst the notion that clinical practice should be evidence-based is well accepted, health and policy decision-making has only recently recognised a similar need to ground decisions on research evidence rather than on 'values and resource considerations'. Where robust evidence has not routinely been available, it is perhaps not surprising that policy-makers fall back on their own values. But there is also, as Kane observes, something about the process of policy-making, where action is often taken at an unexpected point in time, by politicians, on the basis of limited information that prevents policy-making being a clear, linear process. Rather, decisions get taken in turbulent environments, influenced as much by good advocacy as independent analysis. Too frequently, the relevant issues are only identified at the point at which action is about to be taken. Thus, research tends to trail in the wake of policy-making, rather than forging the way ahead of it.

Kane asserts that action is propelled by five broad factors: values, resources, failures and crises, the canvassed views of selected focus groups and representa-

[25] Wall *et al* 1999. See also the Department of Health's National Research Register at www.doh.gov.uk/.
[26] See for example, Hagell and Bourke Dowling 1999 and Badger *et al* 1999.
[27] DoH 2000.
[28] Kane 2002: 215.
[29] As Bindman, one of the researchers in the DoH programme, has observed, there were regular feedback sessions between the researchers and the policy makers. Yet, it remains hard to discern what impact the research had, particularly where the direction of reform has run counter to the research findings.
[30] Kane 2002: 225.

tions from pressure groups.[31] He argues that these factors can be found at the heart of almost all recent and proposed changes to mental health policy and legislation in the UK. Curiously, whilst responding to user opinion and increasing the involvement of people who use services are seen as important objectives, they seem not to have had an influence acceptable to users and user-groups in respect of the Draft Bill 2002.[32] This is regrettable, as is the seeming rejection of the views of the key professional groups for, as Kane observes, any law reform needs to ensure that the underlying policy is adopted at 'ground level' where the detail or spirit of the policy is to be implemented. Perhaps again this is a field where the mores do not apply, for the government's agenda appears resolute even though its objectives conflict with those prevailing in a different community of interests.

There may be nothing unusual in this. Kane cites work that has examined the influence of research on policy-makers in the United States of America.[33] Whilst policy-makers reported a positive attitude towards research findings, 44 per cent of interviewees recounted instances where they purposely disregarded relevant information in making policy decisions. On a more positive note, this US study did find that research was not wholly irrelevant, for its findings tended to be integrated by the policy-makers with their pre-existing frame of reference; the impact, if one occurred, was thus at a conceptual level.

Another way of asking whether law is or might be informed by research would be to speculate about whether the implications of this study have had, or are likely to have, any impact on the structures or activities of other multi-disciplinary or multi-party decision-making bodies. At the end of chapter four questions were raised about the likely consequences of the proposed structural arrangements under the Draft Bill 2002 for admitting someone to compulsory assessment. It was argued that, on the basis of this research, it would appear that the proposals would be likely to make it initially more difficult to gain agreement between three parties that admission was necessary. This was because the decisions were to be made individually. But, where risk was an issue, patients would also be more likely to be assessed in hospital than in the community; that is, any doubt would propel the professionals towards hospital-based assessment (somewhat contrary to the government's intentions). Resolving risk in this way has, of course, more certain if not greater implications for the liberty of individuals, rather than asking the community to bear the brunt of a perceived risk which may, in the event, not materialise.

In respect of the proposed tribunal arrangements, which are based closely on the recommendations of the Richardson Committee, the new structure has been influenced primarily by issues of natural justice (informed by other research findings[34]), concerns about human rights challenges and the burgeoning

---

[31] Kane 2002: 221.
[32] See above Alliance press statement 'Unique and United'.
[33] Caplan *et al* 1975.
[34] See especially Perkins 2002; Richardson and Machin 1999, 2000.

caseload of judicial reviews in this field.[35] However, the potential absence of a clinician from the tribunal, with the latter having access to a panel of clinicians for expert advice, may assist the tribunal not to be inappropriately over-whelmed by clinical considerations. To speculate any further, in the absence of a firm commitment to a new Act, would be premature.

However, it would also be possible to apply the messages of this research to other decision-making bodies in order to gain some possible insight into their activities. Two different models might be pertinent in illustrating the range of possibilities. First, multi-disciplinary panels. These are very much in vogue;[36] yet, little is known about whether their decisions and recommendations achieve consensus and/or broadly informed decision-making as a result of their neces-sarily unwieldy nature. On the basis of this study it looks unlikely; their propo-nents however, may see their advantages more in terms of an efficient method of information sharing than as a basis for 'good' decision-making. Second, one might speculate about the meaning of dissenting judgments in cases involving the House of Lords. Where their Lordships hear identical submissions, and base their decisions on the same body of existing law, how is it that decisions are not always unanimous? The answer to that question should now be clear. But, the significance of dissenting judgments now also appears all the greater, since these will have emerged after sometimes lengthy periods of discussion and the sharing of draft judgments. Given that the options available to their Lordships range from a mere assent with the leading judgment, or an assent plus a rider, through to a dissenting judgment, can a fully argued dissent reflect anything other than irreconcilable breakdown?[37] And, if agreement is reached after a lengthy delay between hearing the case and delivering the judgment, what is the significance of this?[38]

4. MOVING TOWARDS A MORE GROUNDED LAW?

Rules acquire some of their value from the notion that they are capable of achieving their objectives. This premise has been examined and challenged else-where.[39] Similarly, whether it is possible to design law that better achieves its

---

[35] See ch 5.

[36] See, for example, Home Office 2002; for the advent of Education Panels for appeals against school exclusions, see Harris *et al* 2000; and on the role of Discretionary Lifer Panels, which con-sider the release of prisoners on discretionary life sentences, see Padfield and Leibling 2000.

[37] See for example, their Lordships judgments in *R v Bournewood Community Mental Healthcare NHS Trust ex parte L (Secretary of State for Health and Others Intervening)* [1998] where there they were not only split 3/2 but also remarkably split on the issues in terms of their rea-soning.

[38] For example, the s 117 judgment in *R v Manchester City Council ex parte Stennett and two other actions* [2002] took over two months from hearing to unanimous judgment.

[39] See for example, Baldwin 1990; McBarnet and Whelan 1991; and in the financial sector, Black 1998.

objectives has also been reviewed.[40] These arguments will not be rehearsed here. However, a number of more nuanced questions that arise on the basis of this study will be addressed.

First, how can one achieve better legal education amongst non-legal practitioners? Knowledge of the law per se would seem a prerequisite.[41] At present, ASWs receive some three months of training in mental health law and practice; section 12(2) approved psychiatrists some two days; and Mental Health Act Commissioners a varying amount of formal and informal training.[42] Yet, a recent study did not find substantial differences in their levels of legal knowledge.[43] Equally, others have reported very poor absolute levels of legal knowledge amongst non-legal practitioners.[44] Moreover, poor knowledge or understanding of law is not confined to coal-face practitioners; even amongst the most senior of policy-makers, knowledge of the terms of legislation can be disappointing.[45] It may be that the method of education is inappropriate, or that we expect too much of non-lawyers working in environments where recourse to legal argument does not seem a priority. However, on the basis of the available research, practitioners should arguably be educated about principles and objectives, even if not the detail of law, were it possible to make the latter clear. And it should be done experientially, so that the lessons can be integrated into daily practices; a form of state related learning.[46] And, if law is to be inconsistent with or absent of overarching objectives then it is unlikely to achieve its aims consistently, or at all. In such circumstances establishing a Mental Health Tribunal to authorise all uses of longer-term compulsion may have a 'criteria-focussing effect' on practitioners' legal education, as well as addressing its underlying purpose of ensuring that all such detentions are subject to quasi-judicial authorisation and are therefore ECHR compliant.

Second, practice in the field of mental health does not nest easily with other areas of clinical practice. There, intervention aims at the patient's good but may risk doing some harm (for example, the high level of hospital acquired 'iatrogenic' disease); in contrast, in mental health practice the law permits practitioners to intervene solely for the safety of other persons and will, where compulsion is used, do the patient harm, if only to the patient's sense of autonomy. Under the Draft Bill 2002, the curious concept of giving medical treatment to a patient

---

[40] Cotterrell 1992; Eastman and Peay (eds) 1999 esp pp 24–36.

[41] Other critical elements would include practitioners' attitudes, objectives, priorities and thinking processes (alone and in conjunction with others) in respect of law.

[42] CCETSW 1992; NHS Executive 1996. Once appointed, Mental Health Act Commissioners receive training at team meetings; members would attend meetings with a significant training component on average twice a year (see Peay *et al* 2001).

[43] Peay *et al* 2001.

[44] See, for example, Humphreys 1998.

[45] See the letter from Professor Louis Appleby, National Clinical Director for Mental Health Services, DoH to the Guardian 1 August 2002.

[46] State related learning is perhaps best summarised by the statement 'I only remember stories heard when I am drunk, when I am next drunk.' See also Peay *et al* 2001, which points to the importance of using the law regularly as a factor in retaining knowledge of it.

who posed a substantial risk of causing serious harm to other persons, solely for the benefit of those other persons, would have built on this role of clinician as dispenser of interventions with no necessary benefit to the patient being treated. Any new law adopting this approach would therefore be likely to be doubly unfamiliar to clinicians, being outside their terms of reference as doctors, and outside their terms of reference as experienced psychiatrists. In such circumstances, would clinicians regard doing good to others (a public health function blurring into that of custodian) as more important than respecting the principle of autonomy? Similarly, the British Association of Social Workers (BASW) regarded their function under the 1983 Act as critical and in keeping with their professional expertise. However, they have argued that the role of 'approved mental health professional' under the Draft Bill 2002 would, in effect, have required them to act as hired muscle for the Secretary of State and would likely be in breach of the BASW Code of Ethics.[47] If this were indeed not a social work role, it would be excluded from the BASW indemnity insurance; members would have been advised accordingly.

What ethical justifications will then be used by mental health practitioners in activities where the main, or even sole, purpose is the benefit not of the patient, but of others? Ethical tensions will inevitably result. Predicting whether and how any law might be applied is therefore even more problematic. As Bynoe and Holland have argued, when law is regarded by psychiatrists as something 'out there' rather than fully integrated into practice, it will be at odds with the clinician's traditional approach of persuading patients to cooperate.[48] And, whilst such law may be seen as offering reinforcement to their authority it will be at odds with their daily practices. When the overriding ethic of medical treatment is 'treatment with the patient's consent', how do practitioners work outside their routine and ethically grounded decision-making structures? Add in the competing demands of risk and legal obligations and duties and there is a powerful cocktail of issues that require a sober hand to juggle. Will any resulting compliance be rooted merely in the fear that 'things might go wrong'? Would it be better to narrow the gulf between public policy objectives and clinical objectives (that is, by arguing that public policy in relation to the use of compulsion ought to be brought into line with public policy in mental health generally) rather than by dragging protesting clinicians in a direction they do not want to go, to a place they do not want to be, motivated largely by fear?

Third, can the law be better designed to achieve the conflicting imperatives of lawyers, policy makers and working practitioners? Would a more detailed law covering all of the angles be better? At this point one's thoughts might turn to parallels with the development of ever-more and ever-better technology, as for example in the game of cricket. Cricket umpires have found themselves most recently subject to the role of the third umpire; this umpire has the advantage of

---

[47] BASW 2001.
[48] Bynoe and Holland 1999:102.

slow motion television replays from a number of different angles in potentially controversial decisions. This innovation is not seen as a challenge to the traditional two-umpire role. It is designed to assist them to reach a decision where error is minimised. But ironically, even technology has its limits. A freeze-frame approach can still miss the vital second in a potential run-out and thus, even the third umpire may have to leave the benefit of the doubt to the batsman, where a traditional umpire may have (justly) given a batsman out on the basis of judgement by the naked eye. The parallel with law is three-fold. First, law is unlikely ever to achieve sufficient precision to anticipate every possible variant on the facts; so it will always have to operate with a degree of tolerance, flexibility and discretion. Second, having the underlying objectives and principles of the game agreed (for example, that 'fair play' would require the batsman to walk without having to be told to do so and that the umpire's decision is final) can facilitate adherence to the rules in future situations of conflict. And third, whilst the rules of cricket have remained largely unchanged, the method of adjudication has become more sophisticated, without necessarily decreasing the controversy that surrounds individual decisions. Similarly, the methods of decision-making in mental health law may evolve so as better to respect the rules of natural justice (that is, fair procedures and decision-making practices) without necessarily achieving a consensus that the right decision has been made.

The fourth nuanced question concerns the notion of the 'effectiveness' of law. Effectiveness may mean different things to practitioners with different attitudinal profiles and therefore objectives.[49] It may also mean something different to some clinicians than to policy-makers and politicians. And the greater the 'attitudinal distance' between clinicians and policy-makers, including politicians, the greater the difficulty the latter will have in achieving their objectives through the means of the former. Whilst there are mechanisms within the NHS effectively to direct the use of law through control of the necessary resources, any gap between the framing of law and the attitudes of clinicians will always tend to result in the law swimming against a clinical tide. Knowledge and attitudes are also important as determinants of the predictability of the effect of law. Widely varying knowledge and attitudes are likely to result in varying decisions, justified through diverse decision strategies used to validate desired outcomes.[50]

In an excellent analysis of the factors promoting and impeding change, Scully notes that the successful implementation of change occurs primarily in the development stages, that is between formulation of a plan and final implementation. During this phase resources are assembled and support gathered amongst stakeholders to overcome inertia and resistance.[51] Applying this analysis, it appears that the government has gone about formulating a new Mental Health Act in a way that has alienated not only its usual adversaries, but its

[49] See, for example Cope's 1992 study of clinicians' attitudes to psychopathic disorder.
[50] Peay 1981.
[51] Scully, 2000. See in particular, Eccles and Grimshaw 2000.

traditional supporters also. The prospects are not auspicious for achieving more grounded law; namely, law that feels right to practitioners (or can be made to feel right to them), that can be integrated into their respective conceptual frameworks, that has realistic objectives and does not generate fear in its application or avoidance, and law that meaningfully shares responsibility with patients for the decisions made.

Of course, whilst the efficacy of the law will depend upon the ability and willingness of key practitioners to implement the law in its intended way, achieving grounded law by utilising research is not the end of the matter. The law should be concerned not only with what feels right to practitioners but also what is right. However, this, with its focus on substantive and procedural justice, and on matters of consistency and practicalities, would be the subject of another book. Not this one.

5. THE NEXT MENTAL HEALTH ACT?

At this point, the only matter about which one can be confident is that a new Act is not imminent. In what shape or form legislation will be brought forward is not clear; and, whilst an assurance has been given that it will be forthcoming, it is impossible to ascertain in which direction the government might jump in response to the results of its consultation exercise over the Draft Mental Health Bill 2002 and the Report of the Joint Committee on Human Rights.[52] Reconciling the government's preoccupations with issues of risk and safety, with the concerns of user and carer groups, and with the professionals' objectives, remains a daunting task. And any proposed mental health law looks unlikely to escape the driving force of risk, a force which has pervaded so much of the government's proposed legislation for the 2002/3 session;[53] given the climate, the remit of any legislation is likely to be retrograde.[54]

Another point which bears re-iterating is the notion of consequences. It may be an aphorism to remark that 'when all is said and done, more will be said than done', and, to those exhausted by the process of law reform, this may be true. However, it is equally true to retort that 'what is done, is done'. For patients like Mr Draper, Mr Wright and Hazel Robinson, decisions made about them will have consequences for their liberty and their freedom from unsought medical treatment. Where other decisions might have been made, decisions perhaps with less irrevocable consequences, it would serve all of those involved well to think, and think again, before concluding that there is no other option.

Finally, one of the central lessons of this research is by no means novel. However, it bears restating since it may easily slip from view, or at least from

---

[52] Joint Committee on Human Rights 2002.

[53] There were, for example, six new Bills on criminal justice in the Queen's speech, including measures to tighten the regimes for the release and supervision of sexual and violent offenders.

[54] Fiona Caldicott in Eastman and Peay 1999:2.

the view of those who sit on the side-lines and judge those who apply the law, or determine how they should so do. Application of the law is fundamentally an interpretative exercise. It involves the construction of choices and bearing the consequences of the choices made. Given all that has been said here about uncertainty and complexity, it is wise to end on a cautionary note. Legislators should remain vigilant of the law of unintended consequences, for as Heginbotham and Elson have argued, the translation of public policy into practice or law does not always follow the original intentions of those who formulated the proposals.[55] In October 1998, just as the Richardson Committee commenced its work, the Guardian fortuitously published the following story. It concerned Orca whales in the Baring Strait. Concern had been expressed about the relationship between factory fishing and a desire to protect the Orcas. Orcas eat seals. Seals eat fish. Factory fishing leads to the decline of fish stocks. In this context the seals move on to richer waters, and those that don't are at risk of being eaten by the resident Orcas. As the seals progressively disappear, the Orcas eat the less nutritious sea otters. And, with the consequent decline in sea otters the sea urchins (whom the otters eat) increase. The sea urchins eat more of the kelp. This in turn affects the quantity of mussels and barnacles. With their decline, the bald-headed sea eagle declines. Not the intended consequence. And another problem thus arises.

[55] 1999: 59.

Appendix 1—Selected Sections of the Mental Health Act 1983

Set out below are the key sections of the 1983 Act mentioned in the text. They deal respectively with the definition of mental disorder under s 1, admission for assessment under s 2 (for up to 28 days), admission for treatment under s 3 (for up to six months) and emergency admission under s 4 (for 72 hours). Following these sections are the responsible medical officer's power to renew detention (under s 20) and the power to apply for after-care under supervision for a patient who is about to leave hospital (under s 25A). Finally, sections 58, 62 and 63, which concern the provision of treatment, are reproduced, together with the definition of medical treatment under s 145 of the Act.

No attempt is made to reproduce every section of the Act that might be relevant to the decisions the practitioners took, or every section mentioned in the text. For further details, the reader is referred to Richard Jones' *Mental Health Act Manual* 2002. At the time the research was conducted, practitioners might have had access to either the 1996 (5th edn) or the 1999 (6th edn).

Application of Act: 'mental disorder'

1.-(1) The provisions of this Act shall have effect with respect to the reception, care and treatment of mentally disordered patients, the management of their property and other related matters.

(2) In this Act—

'mental disorder' means mental illness, arrested or incomplete development of mind, psychopathic disorder and any other disorder or disability of mind and 'mentally disordered' shall be construed accordingly;

'severe mental impairment' means a state of arrested or incomplete development of mind which includes severe impairment of intelligence and social functioning and is associated with abnormally aggressive or seriously irresponsible conduct on the part of the person concerned and 'severely mentally impaired' shall be construed accordingly;

'mental impairment' means a state of arrested or incomplete development of mind (not amounting to severe mental impairment) which includes significant impairment of intelligence and social functioning and is associated with abnormally aggressive or seriously irresponsible conduct on the part of the person concerned and 'mentally impaired' shall be construed accordingly;

'psychopathic disorder' means a persistent disorder or disability of mind (whether or not including significant impairment of intelligence) which results in abnormally aggressive or seriously irresponsible conduct on the part of the person concerned:

and other expressions shall have the meanings assigned to them in section 145 below.

(3) Nothing in subsection (2) above shall be construed as implying that a person may be dealt with under this Act as suffering from mental disorder, or from any form of mental disorder described in this section, by reason only of promiscuity or other immoral conduct, sexual deviancy or dependence on alcohol or drugs.

Admission for assessment

2.-(1) A patient may be admitted to a hospital and detained there for the period allowed by subsection (4) below in pursuance of an application (in this Act referred to as 'an application for admission for assessment') made in accordance with subsections (2) and (3) below.

(2) An application for admission for assessment may be made in respect of a patient on the grounds that—

    (a) he is suffering from mental disorder of a nature or degree which warrants the detention of the patient in a hospital for assessment (or assessment followed by medical treatment) for at least a limited period; and

    (b) he ought to be so detained in the interests of his own health or safety or with a view to the protection of other persons.

(3) An application for admission for assessment shall be founded on the written recommendations in the prescribed form of two registered medical practitioners, including in each case a statement that in the opinion of the practitioner the conditions set out in subsection (2) above are complied with.

(4) Subject to the provisions of section 29(4) below, a patient admitted to hospital in pursuance of an application for admission for assessment may be detained for a period not exceeding 28 days beginning with the day on which he is admitted, but shall not be detained after the expiration of that period unless before it has expired he has become liable to be detained by virtue of a subsequent application, order or direction under the following provisions of this Act.

Admission for treatment

3.-(1) A patient may be admitted to hospital and detained there for the period allowed by the following provisions of this Act in pursuance of an application (in this Act referred to as 'an application for admission for treatment') made in accordance with this section.

(2) An application for admission for treatment may be made in respect of a patient on the grounds that—

    (a) he is suffering from mental illness, severe mental impairment, psychopathic disorder or mental impairment and his mental disorder is of a nature or degree which makes it appropriate for him to receive medical treatment in a hospital; and

(b) in the case of psychopathic disorder or mental impairment, such treatment is likely to alleviate or prevent a deterioration of his condition; and

(c) it is necessary for the health or safety of the patient or for the protection of other persons that he should receive such treatment and it cannot be provided unless he is detained under this section.

(3) An application for admission for treatment shall be founded on the written recommendations in the prescribed form of two registered medical practitioners, including in each case a statement that in the opinion of the practitioner the conditions set out in subsection (2) above are complied with; and each such recommendation shall include—

(a) such particulars as may be prescribed of the grounds for that opinion so far as it relates to the conditions set out in paragraphs (a) and (b) of that subsection; and

(b) a statement of the reasons for that opinion so far as it relates to the conditions set out in paragraph (c) of that subsection, specifying whether other methods of dealing with the patient are available and, if so, why they are not appropriate.

Admission for assessment in cases of emergency

4.-(1) In any case of urgent necessity, an application for admission for assessment may be made in respect of a patient in accordance with the following provisions of this section, and any application so made is in this Act referred to as 'an emergency application'.

(2) An emergency application may be made either by an approved social worker or by the nearest relative of the patient; and every such application shall include a statement that it is of urgent necessity for the patient to be admitted and detained under section 2 above, and that compliance with the provisions of this Part of this Act relating to applications under that section would involve undesirable delay.

(3) An emergency application shall be sufficient in the first instance if founded on one of the medical recommendations required by section 2 above, given, if practicable, by a practitioner who has previous acquaintance with the patient and otherwise complying with the requirements of section 12 below so far as applicable to a single recommendation, and verifying the statement referred to in subsection (2) above.

(4) An emergency application shall cease to have effect on the expiration of a period of 72 hours from the time when the patient is admitted to the hospital unless—

(a) the second medical recommendation required by section 2 above is given and received by the managers within that period; and

(b) that recommendation and the recommendation referred to in subsection (3) above together comply with all the requirements of section 12 below (other than the requirement as to the time of signature of the second recommendation).

(5) In relation to an emergency application, section 11 below shall have effect as if in subsection (5) of that section for the words 'the period of 14 days ending with the date of the application' there were substituted the words 'the previous 24 hours'.

Duration of authority

20.-(1) Subject to the following provisions of this Part of this Act, a patient admitted to hospital in pursuance of an application for admission for treatment, and a patient placed under guardianship in pursuance of a guardianship application, may be detained in a hospital or kept under guardianship for a period not exceeding six months beginning with the day on which he was so admitted, or the day on which the guardianship application was accepted, as the case may be, but shall not be so detained or kept for any longer period unless the authority for his detention or guardianship is renewed under this section.

(2) Authority for the detention or guardianship of a patient may, unless the patient has previously been discharged, be renewed—

    (a) from the expiration of the period referred to in subsection (1) above, for a further period of six months;

    (b) from the expiration of any period of renewal under paragraph (a) above, for a further period of one year,

and so on for periods of one year at a time.

(3) Within the period of two months ending on the day on which a patient who is liable to be detained in pursuance of an application for admission for treatment would cease under this section to be so liable in default of the renewal of the authority for his detention, it shall be the duty of the responsible medical officer—

    (a) to examine the patient; and

    (b) if it appears to him that the conditions set out in subsection (4) below are satisfied, to furnish to the managers of the hospital where the patient is detained a report to that effect in the prescribed form;

and where such a report is furnished in respect of a patient the managers shall, unless they discharge the patient, cause him to be informed.

(4) The conditions referred to in subsection (3) above are that—

    (a) the patient is suffering from mental illness, severe mental impairment, psychopathic disorder or mental impairment, and his mental disorder is of a nature or degree which makes it appropriate for him to receive medical treatment in a hospital; and

    (b) such treatment is likely to alleviate or prevent a deterioration of his condition; and

    (c) it is necessary for the health or safety of the patient or for the protection of other persons that he should receive such treatment and that it cannot be provided unless he continues to be detained;

but, in the case of mental illness or severe mental impairment, it shall be an alternative to the condition specified in paragraph (b) above that the patient, if discharged, is unlikely to be able to care for himself, to obtain the care which he needs or to guard himself against serious exploitation.

(5) Before furnishing a report under subsection (3) above the responsible medical officer shall consult one or more other persons who have been professionally concerned with the patient's medical treatment.

(6) Within the period of two months ending with the day on which a patient who is subject to guardianship under this Part of this Act would cease under this section to be so liable in default of the renewal of the authority for his guardianship, it shall be the duty of the appropriate medical officer—

(a) to examine the patient; and

(b) if it appears to him that the conditions set out in subsection (7) below are satisfied, to furnish to the guardian and, where the guardian is a person other than a local social services authority, to the responsible local social services authority a report to that effect in the prescribed form; and where such a report is furnished in respect of a patient, the local social services authority shall, unless they discharge the patient, cause him to be informed.

(7) The conditions referred to in subsection (6) above are that—

(a) the patient is suffering from mental illness, severe mental impairment, psychopathic disorder or mental impairment and his mental disorder is of a nature or degree which warrants his reception into guardianship; and

(b) it is necessary in the interests of the welfare of the patient or for further protection of other persons that the patient should remain under guardianship.

(8) Where a report is duly furnished under subsection (3) or (6) above, the authority for the detention or guardianship of the patient shall be thereby renewed for the period prescribed in that case by subsection (2) above.

(9) Where the form of mental disorder specified in a report furnished under subsection (3) or (6) above is a form of disorder other than that specified in the application or admission for treatment or, as the case maybe, in the guardianship application, that application shall have effect as if that other form of mental disorder were specified in it; and where on any occasion a report specifying such a form of mental disorder is furnished under either of those subsections the appropriate medical officer need not on that occasion furnish a report under section 16 above.

(10) In this section 'appropriate medical officer' has the same meaning as in section 16(5) above.

Application for supervision

25A.-(1) Where a patient—
>   (a) is liable to be detained in a hospital in pursuance of an application for
>   admission for treatment; and
>   (b) has attained the age of 16 years,

an application may be made for him to be supervised after he leaves hospital, for
the period allowed by the following provisions of this Act, with a view to securing that he receives the after-care services provided for him under section 117
below.

(2) In this Act an application for a patient to be so supervised is referred to as
a 'supervision application'; and where a supervision application has been duly
made and accepted under this Part of this Act in respect of a patient and he has
left hospital, he is for the purposes of this Act 'subject to after-care under supervision' (until he ceases to be so subject in accordance with the provisions of this
Act).

(3) A supervision application shall be made in accordance with this section
and sections 25B and 25C below.

(4) A supervision application may be made in respect of a patient only on the
grounds that—
>   (a) he is suffering from mental disorder, being mental illness, severe men-
>   tal impairment, psychopathic disorder or mental impairment.
>   (b) there would be a substantial risk of serious harm to the health or
>   safety of the patient or the safety of other persons or of the patient
>   being seriously exploited, if he were not to receive the after-care ser-
>   vices to be provided for him under section 117 below after he leaves
>   the hospital; and
>   (c) his being subject to after-care under supervision is likely to help to
>   secure that he receives the after-care services to be so provided.

(5) A supervision application may be made only by the responsible medical
officer.

(6) A supervision application in respect of a patient shall be addressed to the
Health Authority which will have the duty under section 117 below to provide
after-care services for the patient after he leaves hospital.

(7) Before accepting a supervision application in respect of a patient a Health
Authority shall consult the local social services authority which will also have
that duty.

(8) Where a Health Authority accept a supervision application in respect of a
patient the Health Authority shall—
>   (a) inform the patient both orally and in writing—
>   (i) that the supervision application has been accepted; and
>   (ii) of the effect in his case of the provisions of this Act relating to a
>   patient subject to after-care under supervision (including, in par-
>   ticular, what rights of applying to a Mental Health Review
>   Tribunal are available);

(b) inform any person whose name is stated in the supervision application in accordance with sub-paragraph (i) of paragraph (e) of section 25B(5) below that the supervision application has been accepted; and

(c) inform in writing any person whose name is so stated in accordance with sub-paragraph (ii) of that paragraph that the supervision application has been accepted.

(9) Where a patient in respect of whom a supervision application is made is granted leave of absence from a hospital under section 17 above (whether before or after the supervision application is made), references in—

(a) this section and the following provisions of this Part of this Act; and

(b) Part V of this Act,

to his leaving hospital shall be construed as references to his period of leave expiring (otherwise than on his return to the hospital or transfer to another hospital).

Treatment requiring consent or a second opinion

58.-(1) This section applies to the following forms of medical treatment for mental disorder—

(a) such forms of treatment as may be specified for the purposes of this section by regulations made by the Secretary of State;

(b) the administration of medicine to a patient by any means (not being a form of treatment specified under paragraph (a) above or section 57 above) at any time during a period for which he is liable to be detained as a patient to whom this Part of this Act applies if three months or more have elapsed since the first occasion in that period when medicine was administered to him by any means for this mental disorder.

(2) The Secretary of State may by order vary the length of the period mentioned in subsection (1)(b) above.

(3) Subject to section 62 below, a patient shall not be given any form of treatment to which this section applies unless—

(a) he has consented to that treatment and either the responsible medical officer or a registered medical practitioner appointed for the purposes of this Part of this Act by the Secretary of State has certified in writing that the patient is capable of understanding the nature, purpose and likely effects of that treatment and has consented to it; or

(b) a registered medical practitioner appointed as aforesaid (not being the responsible medical officer) has certified in writing that the patient is not capable of understanding the nature, purpose and likely effects of that treatment or has not consented to it but that, having regard to the likelihood of its alleviating or preventing a deterioration of his condition, the treatment should be given.

(4) Before giving a certificate under subsection (3)(b) above the registered medical practitioner concerned shall consult two other persons who have been professionally concerned with the patient's medical treatment, and of those

persons one shall be a nurse and the other shall be neither a nurse nor a registered medical practitioner.

(5) Before making any regulations for the purposes of this section the Secretary of State shall consult such bodies as appear to him to be concerned.

Urgent treatment

62.-(1) Sections 57 and 58 above shall not apply to any treatment—

    (a) which is not immediately necessary to save the patient's life; or

    (b) which (not being irreversible) is immediately necessary to prevent a serious deterioration of his condition; or

    (c) which (not being irreversible or hazardous) is immediately necessary to alleviate serious suffering by the patient; or

    (d) which (not being irreversible or hazardous) is immediately necessary and represents the minimum interference necessary to prevent the patient from behaving violently or being a danger to himself or to others.

(2) Sections 60 and 61(3) above shall not preclude the continuation of any treatment or of treatment under any plan pending compliance with section 57 or 58 above if the responsible medical officer considers that the discontinuance of the treatment or of treatment under the plan would cause serious suffering to the patient.

(3) For the purposes of this section treatment is irreversible if it has unfavourable irreversible physical or psychological consequences and hazardous if it entails significant physical hazard.

Treatment not requiring consent

63. The consent of a patient shall not be required for any medical treatment given to him for the mental disorder from which he is suffering not being treatment falling within section 57 or 58 above, if the treatment is given by or under the direction of the responsible medical officer.

Interpretation

145.-(1) In this Act, unless the context otherwise requires—

. . .

'medical treatment' includes nursing, and also includes care, habilitation and rehabilitation under medical supervision

Appendix 2—Methodology

The three cases used in the study (admission, discharge and compulsory treatment) were made up of the substantial mental health records reproduced in chapters one–three and customised videos involving some of the parties in the cases.

In summary, the cases raised the following scenarios:

1.1 Admission Case

This concerned a consultant psychiatrist and an ASW visiting a young black patient, Robert Draper, who was previously known to services and about whom there had been complaints by his neighbours. There was evidence to suggest that the patient might be psychotic; the patient refused admission to hospital for assessment or treatment.

1.2 Discharge Case

This case involved a consultant psychiatrist, a nurse and a close relative of the patient. The patient, Clive Wright, was detained in a local psychiatric hospital, but had previously been in Broadmoor, following an incident of arson in the same local hospital. The Responsible Medical Officer (RMO) had to consider whether to discharge the patient from detention under section 3, against the wishes of the relative and in the light of media interest in the case, or whether to renew his detention under section 20.

1.3 Compulsory Treatment Case

This concerned Hazel Robinson, a patient with a long history of intermittent depression. She had given birth 10 weeks prior to the current incident and was also suffering from severe puerperal depression. Her psychiatrist advised electro-convulsive therapy (ect); the patient's partner wished her to have medication; and her mother was very strongly opposed to ect on the grounds that it was not what her daughter would have wanted. The patient was not eating, drinking or sleeping adequately.

1.4 Design of Decision Points

The research exercise for the admission and discharge cases required ASWs and psychiatrists to reach an individual decision and then to make a joint decision as to what should happen next. For the compulsory treatment case, psychiatrists and SOADs similarly had to make individual and then joint decisions, but in this case about both clinical and legal issues. The exercises were not designed exactly to mirror the real-life decision-making setting, but rather acted as a device to parallel aspects of the real-life context, in order to facilitate a study of decision practices. Thus, for the admission scenario, in real-life other parties might be involved more actively in the decision, for example the patient's GP could act as the required second doctor for a decision to admit under section 2 or section 3. Similarly, in the decision to renew compulsion, the RMO is obliged to consult with 'one or more other persons who have been professionally concerned with the patient's medical treatment';[1] this could be for example, a nurse or it could be a hospital-based ASW.

Participants were sent the case histories prior to the exercise, but watched the videos in pairs at the research sites. These were the LSE in London and a hotel in the centre of Manchester. In this sense, both parties were away from their work-base and their colleagues. In a paradoxical sense, this mirrored the situation in which many of these decisions would naturally be taken, that is, in a patient's home, or in car parks or streets adjacent to the patient's where-abouts.

For all three cases the participants recorded their initial decision (based on their reading of the case papers) on a form that combined potential outcomes and confidence scales. The participants had to rank a number of possible legal options and then attach a confidence level to their first ranked option. Further decisions charting potential outcomes and confidence levels were made during and after presentation of the relevant video. Finally, the paired participants reached a joint decision following an uninterrupted discussion between them and recorded their individual level of confidence in it; this constituted the outcome of the case. The participants were then questioned about their decision-making strategies and outcomes in front of one another.

2. PARTICIPANTS

The participants were drawn from those practising within a reasonable distance of London and Manchester. In total, 106 people took part

---

[1] S 20(5), 1983 Act.

—52 Psychiatrists from the Faculty of General and Community Psychiatry of the Royal College (7 of these were also qualified SOADs)
—14 SOADs (who were all psychiatrists of consultant status)
—40 ASWs

The same 40 psychiatrists and 40 ASWs took part in the admission and the discharge cases. The compulsory treatment case involved 14 psychiatrists and 14 SOADs (two of whom had already undertaken the admission and discharge cases as psychiatrists), making 54 pairs in total.

3. CONSTRUCTING AND PILOTING THE CASES

The starting point for the production of the case materials was the videos. These had already been produced for training purposes by the Royal College of Psychiatrists,[2] but permission was obtained to edit and adapt them for the research. The original videos had been produced in conjunction with a professional production company, using financial support from the Department of Health, and were of a high standard. They had not been widely circulated at the time the research was conducted.

Having watched the videos repeatedly and thereafter drawn-up a credible picture of what the patients' lives and psychiatric histories might have been before the point in time at which the videos were set, the patient's case histories were written from scratch. In essence, this entailed 'writing the book of the film'. In so doing, three matters were critical. First, that the materials were as realistic as possible; second, that the issues were appropriately pitched so that the decisions were not straightforward; and finally, that the issues could be substantiated on the materials.

One illustration of how this was achieved in practice will suffice. For Mr Draper, included in his forensic history was a conviction for the possession of a Swiss army knife for which he received a six-month suspended sentence. This 'fact' was designed to be open to a number of interpretations that might cause his then current presentation to be seen in either a more or less serious light. For example, some participants might interpret this fact as being evidence that he has a tendency to carry weapons or as merely an inconsequential part of the daily cultural experience of many young Afro-Caribbean men living in London in the early 1990s.

The decision-making exercises, together with the case materials and videos, were piloted with volunteers who had the necessary professional experience to mirror those who would constitute the participants. The volunteers were debriefed with respect to flaws in the materials and the exercise, and both were amended accordingly.

---

[2] RCP 1997.

This process was time-consuming. However, by the end it appeared that the exercises were of adequate quality and sufficient realism. This was a crucial stage in the research since one of the primary criticisms of vignette exercises is that participants always remain aware that they are not dealing with real cases, and that their decision-making is thereby subtly influenced. The final validity of the exercises was cross-checked with the views of the participants in the debriefing process.

4. FIELDWORK

4.1 Venues and Samples

The exercise took place in two venues during 1999; at the LSE in June–August and in Manchester in September–October. Both the psychiatric and ASW samples invited to take part were drawn from amongst those included in a prior national survey of knowledge and attitudes about mental health law.[3] Since the original samples in the national survey were statistically representative, the use of this data-base facilitated the 'representativeness' of those approached to take part in the exercises. The sample of SOADs was drawn from names and addresses provided by the Mental Health Act Commission (MHAC).

Potential participants were initially approached by letter with an outline explanation of the exercise. The letter also stressed the importance of the study for law reform. It was made clear that the exercise was linked to the national survey, that travelling expenses would be paid and that there was a 'mystery' incentive for taking part. This incentive was subsequently revealed to be entry into a prize draw for a week-end for two in a Heritage hotel.

Of those contacted by letter some 200 either did not want to participate or were not section 12(2) approved (for the psychiatric sample). A number either did not respond at all or their letters were returned as 'not known at this address'; this is a regrettable consequence of having to use lists that, whilst maintained by the RCP for their practising psychiatrists, were not fully up-to-date. However, an almost equal number to those who actively refused to take part, offered to take part, namely, 199 people. From amongst this group appointments were secured for 116 people, selected on the basis of their availability and the logistics of pairing section 12(2) psychiatrists with either an ASW or a SOAD. At short-notice nine pairs were cancelled when either one or both of the parties were unable to attend. In all cases these participants were enthusiastic about re-scheduling and some were subsequently included at a later date.

Although the sample was never intended to be representative, and indeed, qualitative research of this kind does not depend for its validity upon statistically representative samples, the take-up rate made it unlikely that any obvious

---

[3] Peay *et al* 2001; Roberts *et al* 2002.

bias applied to those who responded positively. However, the sample was partially self-selected and therefore the participants may have had some characteristics in common; off-the-cuff remarks made by the participants indicated some had an enthusiasm for taking part in research whilst others were tortured souls whose own doubts about their facility with the Act led them to participate in the hope that they might learn something. Finally, the geographical bias, with its concomitant resource profile for 'London' and 'Manchester', cannot be discounted; it may have introduced an additional selection effect.[4] These are imponderables. Whilst no claims were made about the sample being statistically representative, there was a very limited use of inferential statistics in the analysis of the data. This, together with the relevant confidence levels, gave some indication that the results could be generalisable to the whole population of ASWs and psychiatrists; however, the large health warning above about the nature of the samples should not be forgotten.

Whilst the two venues were originally identified for reasons of convenience and to include a non-London sample, participants in fact came from considerable distances to take part. The 'London sample' included people from places as far apart as Kings Lynn and Chichester, whilst the 'Manchester sample' drew in people from, amongst other places, Birmingham, Dudley, Leicester, Liverpool, Sheffield, Rochdale and Wales as well as from two of the Special Hospitals, namely Rampton and Ashworth.

Of the 40 pairs of ASWs and psychiatrists who completed both the admission and the discharge cases, 17 took part in London and 23 in Manchester. For the compulsory treatment case the 14 pairs of psychiatrists and SOADs were split equally between London and Manchester.

The 106 participants came with a range of backgrounds. The ASWs had both conventional experience (as members of a community mental health team, or as 'generic' social workers, or as hospital-based social workers) and out-of-hours experience (which meant that they undertook emergency night-time and weekend work). The psychiatric sample included Specialist Registrars about to commence Consultant posts and Consultants with up to 25 years in clinical practice; many of these also had experience as members of the MHAC. There was a particularly good response from the sample of SOADs. Fortuitously, therefore, the pairs included both less experienced psychiatrists with highly experienced ASWs, and highly experienced Consultants with newly approved ASWs.

4.2 Procedures

Each participant was sent the written materials in advance of the exercise. On arrival at the venue the pairs were warmly greeted and offered refreshments, but

---

[4] See Bindman *et al* 2000.

they were told little about the exercise, other than that they would be de-briefed at the end. They were instructed not to discuss the cases at that stage with their partner or indeed, even to look at how the other party was completing his or her decision-form and confidence-scales, although they were warned that they would ultimately be required to reach a joint decision. In these initial stages, the atmosphere at the exercises was somewhat reminiscent of that which pervades the examination hall; namely, tense and quiet.

Once the videos had been shown and each party had recorded their individual decisions, the pairs in the admission and discharge cases were then invited to discuss 'what should happen next?' They were asked to adopt the position of either the duty psychiatrist or the emergency team ASW for the admission case, or that of the RMO or a hospital-based social worker for the discharge case.

These discussions took place uninterrupted until such time as it was evident that the pairs had reached and recorded a joint decision as to what to do. Then each party was questioned in the presence of the other. Further or different hypothetical facts were also introduced in order to elucidate particular issues with particular pairs. All of the discussions were tape-recorded. The admission/discharge exercises took approximately two and a quarter hours to complete for each pair.

For the compulsory treatment case for the individual decisions both participants were asked to adopt the perspective of the RMO. Thereafter, for the joint decisions, one of them acted as the RMO and if that person wished to draw on the services of a SOAD (for example, if a decision was made to administer non-consensual ect), the real SOAD was then asked to adopt that perspective. This exercise took, on average, one hour to complete.

The final questioning session of each exercise represented a cross between role play, an interview and appearing on 'Hypotheticals', the round-table ethical 'what if?' programme. A Socratic approach was adopted in order to refine an understanding of the participants' decision-making. The method of cross-questioning adopted must, at times, have appeared like a cross-examination. Words, groups of words, or the relationships between different words and groups of words in the Act, or clinical constructs relevant to them, were picked over in much greater detail than would ever occur in everyday practice. Indeed, the very different tone and content of the uninterrupted discussions which had preceded this emphasised the point. And yet nearly all the participants commented that the exercise had been of great use in helping them to understand what it was that they do when using the Act.

What then was the true relevance of these post-decision examinations, with their emphasis on detail and logic, for real decision-making? In short, their purpose was not to catch people out, or to indulge in philosophical debate, but rather to understand what were the justifications for positions taken. At times, trying to find out the real reason for a view led to that reason seeming illogical to all present. However, illogicality per se by the subject was rarely the end of the matter, since the manifest incongruity between clinical constructs and the relevant legal constructs often made logicality impossible. A different, but very common, type of explanation lay in the wish of the participants to achieve something that the Act was poorly designed to achieve, or even frankly contradicted, but which seemed clinically 'the best thing to do'.

Finally, many of those taking part commented on the usefulness of the exercises for training. Indeed, the sessions were regarded as much more instructive than the single profession didactic training these professionals had experienced. Their inter-disciplinary nature, together with the exposure to the other party's thinking processes, was highlighted as an aid to understanding the working perspectives of the respective professions. Moreover, whilst many of the participants were clearly nervous about the exercise, they also said that they had 'enjoyed' the necessarily challenging and sometimes apparently persecutory questioning. The benefit seemed to derive from having to articulate and justify their own reasoning processes in a way they had not previously been called upon to do. As one psychiatrist commented succinctly 'it makes you think about your knee-jerk responses'.

4.3 Validity and Reality Checks

After the exercises were complete all participants were asked:

(a) whether they had worked together before
(b) whether they had seen any of the videos before
(c) whether, taking the written materials and the videos together, the exercise felt as if they were doing a real case.

One pair had worked together before, and another knew of one another because the SOAD had provided a second opinion service to the psychiatrist's hospital, although they had not dealt directly with one another.

Eight of the 106 participants thought they had seen at least one of the videos before, although they were, of course, naive to the written materials which formed their core; of the eight familiarised participants, one had taken part in the production of the videos and another had used them in her capacity as a Mental Health Act trainer.

Almost without exception, the participants said that the exercises did feel very real to them. They particularly emphasised the quality of the written materials. One or two people remarked that the admission video jarred with its occasional incorporation of what was regarded as bad practice (the videos had originally been produced as training exercises and had necessarily included examples of bad practice) and that Mr Draper did not appear as 'ill' as they had anticipated he might be on the basis of their reading of the papers. Further, two people said that they found it hard to accept (although it is not uncommon in reality) that a patient alleged to have committed arson would have spent a decade in Broadmoor on a section 3 (that is, not as a restricted patient). Two

ASWs lamented the absence in the materials of proper discharge planning or risk assessment, although recognising that this was not at all atypical. However, such critical comment was rare.

5. A DEFENCE OF THE HYPOTHETICAL METHODOLOGY

Adopting a vignette methodology is not at all uncommon in the decision-making literature (see chapter four). It is invariably criticised for a lack of reality and validity, with the argument being made that participants are always aware that these are just hypothetical cases. The methodology adopted by this study was highly unusual, both in its use of extensive materials and because the participants were required to interact with other professionals in a way that endeavoured to mirror aspects of their real life practices. In short, the methodology was designed to achieve high ecological validity. In that the participants emphasised that they felt like they were doing real cases, the methodology achieved this objective.

However, another pertinent question remains. Even though the participants said that they felt that they were doing real cases, is it likely that they did them as they really would? A number of factors suggest a positive answer. First, it was evident from the content of the discussions that participants treated the cases in a professional manner. Indeed, it was occasionally necessary to intervene in order to stop the participants from truly role-playing, that is, introducing new facts beyond those they had been given. People 'got into the exercise' and would occasionally even ask questions such as 'what did happen to Mr Draper?' Second, whilst there was the manifest disadvantage that participants could not interact with the parties in the case and pursue their own lines of questioning, it is not uncommon for decisions about use of the Act to be made on the basis of unsatisfactory or necessarily limited information. Indeed, although some participants wanted to obtain further information before committing themselves to use of the Act, or use of a particular section, most participants nonetheless did arrive at decisions in which they expressed high levels of confidence. Had their appreciation of the exercise been that it was wholly unrealistic, there would not have been the very positive and confident feedback which the overwhelming number of participants expressed. Third, and perhaps even more persuasively, is it really likely that, in responding to the cases, participants would have naturally developed on-the-spot and tailored ways of thinking and expressing themselves that were substantially at variance with how they would usually operate? Indeed, is it possible for participants, faced with a case very close to the types of case encountered by them daily, to switch into an entirely fictional psychological mode in dealing with it? Hence, although their thresholds for given levels of intervention could arguably vary between real and hypothetical situations, there is little reason to think that participants would invent ways of thinking that were alien to them. So, although the decision-outcomes for each subject and pair might be open to the criticism of artificiality, the same cannot be said of the ways of thinking and the decision-strategies used. Fourth, whilst the outcome data may be vulnerable to the criticism of artificiality, even this is somewhat misdirected since it is the variability of outcomes between pairs rather than the actual decisions taken which is of particular interest. And in order to discredit conclusions related to variability of outcome it would be necessary to argue that artificiality impacted very differently on different participants and pairs. Thus, given the study's substantially qualitative nature, it is unlikely to be invalidated by the hypothetical aspects of the methodology, since it is the nature of the participants' thinking and reasoning processes, and individual and paired decision-making practices, which were the primary foci of the study.

However, there is one final methodological rider. The field-work element of the research was conducted shortly after the publication of *'Law without Enforcement: Integrating Mental Health and Justice'*.[5] Can a research perspective be divorced from the views and experience of the researchers? Indeed, at the time the fieldwork was conducted I was also sitting as a member of the Richardson Committee, the Expert Scoping Group established to advise the Minister on the scope of mental health law reform.[6] So, having been intimately involved in both this and the design and construction of the exercises, were the lines of questioning pursued partial? Indeed, is the 'Hawthorn' effect, that the process of measurement affects that being measured, inevitable? Simply put, does one find what one wants to find? This is a real concern. However, the range of responses within and across the professional groups encountered and reported in chapters one–three tend to refute that concern. Unless Janus faced in-view, whatever Hawthorn effect there was, was not unidirectional.

6. ANALYSES

The results of the decision study are displayed in tabular form in Appendix 3. Whilst the decision-outcomes largely speak for themselves, some statistical analysis was conducted to investigate the level of agreement in admission and discharge decisions.[7] Two findings of significance emerge; first, in respect of their individual decisions concerning Mr Draper, the response profiles of the psychiatrists and the ASWs are significantly different ($p<.015$), with the psychiatrists preferring a section 3 admission and the ASWs preferring some non-compulsory intervention in the immediate future. Second, the dominance of ASWs in the paired-decisions for Mr Draper, and of the psychiatrists in respect of Mr Wright, are clear. For the Draper outcomes, a binomal test showed that the probability of a distribution with ASWs prevailing in 22 pairs and

---

[5] Eastman and Peay (eds) 1999.

[6] Richardson 1999.

[7] For this work I am indebted to George Gaskell and Nicholas Allum of the Methodology Institute at the LSE.

psychiatrists prevailing in 9 pairs was P<.03; the null hypothesis, that there was an equal probability of each group prevailing in cases of disagreement, can thus be rejected. Similarly for the Wright outcomes, where 22 psychiatrists prevailed in pairs where disagreement occurred and 6 ASWs prevailed, a binomal tests showed a probability of distribution of P<.012, again indicating that chance could be rejected as a putative explanation.

ALCESTE textual analysis of the uninterrupted discussions between the ASWs and the psychiatrists in the cases of Mr Draper and Mr Wright was also undertaken.[8] *ALCESTE* is a 'tool for determining the main word distribution patterns within a text or discourse.'[9] Here is not the place for details of the computer programme; however, one factor is important. The output from the analysis does not depend on the researcher's prior expectations or prejudices about the content of the material. It is not, therefore, like a visual inspection of a narrative, where one's eye can alight on those issues that seem most pertinent to one's argument, whilst neglecting other and perhaps contradictory information.

ALCESTE works by breaking-down text into smaller sets of statements as a function of word distribution patterns. Correspondence analysis (a statistical classification procedure) is then used to establish the most characteristic words in the texts.[10] Through this process it was possible to demonstrate (perhaps unsurprisingly) that statements referring to Mr Draper's condition were more likely to be associated with psychiatrists speaking, whereas statements referring to issues of case management were more often raised by ASWs. For Mr Wright, the analysis is arguably more striking, with a clear distinction being established between the discourse of the ASWs and that of the psychiatrists. Discourse concerning Mr Wright's current condition and issues of risk were more often articulated by the psychiatrists, with the ASWs' speech patterns being more concerned with general discharge issues and how the case should be managed if Mr Wright were to be discharged. Thus, the distinction between whether and how type questions about discharge emerged, with the former being notably associated with issues of risk, as well as issues of health.

[8] I am very grateful to Caroline Roberts at the LSE for this work.
[9] Reinert 1998.
[10] Greenacre and Blasius 1994.

Appendix 3—Decision Outcomes

Table 1. Decisions by individual preference on the basis of the papers *and* following the video, with percentage confidence levels, *also* by joint outcome

Pair	Pap A	Pap P	Con A	Con P	Vid A	Vid P	Con A	Con P	Out	Con A	Con P	Who wins
1.	4	4	70	75	6	4	70	75	4	70	75	P
2.	3	4	75	25	3	4	75	35	3	75	35	A
3.	6	6	75	80	2	6	75	75	6	75	90	A
4.	4	3	75	75	4	3	75	75	3	75	90	P
5.	6	3	48	75	6	3	55	80	6	60	70	A
6.	3	4	50	80	6	4	75	88	4	75	95	P
7.	4	3	75	50	6	4	65	60	4	80	75	A
8.	3	4	52	90	3	4	60	60	6	20	5	A
9.	1	2	75	85	1	3	50	85	6	50	5	A
10.	4	4	50	80	6	4	15	90	4	30	100	P
11.	4	3	85	90	5	1	80	60	3	70	75	A/P
12.	4	4	60	63	4	5	50	80	4	75	80	A
13.	6	4	80	90	6	4	80	90	6	90	75	A
14.	6	4	50	75	4	4	30	80	6	70	80	A/P
15.	3	4	50	75	3	6	25	75	3	75	75	A
16.	2	2	75	75	3	3	75	75	3	85	75	A/P
17.	2	4	25	75	6	4	75	75	6	75	80	A
18.	6	4	75	80	6	4	75	80	6	100	70	A
19.	1	3	78	75	1	3	70	80	6	95	80	A
20.	3	3	75	75	3	6	70	70	6	70	70	P
21.	2	4	65	80	1	4	35	95	4	35	95	P
22.	4	2	75	70	4	3	75	40	3	90	75	P
23.	3	6	80	80	6	6	60	80	6	70	80	P
24.	6	4	75	60	6	4	90	70	6	90	75	A
25.	3	6	55	75	3	4	72	75	3	80	50	A
26.	3	4	75	78	3	4	50	100	6	50	96	A
27.	6	3	66	75	6	3	80	95	6	93	90	A
28.	6	2	69	85	6	4	80	100	2	75	60	A
29.	4	2	50	79	6	3	25	75	2	50	25	A
30.	6	6	100	90	6	3	75	90	6	84	40	A
31.	2	4	17	83	6	4	35	87	6	72	45	A
32.	2	3	25	46	2	6	50	63	6	25	70	A/P
33.	2	6	78	75	1	6	82	70	6	80	90	A/P
34.	6	6	60	50	6	6	52	53	6	68	60	A/P
35.	3	3	55	90	3	3	75	100	3	100	100	A/P
36.	2	3	75	70	6	3	70	100	6	100	85	P
37.	3	3	50	90	3	6	75	50	3	75	90	A
38.	3	3	75	75	3	6	50	50	3	80	80	A/P
39.	3	3	87	75	3	3	50	90	3	75	90	A/P
40.	2	4	50	90	3	4	20	60	3	75	70	A

Where: Nos 1–17 = London sample; 18–40 = Manchester sample

And where: A = ASW; P = Psychiatrist; Pap = After papers; Con = Confidence level as a percentage; Vid = After video; Out = joint decision after discussion

And for decisions where: 1 = no immediate action; 2 = informal admission; 3 = s 2; 4 = s 3; 5 = s 4; 6 = other

DISCHARGE CASE—CLIVE WRIGHT

Table 2. Decisions by individual preference on the basis of the papers *and* following the video with percentage confidence levels; *also* by joint outcome

Pair	Pap A	Pap P	Con A%	Con P%	Vid A	Vid P	Con A%	Con P%	OUT	Con A%	Con P%	Who wins
1.	8	10	80	60	8	11	80	60	9	50	75	P
2.	11	8	75	25	11	9	75	15	8	75	75	A
3.	8	10	75	70	8	10	75	55	10	50	50	P
4.	11	10	75	75	11	10	75	75	10	90	83	A/P
5.	11	11	47	60	11	11	54	58	8	43	70	A/P
6.	9	9	42	48	11	8	50	50	8	63	68	P
7.	8	10	88	50	8	8	88	65	8	95	54	A/P
8.	10	10	78	38	10	10	70	75	10	78	90	A/P
9.	11	10	25	50	11	9	25	63	10	75	62	A/P
10.	10	11	25	64	11	11	20	85	11	75	85	P
11.	8	8	75	85	8	8	75	80	8	90	90	P
12.	10	8	33	48	8	8	52	55	8	84	56	A/P
13.	8	8	85	70	8	9	85	24	8	85	73	A
14.	11	9	38	46	11	9	48	45	11	50	55	A
15.	11	8	25	75	11	8	50	100	8	40	100	P
16.	10	11	60	50	10	11	60	50	11	75	50	A/P
17.	8	8	75	75	9	8	70	68	8	80	75	P
18.	8	11	75	75	8	11	100	75	11	75	75	P
19.	10	10	54	62	9	10	54	74	9	85	75	A/P
20.	8	9	65	60	8	9	68	50	8	70	75	A
21.	8	8	88	90	8	8	88	94	8	88	96	P
22.	10	9	50	53	10	11	75	38	11	75	68	P
23.	10	9	78	60	8	11	58	50	11	70	50	A/P
24.	8	11	45	60	8	9	60	45	8	60	71	A
25.	10	8	50	50	11	8	70	75	8	20	75	P
26.	11	8	50	75	11	8	40	83	8	50	83	P
27.	10	9	90	90	11	9	75	90	10	64	80	A/P
28.	9	9	82	100	9	10	58	100	10	40	100	P
29.	11	8	75	50	11	8	75	75	8	15	50	P
30.	11	8	75	65	11	8	75	80	8	50	92	P
31.	9	11	23	70	9	11	25	80	8	75	73	P
32.	8	9	75	80	8	9	75	52	8	75	88	A
33.	9	10	82	100	9	9	81	97	9	87	97	A/P
34.	9	11	81	53	9	10	81	53	8	80	75	P
35.	9	8	50	90	8	8	53	95	8	100	100	P
36.	11	11	100	62	11	11	100	65	11	75	69	P
37.	10	8	75	50	10	8	50	50	8	25	79	P
38.	9	10	75	75	9	8	75	62	8	100	78	P
39.	9	10	48	55	8	9	53	75	11	75	90	P
40.	8	8	70	50	8	8	78	75	8	88	87	A/P

Where: Nos 1–17 = London sample; 18–40 = Manchester sample

And where: A = ASW; P = Psychiatrist; Pap = After papers; Con = Confidence level; Vid = After video; Out = joint decision after discussion

And where for decisions: 7 = no immediate action; 8 = renew s 3; 9 = discharge into community; 10 = do not renew but assume patient will remain as an informal patient in hospital; 11 = other

ASSESSMENTS OF 'NATURE OR DEGREE'

Table 3. Assessments of seriousness of disorder by 'nature or degree'—conjunctively— London sample

	ASW (D)	ASW (W)	PSY (D)	PSY (W)
1.	6	4.5	4.5	3
2.	5	2	5	3.5
3.	5	8.5	5	7
4.	7	7	7	9.5
5.	5	5	5.5	5
6.	4	1	3	1.5
7.	5	7	8	4
8.	5.5	5.5	5.5	5.5
9.	7	1.5	6	1.5
10.	7	4	7.5	3.5
11.	7.5	7	7	7
12.	8	10	8	7
13.	5	6	7	6
14.	6	4	6	7.5
15.	7	5	7	5
16.	6	4.5	5.5	5.5
17.	5.5	7.5	6.5	6.5

Where: ASW = Approved Social Worker; PSY = Psychiatrist; (D) = Draper; (W) = Wright
Assessments were made on a 1–10 scale, where 1 = an absence of disorder and 10 = the most serious presentation of the disorder

Table 4. Assessments of the seriousness of disorder by 'nature or degree'—disjunctively— Manchester sample

	ASW–N (D)	ASW–D (D)	ASW–N (W)	ASW–D (W)	PSY–N (D)	PSY–D (D)	PSY–N (W)	PSY–D (W)
1.	7	9	8	3	8	9	8	4
2.	6	6	8	8	6	6	6	7
3.	6.5	5.5	4.5	4	4.5	4.5	7.5	5
4.	4	5.5	7	7	3	4.5	7	7
5.	8	6.5	3.5	3	9.5	8	3.4	4
6.	7	5	8	4	7	7	9	4
7.	7	7	8	1	5	6	8	3
8.	3	1.5	8	1.5	8	7	9.5	3
9.	8	6	8	6	8	6	8	7
10.	7	3.5	9	6	8	6	9	8
11.	8	6	9	4	5	5	8	5
12.	7	4	9	5	6	3	8	5
13.	3	4	4	0	2	4	1.5	0
14.	8.5	5	9	6	9	7	10	7
15.	5.5	6	7	4	6	6	8	3
16.	9.5	6.5	9	6.5	8	6.7	9	5.6
17.	6	7.5	8	7.5	6	9	8	8
18.	5.5	6	9	6	7.5	8	9	6
19.	5	5	8	3	6	8	5	4
20.	4.5	5.5	8	8	6	6.5	9	8
21.	4.5	7.5	7.5	8	8	5	7	4.5
22.	5	4.5	9.5	6	5.5	7	4.5	4.5
23.	5.5	7.5	8.5	6	6	7.5	8	3.5

Where: ASW = Approved Social Worker; PSY = Psychiatrist; N(D)—Nature Draper; D(D)—Degree Draper; N(W)—Nature Wright; D(W)—Degree Wright
Assessments were made on a 1–10 scale, where 1 = an absence of disorder and 10 = the most serious presentation of the disorder

COMPULSORY TREATMENT CASE—HAZEL ROBINSON

Table 5. Decisions by individual preference on the basis of the papers *and* following the video with percentage confidence levels; *also* by joint outcome

	RMO–P	SO–P	RMO CON %	SO–CON %	RMO–V	SO–V	RMO CON %	SO–CON %	OUT	RMO CON %	SO–CON %
1.	13	14	75	75	17	13	75	75	18	20	25
2.	12	15	75	75	12	15	75	100	16	50	100
3.	16	15	80	90	16	15	85	95	16	85	95
4.	12	(XX)	100	(XX)	12	(XX)	100	(XX)	16	100	(XX)
5.	16	13	100	90	13	13	100	95	16	100	85
6.	15	16	90	75	15	16	100	75	16	100	50
7.	14	14	60	50	14	14	75	75	18	75	75
8.	17	14	80	95	17	14	70	95	16	75	90
9.	13	16	75	75	13	16	75	100	16	100	100
10.	14	12	78	75	14	12	85	75	16	88	71
11.	12	16	50	85	12	16	50	85	16	75	100
12.	16	12	75	73	16	12	50	75	18	75	73
13.	13	16	75	75	13	16	75	75	16	75	75
14.	17	15	60	80	16	14	60	80	16	55	90

Where: Numbers 1–7 = London sample; 8–14 = Manchester sample

[NOTE: For pair 4 the SOAD forms are missing. The recorded discussion reveals agreement with the RMO]

And where: RMO = Responsible Medical Officer; SO = Second Opinion Appointed Doctor; Pap = After papers; CON = Confidence level; Vid = After video; OUT = joint decision after discussion

And where for decisions: 12 = no immediate compulsory treatment; 13 = compulsory re-hydration under s 63; 14 = compulsory medication under s 63; 15 = 'emergency' ECT under s 62 (whilst simultaneously requesting a SOAD visit); 16 = ECT under s 58 with SOAD authorisation; 17 = other; 18 = no ECT authorised

Case List

A and others v Secretary of State for the Home Department (2002) CA 25 October 2002

Airedale NHS Trust v Bland [1993] AC 789; [1993] 2 WLR 316; [1993] 1 All ER 821

AG v English (David) [1983] 1 AC 116; [1982] 3 WLR 278; [1982] 2 All ER 903

Anderson, Reid and Doherty v The Scottish Ministers and the Advocate General for Scotland (2001) Privy Council 15 October 2001

B v Barking Havering and Brentwood Community Healthcare NHS Trust, ex parte Barker [1999] 1 FLR 106

B v Croyden Health Authority [1995] Fam 133; [1995] 2 WLR 294

Benjamin and another v United Kingdom (2002) ECHR 26 September 2002

Bolam v Friern Hospital Management Committee [1957] 1 WLR 582; [1957] 2 All ER 118

F v West Berkshire Health Authority [1990] 2 AC 1; [1989] 2 WLR 1025; [1989] 2 All ER 545

Johnson v United Kingdom (1997) 27 EHRR 196; (1998) 40 BMLR 1

Kawka v Poland (2001) ECHR Application no. 25874/94, Judgment 9th January

Lessard v Schmidt 349 F Supp (1972 case)

R v Bournewood Community Mental Healthcare NHS Trust ex parte L (Secretary of State for Health and Others Intervening) [1998] 3 ALL ER 289 (HL); [1998] 3 WLR 107; [1999] 1 AC 458

R v Canons Park Mental Health Review Tribunal, ex parte A [1994] 3 WLR 630; [1994] 2 All ER 659; [1995] QB 60

R v Hallstrom, ex parte W (no 2); R v Gardner, ex parte L [1986] QB 1090; [1986] 2 WLR 883; [1986] 2 All ER 306

R v Howe [1987] 1 All ER 771

R v Lloyd [1967] 1 QB 175

R v Manchester City Council ex parte Stennett and two other actions [2002] UKHL 34; [2002] 3 WLR 584; [2002] 4 All ER 124

R v Mental Health Review Tribunal for the South Thames Region, ex parte Smith Times 9 Dec 1998

R v Riverside Mental Health Trust ex parte Huzzey (1998) 43 BMLR 167

Re B (Consent to Treatment: Capacity); sub nom. B v An NHS Hospital Trust [2002] EWHC Fam 429; [2002] 2 All ER 449

Re C (Adult: Refusal of Medical Treatment) [1994] 1 WLR 290; [1994] 1 All ER 819

Re MB (Medical Treatment) [1997] 2 FLR 426; (1997) 38 BMLR 175

Re S-C (Mental Patient: Habeas Corpus) [1996] QB 599; [1996] 2 WLR 146; [1996] 1 All ER 532 CA

Re T (Consent to Medical Treatment) (Adult Patient) [1993] Fam 95; [1992] 3 WLR 782; [1992] 4 All ER 649

R (on the application of B) v Mental Health Review Tribunal (2002) Administrative Court 22nd July 2002

R (on the application of DR) v Mersey Care NHS Trust (2002) Administrative Court 7 August 2002

R (on the application of H) v Mental Health Review Tribunal for North and East London Region [2001] EWCA Civ 415; [2002] QB 1; [2001] 3 WLR 512

R (on the application of IH) v Secretary of State for the Home Department and the Secretary of State for Health [2002] EWCA Civ 646

R (on the applications of KB, MK, JR, GM, LB, PD, and TB) v MHRT and the Secretary of State for Health [2002] EWHC 639 Administrative Court

R (on the application of the Kurdistan Workers Party and others) v Secretary of State for the Home Department [2002] EWHC 644

R (on the application of M) v Secretary of State for Health (2002) Administrative Court 5 July 2002

R (on the application of Wilkinson) v Broadmoor Hospital; sub nom R (on the application of Wilkinson) v Responsible Medical Officer Broadmoor Hospital, the Mental Health Act Commission Second Opinion Appointed Doctor and the Secretary of State for Health [2001] EWCA Civ 1545; [2002] 1 WLR 419

R (on the application of Wooder) v Feggetter [2002] EWCA Civ 554; [2002] 3 WLR 591

Reid v Secretary of State for Scotland [1999] 1 All ER 481

Thameside and Glossop Acute Services NHS Trust v CH (A Patient) [1996] 1 FLR 762

Varbanov v Bulgaria (2000) Application 31365/95, Judgment 5 October

Wassink v The Netherlands (1990) Series A, No 185–A, September 27th

Winterwerp v The Netherlands (1979) 2 EHRR 387

X v United Kingdom (1981) 4 EHRR 188

SI 2001/3712 Mental Health. The Mental Health Act 1983 Remedial Order 2001. In force 26 Nov 2001

Bibliography

AFFLECK, G G, PESKE, M A and WINTROB, R M (1978), 'Psychiatrists Familiarity with Legal Statutes Governing Emergency Involuntary Hospitalisation', 135 *American Journal of Psychiatry* 205–09.

APPELBAUM, P (2001), 'Thinking Carefully About Outpatient Commitment', 52 *Psychiatric Services* 347–50.

—— and GRISSO, T (1995), 'The MacArthur Treatment Competence Study: I. Mental Illness and Competence to Consent to Treatment', 19 *Law and Human Behavior*, 105–26

APPLEBY, L (1999), *Safer Services*. Report of the National Confidential Inquiry into Suicide and Homicide by People with Mental Illness. (London, Department of Health).

—— SHAW, HJ, SHERRATT, J and AMOS, T (2001), *Safety First: Five Year Report of the National Confidential Inquiry into Suicide and Homicide by People with Mental Illness* (London, Department of Health).

ARCE, R, FAINA, F and SABRAL, J (1996), 'From Juror to Jury Decision-Making: A Non-Model Approach', in Davies, G, Lloyd-Bostock, S, McMurrann, M and Wilson, C (eds), *Psychology, Law and Criminal Justice* (Berlin, de Gruyter).

ASHWORTH, A (1999), *Principles of Criminal Law* 3rd edn (Oxford, Oxford University Press).

—— (2002), *Human Rights, Serious Crime and Criminal Procedure* Hamlyn Lectures 53rd Series (London, Sweet and Maxwell).

AUDINI, B and LELLIOTT, P (2002), 'Age, gender and ethnicity of those detained under Part II of the Mental Health Act 1983' *British Journal of Psychiatry* 180:222–26.

BADGER, D, NURSTEN, J, WILLIAMS, P and WOODWARD, M (1999), *Systematic Review of the International Literature on the Epidemiology of Mentally Disordered Offenders* (NHS Centre For Reviews and Dissemination, University of Reading: University of York, CRD, Report 15).

BAKER, E (1997), 'The Introduction of Supervision Registers in England and Wales: A Risk Communication Analysis', 8 *Journal of Forensic Psychiatry*, 15–35.

BALDWIN, R (1990), 'Why rules don't work' 53 *Modern Law Review* 321–37.

BARON, J (1994), *Thinking and Deciding* 2nd edn (Cambridge, Cambridge University Press).

BARTLETT, A and PHILLIPS, L (1999), 'Decision Making and Mental Health Law', in Eastman, N and Peay, J (eds), below.

BARTLETT, P, and SANDLAND, R (2000), *Mental Health Law: Policy and Practice* (London, Blackstone Press Ltd).

BEAN, P (1980) *Compulsory Admissions to Mental Hospitals* (Chichester, John Wiley).

BINDMAN, J (2002), 'Involuntary outpatient treatment in England and Wales' 15 *Current Opinion in Psychiatry* 595–98.

BINDMAN, J, THORNICROFT, G and TIGHE, J (2000), *A Study of the Use of the Mental Health Act 1983 in Eight Sites* (A Report on Module B to the Department of Health. (Royal College of Psychiatrists, College Research Unit).

BINDMAN, J, REID, Y, THORNICROFT, G, SZMUKLER, G and TILLER, J (2001), *A Study of Experiences of Hospital Admission* (Report of a Study Commissioned by the Department of Health Research and Development Division, London).

—— TIGHE, J, THORNICROFT, G and LEESE, M (2002), 'Poverty, poor services and compulsory psychiatric admission in England'. 37 *Social Psychiatry and Psychiatric Epidemiology* 341–45.

BLACK, J (1998), 'Using Rules Effectively'. In McCrudden, C (ed) *Regulation and Deregulation: Policy and Practice in the Utilities and Financial Services Industries* (Oxford, Oxford University Press).

BLOCK, B (1991), *Decision Making in the Magistrates' Court* (Unpublished dissertation submitted for MA in Criminal Justice, Law Department, Brunel University, West London).

BLOM-COOPER, L, HALLY, H and MURPHY, ER (1995), *The Falling Shadow. One Patient's Mental Health Care 1978–93* (London, Duckworth).

BOWEN, P (2000), 'Reform of the Mental Health Act 1983: Convention Implications of the Green Paper', *Journal of Mental Health Law* 99–120.

BRAY, R and KERR, N (1982), 'Methodological considerations in the study of the psychology of the courtroom', in Kerr and Bray (eds) *The Psychology of the Courtroom* (London, Academic Press).

BRINDLE, D (2002), 'Missed Targets: New funds for mental health "hijacked" ' (*Guardian* 5 June 2002).

BRITISH ASSOCIATION OF SOCIAL WORKERS (2001), *The White Paper 'Reforming the Mental Health Act' Alternative Proposals* (Mental Health Special Interest Group, 16 Kent Street, Birmingham).

BUCHANAN, A (2002), 'Who does what? The relationships between generic and forensic psychiatric services', in Buchanan, A (ed), *Care of the Mentally Disordered Offender in the Community* (Oxford, Oxford University Press).

—— and LEESE, M (2001), 'Detention of People with Dangerous Severe Personality Disorder: A Systematic Review', 358 *The Lancet* 1955–59.

BUDD, T (1999), *Violence at Work: Findings from the British Crime Survey* (London, Home Office).

BURNEY, E and PEARSON, G (1995), 'Mentally Disordered Offenders: Finding a Focus for Diversion', 34 *The Howard Journal* 291–313.

BUSTON, K, PARRY-JONES, W, LIVINGSTON, M, BOGAN, A and WOOD, S (1998), 'Qualitative Research', 172 *British Journal of Psychiatry* 197–99.

BYNOE, I and HOLLAND, A (1999), 'Law as a Clinical Tool: Practising Within and Outwith the Law', in Eastman, N and Peay, J (eds), below.

CALDICOTT, F and MANN, S (1994), 'College Committed to Improving Training', 308 *British Medical Journal* 408–9.

CAPLAN, N, MORRISON, A and STAMBAUGH, R (1975), *The Use of Social Science Knowledge in Policy Decisions at the National Level* (Ann Arbor, USA, Institute of Social Research, University of Michigan).

CAVADINO, P (1999), 'Diverting Mentally Disordered Offenders from Custody', in Webb, D and Harris, R (eds), *Mentally Disordered Offenders: Managing People Nobody Owns* (London, Routledge).

CENTRAL COUNCIL FOR EDUCATION AND TRAINING IN SOCIAL WORK (1992), *Requirements and guidance for the training of social workers to be considered for approval in England and Wales under the Mental Health Act 1983* (Rev edn London, CCETSW 1003, CCETSW paper: no 19.19).

COHEN, D (2002), *Methodological and Conceptual Failings of Anti-psychotic Drug Trials* (Paper presented at the XXVII International Congress of Law and Mental Health, Amsterdam, The Netherlands, 8–12 July 2002).

COOKE, A, HARPER D and KINDERMAN, P (2002), *Results of a Survey of DCP Members' Opinions about Proposed Reforms to the 1983 Mental Health Act* (Paper presented to the 'Make Up Your Mind' RCP/Law Society joint conference London, June 2002).

COPE, R (1992), 'A Survey of Forensic Psychiatrists' Views on Psychopathic Disorder' 4 *Journal of Forensic Psychiatry* 215–35.

CORBETT, C (1987), 'Magistrates' and Court Clerks' Sentencing Behaviour: an Experimental Study', in Pennington, D and Lloyd-Bostock, S (eds), *The Psychology of Sentencing: Approaches to consistency and disparity* (Centre for Socio-Legal Studies, University of Oxford).

CORKERY, J (1992), 'The Use of Vignettes in Sentencing Studies of English Magistrates', 20 *International Journal of the Sociology of Law* 253–70.

COTTERRELL, R (1992), *The Sociology of Law* 2nd edn (London, Butterworths).

CRICHTON, J and SHEPPARD, D (1996), 'Psychiatric Inquiries: Learning the Lessons', in Peay, J (ed) below.

CRISP, A (ed) (2001), *Every Family in the Land—Understanding Prejudice and Discrimination Against People with Mental Illness* (London, Royal Society of Medicine).

DAWES, R (1988), *Rational Choice in an Uncertain World* (San Diego, California, Harcourt Brace Jovanovich).

DAWSON, J (2003), 'Randomised Controlled Trials of Mental Health Legislation', *Medical Law Review* (forthcoming).

—— ROMANS, S, GIBBS, S and RATTER, N (2003), 'Ambivalence about Community Treatment Orders', *International Journal of Law and Psychiatry* (forthcoming).

DEPARTMENT OF HEALTH, NHS EXECUTIVE (1994), *Guidance on the Discharge of Mentally Disordered People and Their Continuing Care in the Community*, Health Service Guidelines HSG (94) 27, LASSL (94) 4.

DEPARTMENT OF HEALTH (1995), *Mental Health Act 1983 Memorandum on Parts 1 to VI, VIII and X* (London, The Stationery Office Ltd).

—— (1999), *Reform of the Mental Health Act 1983*, Proposals for Consultation Cm 4480 (London, The Stationery Office Ltd).

—— (1999a), *Effective Care Co-Ordination in Mental Health Services: Modernising the Care Programme Approach: a Policy Booklet.*

—— (1999b), *Mental Health National Service Framework* (London, Department of Health).

—— (2000), *Shaping the New Mental Health Act: Key Messages from the Department of Health Research Programme* (London, Department of Health).

—— (2002), *Draft Mental Health Bill Cm 5538–I; Explanatory Notes Cm 5538–II; Mental Health Bill Consultation Document CM 5538–III* (London, The Stationery Office Ltd).

DEPARTMENT OF HEALTH AND HOME OFFICE (2000), *Reforming the Mental Health Act. Part I: The New Legal Framework Cm 5016–I; Part II: High Risk Patients Cm 501–II* (London, The Stationery Office Ltd).

DEPARTMENT OF HEALTH AND NATIONAL STATISTICS (2002), *Inpatients Formally Detained in Hospitals Under the Mental Health Act 1983 and Other Legislation. NHS Trusts, High Security Psychiatric Hospitals and Private Facilities: 2000–01* (London, Government Statistical Service).

DEPARTMENT OF HEALTH AND SOCIAL SECURITY (1976), *A Review of the Mental Health Act 1959* (London, Her Majesty's Stationery Office).

—— (1978), *Review of the Mental Health Act 1959*. Cmnd 7320 (London, Her Majesty's Stationery Office).

DEPARTMENT OF HEALTH AND WELSH OFFICE (1993), *Code of Practice, Mental Health Act 1983*. Published August 1993 pursuant to s 118 of the Act (London, Her Majesty's Stationery Office).

—— (1999), *Code of Practice, Mental Health Act 1983*. Published March 1999 pursuant to s 118 of the Act (London, Her Majesty's Stationery Office).

EASTMAN, N and PEAY, J (1998), '*Bournewood*: An Indefensible Gap in Mental Health Law', 317 *British Medical Journal* 94–95.

—— —— (eds) (1999), *Law Without Enforcement: Integrating Mental Health and Justice* (Oxford, Hart Publishing).

ECCLES, M and GRIMSHAW, J (2000), *Clinical Guidelines: From Conception to Use* (Oxon, Radcliffe Medical Press).

ELTON, B (1996), *Popcorn* (London, Simon & Schuster Ltd).

EXWORTHY, T (1995), 'Compulsory Care in the Community: A Review of Proposals for Compulsory Supervision and Treatment of the Mentally Ill in the Community', 5 *Criminal Behaviour and Mental Health* 218–41.

FENNELL, P (1977), 'The Mental Health Review Tribunal: A Question of Imbalance', 2 *British Journal of Law and Society* 186–219.

—— (1996), *Treatment without Consent: Law, Psychiatry and the Treatment of Mentally Disordered People Since 1845* (London, Routledge).

—— (2001), 'Reforming the Mental Health Act 1983: Joined Up Compulsion', *Journal of Mental Health Law* 5–20.

—— and YEATES, V (2002), 'To Serve which Master?—Criminal Justice Policy, Community Care and the Mentally Disordered Offender', in Buchanan, A (ed), *Care of the Mentally Disordered Offender in the Community* (Oxford, Oxford University Press).

FERENCZ, N and McGUIRE, J (2000), 'Mental Health Review Tribunals in the UK: Applying a Therapeutic Jurisprudence Perspective', Spring 2000 *Court Review* 48–52.

FITZMAURICE, C and PEASE, K (1986), *The Psychology of Judicial Sentencing* (Manchester, Manchester University Press).

GIGERENZER, G (2002), *Reckoning with Risk: Learning to Live with Uncertainty* (London, Penguin).

GLOVER, N (1999), 'L v Bournewood Community and Mental Health NHS Trust', 21 *Journal of Social Welfare and Family Law* 151–57.

GLOVER-THOMAS, N (2002), *Reconstructing Mental Health Law and Policy* (London, Butterworths).

GOFF, LORD (1988), 'The Mental Element in Murder' 104 *Law Quarterly Review* 30–59.

GOROVITZ, S (1982), *Doctors' Dilemmas. Moral Conflict and Medical Care* (Oxford, Oxford University Press).

GOSTIN, L (1983), 'The Ideology of Entitlement: The Application of Contemporary Legal Approaches to Psychiatry', in Bean, P (ed), *Mental Illness: Changes and Trends* (Chichester, John Wiley).

GREENACRE, M and BLASIUS, J (1994), *Correspondence Analysis in the Social Sciences* (London, Academic Press).

GREENHALGH, T and TAYLOR, R (1997), 'Papers That Go Beyond Numbers', 315 *British Medical Journal* 740–43.

GRISSO, T and APPELBAUM, P (1998), *Assessing Competence to Consent to Treatment* (Oxford, Oxford University Press).

GUNN, M (2000), 'Reform of the Mental Health Act 1983: The Relevance of Capacity to Make Decisions', *Journal of Mental Health Law* 39–43.

HADFIELD, B, SHAW, J, PINFOLD, V, BINDMAN, J, EVANS, S, HUXLEY, P and THORNICROFT, G (2001), 'Managing Severe Mental Illness in the Community using the Mental Health Act 1983: A Comparison of Supervised Discharge and Guardianship in England', 36 *Social Psychiatry and Psychiatric Epidemiology* 508–15.

HAGELL, A and BOURKE DOWLING, S (1999), *Scoping Review on the Health and Care of Mentally Disordered Offenders*, NHS Centre for Reviews and Dissemination, Policy Research Bureau (London, University of York CRD Report 16).

HALLIDAY, S (2000), 'The Influence of Judicial Review on Bureaucratic Decision-Making' *Public Law* 110–22.

HARRIS, N, EDEN, K and BLAIR, A (2000), *Challenges to School Exclusion, Appeals and the Law* (London, Routledge).

HASSAN, T B, MACNAMARA, A F, DAVY, A, BING, A and BODIWALA, G G (1999), 'Managing Patients with Deliberate Self Harm who Refuse Treatment in the Accident and Emergency Department', 319 *British Medial Journal* 107–09.

HAWKINS, K (1986), 'On Legal Decision-Making', 43, 4 *Washington and Lee Law Review* 1161–242.

HEGINBOTHAM, C and ELSON, T (1999), 'Public Policy via Law: Practitioner's Sword and Politician's Shield', in Eastman, N and Peay, J (eds) above.

HOGARTH, J (1971), *Sentencing as a Human Process* (Toronto, University of Toronto Press).

HOGGETT, B (1996), *Mental Health Law* 4th edn (London, Sweet and Maxwell).

HOME AFFAIRS SELECT COMMITTEE (2000), *Report on Government Proposals for People with Severe and Dangerous Personality Disorder* (London, Her Majesty's Stationery Office).

HOME OFFICE (2002), *Multi-Agency Public Protection Arrangements: Annual Report 2001–2*.

HOME OFFICE AND DEPARTMENT OF HEALTH (1999), *Managing Dangerous People with Severe Personality Disorder: Proposals for Policy Development*.

HOOD, R (1972), *Sentencing the Motoring Offender: A Study of Magistrates' Views and Practices* (London, Heinemann).

HØYER, G and FERRIS, R (2001), 'Outpatient Commitment. Some Reflections on Ideology, Practice and Implications for Research', *Journal of Mental Health Law* 56–65.

—— KJELLIN, L, ENGBERG M, KALTIALA-HEINO, R, NILSTUN, T, SIGURDJONSDOTTIR, M and SYSE, A (2002), 'Paternalism and Autonomy. A presentation of a Nordic study on the use of coercion in the mental health care system'. 25 *International Journal of Law and Psychiatry* 93–108.

HUMPHREYS, M (1998), 'Consultant Psychiatrists' Knowledge of Mental Health Legislation in Scotland', 38 *Medicine, Science and Law* 237–41.

JACOBY, J, MELLON, L, ROUTLEDGE, E and TURNER, S (1982), *Prosecutorial Decision-Making: A National Study*, National Institute of Justice, US Department of Justice, Washington, DC.

JAMES, D (1999), 'Court Diversion at 10 Years: Can it Work, Does it Work and Has it a Future?', 10 *Journal of Forensic Psychiatry* 507–24.

JOINT COMMITTEE ON HUMAN RIGHTS (2002), *Report on the Draft Mental Health Bill*, Twenty-fifth Report of Session 2001–2. HL paper 181, HC 1294, House of Lords/ House of Commons (London, The Stationery Office Ltd).

JONES, K (1993), *Asylums and After: A Revised History of the Mental Health Services: From the Early 18th Century to the 1990s* (London, Athlone Press).

—— (1972), *A History of the Mental Health Services* (London, Routledge and Kegan Paul).

JONES, R (1999), *Mental Health Act Manual* 6th edn (London, Sweet and Maxwell).

—— (2002), *Mental Health Act Manual* 8th edn (London, Sweet and Maxwell).

KAHNEMAN, D, SLOVIC, P and TVERSKY, A (1982), *Judgment under Uncertainty: Heuristic Biases* (Cambridge, Cambridge University Press).

KANE, E (2002), 'The Policy Perspective: What Evidence is Influential?', in Priebe, S and Slade, M (eds), *Evidence in Mental Health Care* (Andover, Brunner-Routledge).

KIEL, L D and ELLIOTT, E (eds) (1996), *Chaos Theory in the Social Sciences: Foundations and Applications* (Ann Arbor, Michigan, University of Michigan Press).

KJELLIN, L, HØYER, G, ENGBERG, M, KALTIALA-HEINO, R and SIGURDJONSDOTTIR, M (2001), *Legal Status and Patients' Perceptions of being Coerced at Admission to Psychiatric Care in the Four Nordic Countries* Paper presented at the XXVI International Congress on Law and Mental Health, Montreal, July 2001.

KOERNER, B (2002), *First you Market the Disease . . . Then you Push the Pills to Treat it*, The Guardian 30 July 2002.

KULLGREN, G, JACOBSSON, L, LYNOE, N, KOHN, R and LEVAV, I (1996), 'Practices and Attitudes Among Swedish Psychiatrists Regarding the Ethics of Compulsory Treatment', 93 *Acta Psychiatrica Scandinavica* 389–96.

LAW COMMISSION (1995), *Mental Incapacity*, Law Commission Report no 231 (London, Her Majesty's Stationery Office).

LEWIS, O (2000), 'Renewing Detention Whilst a Patient is on Leave of Absence', *Journal of Forensic Psychiatry* 151–57.

—— (2002), 'Protecting the Rights of People with Mental Disabilities: the European Convention on Human Rights' 9, 4, *European Journal of Health Law* 293–320.

LIDZ, C W, MULVEY, F P, APPELBAUM, P S and CLEVELAND, S (1989), 'Commitment: The Consistency of Clinicians and the Use of Legal Standards', 146 *American Journal of Psychiatry* 176–81.

MATTHEWS, E (1999), 'Mental and Physical Illness—An Unsustainable Separation?', in Eastman, N and Peay, J (eds), above.

MCBARNET, D and WHELAN, C (1991), 'The Elusive Spirit of the Law: Formalism and the Struggle for Legal Control' 54 *Modern Law Review* 848–73.

MCCABE, S and PURVES, R (1974), *The Shadow Jury at Work*, Oxford University Penal Research Unit, Occasional Paper no 8.

MCEWAN, J (2000), 'Decision-Making in Legal Settings', in McGuire, J, Mason, T and O'Kane, A (eds), *Behaviour, Crime and Legal Processes: A Guide for Forensic Practitioners* (Chichester, John Wiley and Sons Ltd).

MENTAL HEALTH ACT COMMISSION (1998), *The Threshold for Admission and the Relapsing Patient*, A Discussion Document (Maid Marion House, 56 Houndsgate, Nottingham).

—— (1995), Sixth Biennial Report 1993–95. Laid before Parliament by the Secretary of State for Health Pursuant to s 121(10) of the Mental Health Act 1983 (London, HMSO).

—— (2001), Ninth Biennial Report 1999–2001. Laid before Parliament by the Secretary of State for Health Pursuant to s 121(10) of the Mental Health Act 1983 (London, The Stationery Office).

MILL, J S (1991), *[1859] On Liberty and Other Essays* (ed), Gray, J (Oxford, Oxford University Press).

MILLAN, B (2001), *New Directions: Report of the Review of the Mental Health (Scotland) Act 1984* (Edinburgh, Scottish Executive).

MONAHAN, J, STEADMAN, H, SILVER, E, APPELBAUM, P, ROBBINS, P, MULVEY, E, ROTH, L, GRISSO, T and BANKS, S (2001), *Rethinking Risk Assessment: The MacArthur Study of Mental DIsorder and Violence* (New York, Oxford University Press).

—— LIDZ, C, HOGE, S, MULVEY, E, EISENBERG, M, ROTH, L, GARDNER, W and BENNETT, N (1999), 'Coercion in the Provision of Mental Health Services: The MacArthur Studies', in Morrissey, J and Monahan, J (eds), *Research in Community and Mental Health* Vol 10 Coercion in Mental Health Services—International Perspectives (Stamford Connecticut, JAI Press).

—— BONNIE, R, APPELBAUM, P, HYDE, P, STEADMAN, H and SWARTZ, M (2001), 'Mandated Community Treatment: Beyond Outpatient Commitment', 52 Psychiatric Services 1198–1205.

MORGAN, J, STILT, T and FALKOWSKI, W (1999), 'Application of the Powers of Compulsory Admission to Psychiatric Hospital by GPs, Social Workers and Psychiatrists', 39 *Medicine, Science and Law* 4, 325–31.

MOXON, D, CORKERY, J and HEDDERMAN, C (1992), *Developments in the Use of Compensation Orders in Magistrates' Courts Since October 1988*, Home Office Research Study no 126 (London, Her Majesty's Stationery Office).

NEILL, P (1998), 'The Duty to Give Reasons: The Openness of Decision-Making', in Forsyth, C and Hare, I (eds), *The Golden Metwand and the Crooked Cord. Administrative Law Essays in Honour of Sir William Wade QC* (Oxford, Clarendon Press).

NHS EXECUTIVE (1996), *Approval of Doctors Under Section 12 of the Mental Health Act 1983*, Health Service Guidelines HSG(96)3.

PADFIELD, N and LEIBLING, A (2000), *An Exploration of Decision-Making at Discretionary Lifer Panels*, Home Office Research Study No 213 (London, Home Office, Research and Statistics Directorate).

PARRY-JONES, W (1972), *The Trade in Lunacy* (London, Routledge and Kegan Paul).

PEAY, J (1980), *A Study of Individual Approaches to Decision-Making under the Mental Health Act 1959* (unpublished PhD thesis submitted to the Department of Psychology, University of Birmingham).

—— (1981), 'Mental Health Review Tribunals: Just or Efficacious Safeguards?', 5 2/3 *Law and Human Behavior* 161–86.

—— (1986), 'The Mental Health Act 1983 (England and Wales): Legal Safeguards in Limbo', 14, 3/4 *Law, Medicine and Health Care* 180–89.

—— (1989), *Tribunals on Trial: A Study of Decision Making Under the Mental Health Act 1983* (Oxford, Clarendon Press).

—— (ed) (1996), *Inquiries after Homicide* (London, Duckworth).

—— (1999), 'Thinking Horses not Zebras', in Webb, D and Harris, R (eds), *Managing People Nobody Owns* (London, Routledge).

—— (2000), 'Reform of the Mental Health Act 1983: Squandering an Opportunity?', *Journal of Mental Health Law* 5–15.

PEAY, J (2002), 'Mentally Disordered Offenders, Mental Health and Crime', in Maguire, M, Morgan, R and Reiner, R (eds), *The Oxford Handbook of Criminology* 3rd edn (Oxford, Oxford University Press).

—— ROBERTS, C and EASTMAN, N (2001), 'Legal Knowledge of Mental Health Professionals: Report of a National Survey', *Journal of Mental Health Law* 44–55.

PERCY COMMISSION (1957), *Report of the Royal Commission on the Law Relating to Mental Illness and Mental Deficiency 1954–1957.* Cmnd 169 (London, Her Majesty's Stationery Office).

PERKINS, E (2002), *Decision-Making in Mental Health Review Tribunals* (London, Policy Studies Institute).

—— (2002a), *A New Tribunal?* Paper presented at the joint RCP/Law Soceity Conference 'Make Up Your Mind', (Senate House, University of London, 20–21 June 2002).

PINFOLD, V, ROWE, A, HADFIELD, B, BINDMAN, J, HUXLEY, P, THORNICROFT, G and SHAW, J (2002), 'Lines of Resistance: Exploring Professionals' Views of Compulsory Community Supervision', 11 *Journal of Mental Health* 177–90.

POTAS, I and RICKWOOD, D (1984), *Do Juries Understand?* (ACT, Australian Institute of Criminology).

PRESTON, N, KISELY, S and XIAO, J (2002), 'Assessing the Outcome of Compulsory Psychiatric Treatment in the Community: Epidemiological Study in Western Australia', 324 *British Medical Journal* 1244–49.

PRINS, H (2001), 'Offenders Deviants or Patients', Comments on Part Two of the White Paper, *Journal of Mental Health Law* 21–26.

—— (2002), 'Incapacitating the Dangerous in England and Wales: High Expectations Harsh Reality', *Journal of Mental Health Law* 5–20.

QUIRK, A, LELLIOTT, P, AUDINI, B and BUSTON, K (2000), *A Qualitative Study of the Process of Mental Health Act Assessments*, A Report on Module C to the DoH (Royal College of Psychiatrists, College Research Unit).

REINERT, M (1998), *ALCESTE Users' Manual (English version)* (Toulouse, Image).

RICHARDSON, G (1999), *Review of the Mental Health Act 1983*, Report of the Expert Committee Presented to the Parliamentary Under Secretary of State for Health 15 July 1999. Published November 1999.

—— (2001), 'Reforming Mental Health Law: Principle or Pragmatism', 54 *Current Legal Problems* 415–38.

—— (2002), 'Autonomy, Guardianship and Mental Disorder: One Problem, Two Solutions', 65 *Modern Law Review* 702–23.

—— and MACHIN, D (1999), 'A Clash of Values? MHRTs and Judicial Review' *Journal of Mental Health Law* 3–12.

—— —— (2000), 'Judicial Review and Tribunal Decision Making: A Study of MHRTs', *Public Law* 494–514.

—— and PEAY, J (2000), *Compelling Capacity—An Acceptable Agenda for Law Reform* Paper presented to the XXVth International Congress on Law and Mental Health, Sienna, Italy July 2000.

—— and THOROLD, O (1999), 'Law as a Rights' Protector', in Eastman, N and Peay, J (eds), above.

ROBERTS, C, PEAY, J and EASTMAN, N (2002), 'Mental Health Professionals' Attitudes Towards Legal Compulsion: Report of a National Survey', 1 *International Journal of Forensic Mental Health* 71–82.

ROSE, N (1986), 'Law Rights and Psychiatry', in Miller, P and Rose, N (eds), *The Power of Psychiatry* (Cambridge, Polity Press).

ROYAL COLLEGE OF PSYCHIATRISTS (1997), *Using the Mental Health Act: A Training Resource for Doctors* (London, RCP).

ROYAL COMMISSION (1926), *Report of the Royal Commission on Lunacy and Mental Disorder 1924–26* Cm 2700 (The Macmillan Report).

RUMGAY, J and MUNROE, E (2001), 'The Lion's Den: Professional Defences in the Treatment of Dangerous Patients', *Journal of Forensic Psychiatry* 357–78.

RUSSO, J and SCHOEMAKER, P (1989), *Decision Traps: Ten Barriers to Brilliant Decision-Making and How to Overcome Them* (New York, Simon and Schuster).

SALIZE, H, DREßING, and PEITZ, M (2002), *Compulsory Admission and Involuntary Treatment of Mentally Ill Patients—Legislation and Practice in EU-Member States*, Final Report for the European Commission (Mannheim, Germany, The Central Institute for Mental Health).

SCHWARTZ, H I, APPELBAUM, P S and KAPLAN, R D (1984), 'Clinical Judgments in the Decision to Commit. Psychiatric Discretion and the Law', 41 *Archives of General Psychiatry* 811–15.

SCOTTISH EXECUTIVE (2001), *Reviewing Mental Health Law* (Edinburgh, Scottish Executive).

SCULL, I A (1993), *The Most Solitary of Afflictions: Madness and Society in Britain 1700–1900* (New Haven, Yale University Press).

SCULLY, P (2000), *Resistance to New Pardigms: Hong Kong Guardianship and Medical Treatment Law*, presented to the XXVth International Congress on Law and Mental Health, Sienna, Italy July 2000.

SHEPPARD, D (1996), *Learning the Lessons*, Mental Health Inquiry Reports Published in England and Wales Between 1969 and 1996 and their Recommendations for Improving Practice (London, The Zito Trust).

SIMON, R J (1967), *The Jury and the Defence of Insanity* (Boston, Little, Brown and Co).

SOCIAL SERVICES INSPECTORATE (2001), *Detained: Social Services Inspectorate Inspections of Compulsory Mental Health Admissions*, CI (2001) 1 (London, Department of Health).

STEADMAN, H (2002), *Validating the ICT approach for assessing community violence risk among acute psychiatric inpatients*, Paper presented to the XXVII International Congress on Law and Mental Health, Amsterdam, July 2002.

—— GOUNIS, K, DENIS, D, HOPPER, K, ROCHE, B, SWARTZ, M and ROBBINS, P (2001), 'Assessing the New York City Involuntary Outpatient Commitment Pilot Program', 52 *Psychiatric Services* 330–36.

SURGEON GENERAL (1999), *Mental Health: A Report of the Surgeon General* (Washington, DC, Office of the Surgeon General).

SWARTZ, M, SWANSON, J, WAGNER, R, BURNS, B, HIDAY, V and BORUM, R (1999), 'Can involuntary outpatient commitment reduce hospital recidivism? Findings from a Randomised Trial in Severely Mentally Ill Individuals', 156 *American Journal of Psychiatry* 1968–75.

TYLER, T (1996), 'The Psychological Consequences of Judicial Procedures: Implications for Civil Commitment Hearings', in Wexler, D and Winick, B (eds), *Law in a Therapeutic Key: Developments in Therapeutic Jurisprudence* (Durham, NC, Carolina Academic Press).

UNSWORTH, C (1987), *The Politics of Mental Health Legislation* (Oxford, Oxford University Press).

WADHAM, J and MOUNTFIELD, H (2000), *Blackstone's Guide to the Human Rights Act 1998* 2nd edn (London, Blackstone Press Ltd).

WALL, S, CHURCHILL, R, HOTOPF, M, BUCHANAN, A and WESSELY, S (1999), *A systematic review of research relating to the Mental Health Act 1983* (London, Department of Health).

WALTON, P (2000), 'Reforming the Mental Health Act 1983: An Approved Social Worker Perspective', 22 *Journal of Social Welfare and Family Law* 401–14.

WERTHEIMER, A (1993), 'A Philosophical Examination of Coercion for Mental Health Issues', 11 *Behavioural Sciences and the Law* 239–58.

WORLD HEALTH ORGANISATION (1996), *Mental Health Care Law: Ten Basic Principles*, Division of Mental Health and Prevention of Substance Abuse (Geneva, WHO).

ZIGMOND, A (2000), *Mental Health Legislation: My Patients and Me*, Paper presented at the joint RCP/Law Society Conference 'Make Up Your Mind' (Senate House, University of London 20–21 June 2002).

—— and HOLLAND, A (2000), 'Unethical Mental Health Law: History Repeats Itself', *Journal of Mental Health Law* 49–56.

Index